FPCC

APR 3 0 1990

INVENTORY 98

 St. Louis Community College

Forest Park
Florissant Valley
Meramec

Insructional Resources
St. Louis, Missouri

D1158036

Cynthia Ozick

Twayne's United States Authors Series

Warren French, Editor

University of Wales, Swansea

TUSAS 545

Cynthia Ozick (photograph courtesy of Layle Silbert, 1979).

Cynthia Ozick

By Joseph Lowin

Midrasha Institute of Jewish Studies

Twayne Publishers
A Division of G. K. Hall & Co. • *Boston*

Cynthia Ozick
Joseph Lowin

Copyright 1988 by G. K. Hall & Co.
All rights reserved.
Published by Twayne Publishers
A Division of G. K. Hall & Co.
70 Lincoln Street
Boston, Massachusetts 02111

Copyediting supervised by Barbara Sutton.
Book production by Gabrielle B. McDonald.
Book design by Barbara Anderson.

Typeset in 11 pt. Garamond
by Modern Graphics, Inc., Weymouth, Massachusetts

Printed on permanent/durable acid-free paper
and bound in the United States of America.

Library of Congress Cataloging-in-Publication Data

Lowin, Joseph.
    Cynthia Ozick / by Joseph Lowin.
        p.   cm. — (Twayne's United States authors series ; TUSAS 545)
    Bibliography: p.
    Includes index.
    ISBN 0–8057–7526–9 (alk. paper)
    1. Ozick, Cynthia—Criticism and interpretation.   I. Title.
II. Series.
PS3565.Z5Z75   1988
813'.54—dc19   88–14813
                                                                        CIP

For Judith

כְּשׁוֹשַׁנָּה בֵּין הַחוֹחִים כֵּן רַעְיָתִי בֵּין הַבָּנוֹת:
Song of Songs 2: 2

Mais surtout je voudrais un coeur fait pour le mien,
Qui le sentît, l'aimât, et qui le comprît bien.

Théophile Gautier, "Les Souhaits"

Contents

About the Author

Joseph Lowin received his B.A. from the City College of New York in 1962, studied for two years at the Sorbonne where he was a Fulbright Fellow, and received his Ph.D. in French literature from Yale University in 1968. Lowin recently returned from a year in Israel where he was a Jerusalem Fellow. He has also received research grants from both the National Endowment for the Humanities and the American Council of Learned Societies.

Lowin is currently director of the Midrasha Institute of Jewish Studies and director of the Department of Adult Education Services of the Jewish Education Association of MetroWest, New Jersey. Formerly national director of the Department of Adult Jewish Education at Hadassah, Lowin has held academic and administrative positions at Yale University, the University of Miami, and Touro College and has taught at the 92nd Street Y in New York City. He is currently an Associate in the Columbia University Seminar on the Theory of Literature.

Lowin's articles on French literature have appeared in the *Revue des Lettres Modernes, Revue d'Histoire du Théâtre, Revue des Etudes Juives, Nineteenth Century French Studies,* and *French Review.* Lowin has been a regular contributor to the *Jewish Book Annual* where he has published several articles on the Jewish novel in America and Europe. For *Hadassah Magazine* he writes a monthly column about Hebrew etymology and is a frequent reviewer of Jewish and Israeli fiction.

Preface

"If it were not a pagan rite, I would strew roses at the poet's feet."

I remember having come across a sentence bearing this sentiment many years ago as a first-year graduate student of French literature reading a biography of the poet Paul Verlaine. I recall a feeling of deep pleasure at the thought that one might be fortunate enough to uncover in one's reading an author to whom one would be willing, theoretically, to devote one's life. I recall as well reflecting on the morality of Verlaine's biographer, who, however dedicated to art and beauty he may have been, realized that it was wrong to imitate, even in a secular setting, idolatrous practices. True, I did think then as I do now that the study of literature without enthusiasm is a vain pursuit, but I knew then as I do now that unbridled enthusiasm and lack of critical restraint make for bad scholarship.

I nevertheless resolved to seek out "my" author, an author whose work would be worthy of my close attention but from whom I would maintain dispassionate distance. And then I came across the writings of Cynthia Ozick—a fortunate discovery. Here was a writer who would repay close critical analysis. I recall sitting in the Burgess-Carpenter Library at Columbia University poring over one of her texts over the span of several hours. I was taking such pleasure in this activity that I said to myself, loud enough, I'm embarrassed to say, to be overheard, "I don't want this day to end." And what was the subject of Ozick's narrative being studied by me that day? The dangers of turning the love of literature into idol worship. Here, then, was an author to whom I could dedicate myself. Here also was an author who would constantly be reminding me that it is immoral to make an idol out of a work of art. Thus was born the idea for this book.

The chronological order of the chapters is approximate, intending to give the reader a feeling for the evolution of Ozick's work, from her earliest writings to her latest novel. The reader will not fail to note, however, that the short story "Envy," of 1969 vintage, is discussed before *Trust,* Ozick's first novel, published in 1966, and begun much earlier than that. In addition, the analysis of *The*

Cannibal Galaxy (1983) precedes the discussions of "Usurpation" (1974) and "The Shawl" (1980). A look at the Contents will reveal that the book is organized thematically into pairs of chapters. The first two chapters are introductory and biographical. The next two deal with the theme of pedagogy. The third pair investigates the notion of a Jewish aesthetic, while the fourth couple attempts an analysis of Ozick's transactions with Jewish techniques of rewriting. The final two chapters are about the role of redemption in fiction.

Just as it has been a pleasure to research and write this work, so it is now an even greater pleasure to acknowledge the encouragement and help of those who, sometimes unknowingly, contributed to its completion. The way I now read literary texts, including my very inclination to read these texts, can be traced to the pervasive influence of Henri Peyre, my teacher and literary rebbe at Yale. I record here my debt to a *vieux de la vieille* who remains young through his students, and theirs. Timing is often everything in life. I was fortunate enough to have the right friends at the right time. To Arthur Budick, who read, with pencil in hand, the first-written chapter of this book, and to Doris Oxenhorn, whose vigilant eye spotted for me the exact documents I needed at the exact time I needed them, goes my expression of gratitude. Subsequently in need of further critical feedback on my writing, I submitted three of the chapters of this book for consideration by colleagues who were editing books or annuals on American and Jewish fiction. To Jacob Kabakoff, editor of the *Jewish Book Annual,* to Mark H. Gelber, editor of *Identity and Ethos,* and to Loren Logsdon and Charles W. Mayer, editors of *Since Flannery O'Connor: Essays on the Contemporary American Short Story,* goes this acknowledgment of both their hospitality to my work and their permission to print here, in somewhat revised form, the chapters they published.

Libraries, it will surprise no one, played a large role in the execution of this book. I have long felt that there is no higher calling in the world of intellectual pursuit than that of reference librarians. Without them, I am convinced, we would all be living in huts. It is my pleasure to acknowledge here my considerable debt to the reference librarians of Columbia University's Butler Library, of the Hebrew University's Library at Mount Scopus, and of the Finkelstein Memorial Library in Spring Valley, New York. Much of this book was written in a library of some sort—although many pages were penned at a table of a sidewalk café in Jerusalem. I would like to thank Columbia, the Hebrew University, and especially the Van Leer Institute in Jerusalem for providing me with a long table and an atmosphere conducive to writing. To the Jerusalem Fellows goes an expression of gratitude for giving me the time to execute much of this project.

I have often joked with my children that one of the lessons of the biblical story of the Binding of Isaac is that it is better to be the father than the child. I have been told, however, that some things—especially acknowledgments in a preface—are no laughing matter, and that I should state simply, for all the world to see, my debt to my children, Shari, David, and Benjamin, who were willing and able to make the best of a father's obsession with his writing. It is also particularly pleasant to publicize my debt to my parents, a debt that can be neither counted nor measured. To Judith, my wife, goes the expression of my greatest gratitude. Without her gentle prodding, I would have, several times, given up the idea of finishing this work. To her it is both an honor and a pleasure to dedicate this book.

Joseph Lowin

Midrasha Institute of Jewish Studies

Chronology

1928 Born, 17 April, in New York City. Second child of William and Celia (Regelson) Ozick. Niece of Hebrew poet Abraham Regelson.

1933–1941 Attends P.S. 71 in the Pelham Bay section of the Bronx, New York.

1942–1946 Attends Hunter College High School in Manhattan.

1946–1949 Attends New York University. Is graduated with a B.A. in English, *cum laude*. Phi Beta Kappa.

1950 Receives an M.A. in English literature from Ohio State University. Thesis: "Parable in the Later Novels of Henry James."

1952 Marries Bernard Hallote, lawyer.

1950s Works as advertising copywriter for Filene's Department Store in Boston. First article ("How the [Massachusetts] State House got its gold roof") published in the *Boston Globe*. Writes poetry. Begins an ambitious "philosophical" novel, *Mercy, Pity, Peace, and Love,* abandoned after several years.

1964–1965 Instructor in English at New York University. Daughter Rachel born, 24 September 1965. Several poems published in *Judaism* magazine.

1966 *Trust,* a novel six and a half years in the making, published by New American Library. "The Pagan Rabbi," Ozick's most anthologized short story, appears in the *Hudson Review*.

1968 Fellow, National Endowment for the Arts.

1969 "Envy; or Yiddish in America" published in *Commentary*.

1970 Attends the eighth annual American-Israeli Dialogue on Culture and the Arts at the Weizmann Institute in Israel where she presents a controversial paper on Jewish culture entitled "America: Toward Yavneh."

"Envy" chosen as one of the *Best American Short Stories* of year, the first of five Ozick stories to be honored in this manner.

1971 *The Pagan Rabbi and Other Stories,* Ozick's first collection of stories, published by Knopf. Wins Jewish Book Council Award and B'nai B'rith Jewish Heritage Award.

1972 *The Pagan Rabbi* nominated for National Book Award.

1973 Receives American Academy of Arts and Letters Award for Literature.

1974 "Usurpation," a story, and "All the World Wants the Jews Dead," an essay, published in *Esquire.*

1975 "Usurpation" wins first prize in the *0. Henry Prize Stories* competition for the year, a feat two more Ozick stories will duplicate.

1976 *Bloodshed and Three Novellas* published by Knopf.

1977 "Literature and the Politics of Sex: A Dissent" published in *Ms.* Magazine. *Bloodshed* receives Jewish Book Council Award.

1978 "Letter to a Palestinian Military Spokesman," about the murder by terrorists of her Israeli nephew, Imri, a young musician, appears on the op-ed page of the *New York Times,* 16 March.

1979 "Levitation" published in *Partisan Review.* Selected for *Pushcart Prize* collection. "Judaism and Harold Bloom," an essay, appears in *Commentary.*

1980 "The Laughter of Akiva" and "The Shawl," stories, appear in the *New Yorker.* "Carter and the Jews: An American Political Dilemma," an essay, appears as a whole issue of the *New Leader* magazine. Pays visit to renowned scholar of Jewish mysticism, Gershom Scholem, in Jerusalem.

1982 *Levitation: Five Fictions* published by Knopf. Several poems published in *Literary Review.* Awarded a Guggenheim Fellowship. "The Lesson of the Master," an essay on the pernicious influence of Henry James, appears in the *New York Review of Books.* Attends

International Conference of Jewish Writers, sponsored by Rockefeller Institute, in Bellagio, Italy. Delivers landmark paper, "Bialik's Hint."

1983   "Rosa," a story, published in the *New Yorker*. Receives the American Academy and Institute of Arts and Letters Strauss Living Award. *Art & Ardor*, a collection of essays, *The Cannibal Galaxy*, a novel, published by Knopf.

1984   Recipient of honorary doctorates from Yeshiva University and Hebrew Union College. Awarded the Distinguished Service in Jewish Letters Award by the Jewish Theological Seminary and the Distinguished Alumnus Award by New York University. Nominee, PEN/Faulkner Award. "Rosa" wins first prize for the *O. Henry Prize Stories;* volume's editor calls Ozick one of the three best story writers in America.

1985   Delivers the Phi Beta Kappa Oration at Harvard University.

1986   First recipient of the Michael Rea Award for career contribution to the short story.

1987   Publishes four literary essays in the *New York Times Book Review. The Messiah of Stockholm,* a novel, published by Knopf. Receives honorary doctorate from Hunter College. Several of Ozick's translations from the Yiddish appear in the *Penguin Book of Modern Yiddish Verse.*

1988   "The Suicide Note," an interpretation of Primo Levi's *The Drowned and the Saved,* appears in the *New Republic;* "Sholem Aleichem's Revolution," an appreciation of Yiddish culture, published in the *New Yorker.* Elected a member of the American Academy and Institute of Arts and Letters.

Chapter One

A Drugstore in the Bronx

A novel, to use Stendhal's metaphor, is a mirror. Directed upward, it reflects the sky, clear and serene or cloudy and turbulent; angled downward, it reflects the street, animated and industrious or harsh and degrading. However stylistically innovative it may be, a novel almost always means to reflect its times. Above all, a piece of writing, whether an essay or a poem, a novel or a short story, reflects the life of the person who wrote it.

Cynthia Ozick's writings, her poems and essays, her short stories and novels, give a confusing portrait of the artist. The reader must be careful not to read only at the surface of these texts. It would be superficial, for example, to assume that a writer of irrational fantasies, like Ozick, lives in a world divorced from reality and rationality. The contrary is true. A writer of supernatural tales, Ozick is nevertheless a pure rationalist, not believing for a moment in the magic she has created.

We know this from Ozick's fiction and essays. We also know this because Ozick has written several reminiscences, has had feature articles written about her in popular and professional magazines, and has been interviewed extensively, especially lately, for both scholarly journals and television. The reader is cautioned that it would be injudicious to accept on its face *all* that a writer of fictions has said about his or her work and life. Ozick would be the first to agree that one must trust the tale before the teller. Nevertheless, what writers say they have suffered and celebrated, the pronouncements they have made and the stands they have taken cast light on their work, add nuance to the prism through which they are observed and help us to interpret the images in the mirror.

Childhood

Cynthia Ozick was born in New York City on 17 April 1928, the second of two children. Her parents, Celia (née Regelson) and William Ozick, were the proprietors of the Park View Pharmacy

1

in the Pelham Bay section of the Bronx, which at that time was more like a northern suburb than a part of the city. Her parents came to America from a more severe northern climate, the northwest region of Russia. Most important for an insight into Cynthia Ozick's temperament, they came from the *Litvak* (Lithuanian) Jewish tradition of that region. That is a tradition of skepticism, rationalism, and antimysticism, opposed to the exuberant emotionalism of the Hassidic community that flourished in the *Galitzianer* (Galician) portion of Eastern Europe. This information explains, perhaps, why the Hassidic rebbe in Ozick's story "Bloodshed" is such a reasonable man, almost a *Litvak*. Ozick herself, she does not tire of repeating, is a *mitnagged,* an opponent of mystic religion. In her stories, however, she wallows in mysticism.

Ozick describes the life of her parents with reverence. The whole family (although she does not mention her brother in this context) worked in the drugstore, her parents putting in a fourteen-hour day, often closing the store only at one in the morning, with Cynthia herself serving as delivery girl of prescriptions. Ozick describes her mother's life as a life of total generosity, of lavishness, of exuberance, of untrammeled laughter. Inexactitude, and lack of self-consciousness about it, was her mother's hallmark. Her mother was the complete opposite of the perfectionist Cynthia was to become (although Ozick does confess that in her fiction she often gets her facts wrong, to the consternation of her editors). "She was an optimist who ignored trifles," Ozick writes of her mother. "For her, God was not in the details but in the intent."[1]

Perhaps her mother was more of a *Galitzianer* than Ozick knew. Be that as it may, her mother read voraciously, painted, and wrote, on whatever scrap of paper came to hand, her family's memoirs. Ozick vividly recalls accompanying her mother on subway treks downtown to S. Klein's Department Store on Fourteenth Street where she would participate in New York City's depression-era ritual of looking for bargains that E. L. Doctorow was later to describe as "the Flinging of the Textiles."

Although she grew up in the middle of the depression, a "tender hour," as Ozick now calls it, the young girl was not personally affected by the national trauma. She portrays the family pharmacy as giving a sense of comfort and prosperity. Her father, a discreet, quiet man, a *talmid chochem* (Jewish scholar in Yiddishized Hebrew) who knew both Latin and German from his Russian *Gymnasium*

years, ground and mixed powders, and entered prescriptions meticulously in his record book. It is not without interest that, according to his daughter, he wrote beautiful Hebrew paragraphs and
had a Talmudist's rationalism.

Life, however, was not without its childhood hurts. At the age
of five-and-a-half, Cynthia entered heder, the Yiddish-Hebrew
"room" where, in the America of those years, Jewish pupils were
sent for religious instruction. There she was confronted by Rabbi
Meskin (a name she would later transform into Sheskin in *The
Cannibal Galaxy*). The rabbi told Cynthia's *bobe* (grandmother), who
had accompanied her granddaughter to school, in Yiddish, "Take
her home; a girl doesn't have to study." Ozick dates her feminism
to that time and is especially grateful to her grandmother for bringing her back to school on the very next day and insisting that she
be accepted. Even the rabbi, to whom Ozick appears to bear no
lasting animosity, had occasion to be grateful, for this girl had, as
the rabbi would learn, a *goldene kepele,* a "golden head" that caught
on quickly to the lessons. Ozick owes to both her grandmother and
Rabbi Meskin her knowledge of Yiddish.

At P.S. 71 in the Bronx, the hurt was of a different order. At
home and in heder, the young girl was considered intelligent. In
school, on the contrary, she was unceremoniously made to feel an
idiot. She suffered from not being praised by her teachers, although
she was excellent in the bookish arts, such as grammar, spelling,
reading, and writing. While the Pelham Bay section of the Bronx—
"all cattails and weeds"—is described as "such a lovely place" by
Ozick, she found it "brutally difficult to be a Jew" there. She
remembers having had stones thrown at her and being called a
Christ-killer as she ran past the two churches in her neighborhood.
She was particularly uncomfortable in school, because she would
not, on principle, sing the particularly Christian Christmas Carols,
and was made "a humiliated public example for that."

This feeling of humiliation finds its way into *The Cannibal Galaxy,*
Ozick's novel set in a Jewish all-day elementary school. Speaking
of the novel, she describes how she has universalized her experiences
by making them Jewish. In writing *The Cannibal Galaxy,* she asserts,
"I thought of my own suffering, deeply suffering wormlike childhood in grade school; and of my mother's endurances in grade school
as an immigrant child. Those Irish teachers my mother had, and I
had! I used to think it was because they were Irish Catholic. Now

I know it's because . . . carelessness in a teacher of small children can burn in impotence for life, like a brand or horrible sign."[2]

All was not dreariness in her childhood, however, for there remained the world of books. In "A Drugstore in Winter" Ozick describes how reading and "certain drugstore winter dusks" came together thanks to the "Traveling Library" that arrived in her neighborhood every other week.[3] She recalls that the librarians would come into the Park View Pharmacy after their rounds to take a cup of hot coffee at the fountain. Cynthia would come in behind them, having chosen the two fattest volumes from the boxes of books and magazines offered to her. With these books in her hands, she was transported to another world.

She began her reading career, like everybody else, with fairy tales. From her older brother, who "doesn't like me" and "can't abide me," she received the perfect birthday present—books. From her next-door neighbor, Mrs. Brady, she also received books. These books had a magical effect, transforming her from a doltish schoolgirl into "who I am"—a reader, and perhaps a writer. "Some day, when I am free of P.S. 71," she wrote, "I will write stories. Meanwhile, in winter dusk, in the Park View, in the secret bliss of the Violet Fairy Book, I both see and do not see how these grains of life will stay forever."

Cynthia Ozick owes her metamorphosis into a writer to the fact that her mother's brother, Abraham Regelson, was a Hebrew poet of no mean reputation. She feels that, somehow, he paved the way for her to embark on such a "strange" career. Because of him, she says, "it seemed quite natural to belong to the secular world of literature."[4] She also attributes her freedom to choose such a "frivolous" career as writer to her gender. "My father loved me," she told an interviewer. "But I think one of the reasons I felt free from earliest childhood that I was going to be a writer is that if I had been a boy, I would have had to go be something else. . . . My father did finally see that it was serious, that I was in fact possessed. My mother, on the other hand, always knew it was serious."[5]

School became a serious pursuit for Ozick when she entered Hunter College High School in Manhattan. There she was made to feel part of an elite, a Hunter girl, in a place where academic excellence, where mastery of the poetry of Catullus and Ovid, and Horace and Virgil, set one apart from the *turbam vulgam* (the vulgar crowd). Ozick describes this feeling fleetingly in "An Education," where

Una Meyer excels in Latin, and in *Trust,* by contrasting the heroine's fruitful academic experience with her mother's empty-headed schooling at Miss Jewett's finishing school.

Scholar

Ozick does not dwell as much on her college and university years as she does on her childhood. Nevertheless, in a reminiscence she entitled "Washington Square, 1946," she tells how, eager for the new life awaiting her in college, she arrived a day early at the as yet unpopulated and therefore desolate campus of Washington Square College of New York University in fabled Greenwich Village. It is not this quirk of mistiming, however, into which Ozick reads a portent for the future; rather, she fixes on three phenomena encountered that day and sees them as omens for her entry into society: the pretzel man, the Chock Full O' Nuts coffee shop, and a local newsstand. These three are metaphors for something larger and broader than themselves.[6]

The pretzel man, with his cart, on the top of which are mounted wooden sticks looped with cardboard cylinders taken from toilet paper rolls, is the representative of the derelicts who loiter in Washington Square Park; he is their "loftier brother," the "guardian of the garden of the jettisoned." Will not the heroine of "Rosa," the forlorn Holocaust survivor who smashes up her pathetic shop in Brooklyn only to be exiled to a dank hotel room in Florida, be fashioned out of the rib cage of this pretzel man?

The "Chock Full," as it is called by generations of college students, stands for the University Commons, the college cafeteria where the early part of "An Education" is set. The Commons itself stands for "real life." This is the "marketplace of Washington Square, its bazaar, its roiling gossip parlor, its matchmaker's office and arena." The Commons is the seat of society. In it, two important social activities are carried on: the rousing of political passions and the flashing of engagement rings. The latter activity will find its way as a motif into "An Education." The political activism of Cynthia Ozick—evidenced by many of her speeches and by such articles as "The Whole World Wants the Jews Dead" and "Carter and the Jews: An American Political Dilemma"—seems out of place in the career of a writer who puts the phrase "politics is dung" in the mouth of one of her literary characters. Her activism can be traced to the omen of the Chock Full O' Nuts.

The newsstand, finally, is no ordinary newsstand, attached to an ordinary candystore. It carries not only popular magazines and newspapers but also the *Partisan Review,* the journal of the literary avant-garde. It stands for the world of books and authors. It leads "Young Woman Ozick" to purchase her first nontextbook and to browse through the Village's second-hand bookstores—several scenes of *The Messiah of Stockholm* take place in such a store—with the literary longing of youth. Her college years are Ozick's springtime, a time when she will open up into a burgeoning citizen and writer.

But first she would have to become an old man.

Upon graduation from college, Ozick set out for Columbus, Ohio, where, at Ohio State University, she pursued a graduate degree in English literature. Ostensibly intending originally to stay for a Ph.D. and to seek to combine an academic career with professional writing, she would soon abandon—shades of Una Meyer—her formal schooling, having earned a master's degree, with a thesis on "Parable in the Later Novels of Henry James."

What happened, as she confesses in "The Lesson of the Master," is that she "became Henry James."[7] She explains how she was influenced by the later, older, Henry James to become an exclusive devotee, a worshiper even, of literature, one who, having to choose between ordinary human entanglement—real life—and exclusive devotion to art, chooses art. She chose art over life, she says, to her eternal regret. It was a matter of poor timing. The Master, she explains, teaches his lesson toward the end of his life. Ozick says that she acted on the teaching of her mentor at the wrong time, when she was still a youth. It is not clear by exactly what acts Ozick thinks she obeyed her master, for, at the age of twenty-four in 1952, she married Bernard Hallote, who, upon receiving his degree, would become a lawyer for the city of New York, like the heroine of Ozick's Puttermesser stories.

True, during the first thirteen years of marriage, Ozick devoted herself exclusively to what she called "High Art," working on a "philosophical" novel, *Mercy, Pity, Peace, and Love,* called "MPPL" for short. Ozick would abandon this effort after several years; "a long suck on that Mippel," as she would say wryly. She also spent six and a half years, from 1957 to 1963, on *Trust,* another massive novel, brought out in 1966 by the New American Library, thanks to the tender loving care of her agent, Theron Raines, and, especially, her first editor, the late David Segal.

Ozick underwent a cultural transformation during that time. She became an autodidact, mastering for herself the Jewish textual tradition. Having read, at age twenty-five, Leo Baeck's "Romantic Religion," an essay that "seemed to decode the universe for me," she was further influenced, by Heinrich Graetz's *History of the Jews,* to transform *Trust* from an American into a Jewish novel. "It's history as narration," she says in an interview. "History as pageant almost. . . . I fell into these famous old books by Graetz and then it simply exfoliated from the reading of Graetz. Then I began to read everything."[8] Everything included the writings of Franz Rosenzweig and Martin Buber, two Jewish philosophers, but seemed to exclude imaginative literature. Ozick does not go so far, however, as her hero Enoch Vand, who, at the end of *Trust,* abandons worldliness for the exclusive study of Jewish texts.

Writer of Stature

Cynthia Ozick did not abandon the world. Nor did she abandon writing. She began to wrestle with the term *Jewish writer.* In 1965 she published several poems on Jewish themes in *Judaism* magazine, and produced "The Pagan Rabbi," published in 1966, the same year as *Trust.* In 1965 her daughter Rachel was born, confirming Ozick's return to everyday entanglements. She also produced "Envy; or Yiddish in America," published in *Commentary* in 1969. This story, about the Yiddish literary community in America, was prompted by an invitation from Irving Howe and Eliezer Greenberg to translate several poems from the Yiddish for their 1969 anthology, *A Treasury of Yiddish Poetry.*

By this time Ozick has acquired all the eccentric habits that compose and comfort a writer. Before a recent illness, she wore her clothes to bed, she says, because she wrote at night, beginning at midnight and quitting only when the birds began to chirp noisily in the morning. She was usually incommunicado until noon when she got on the phone and remained there for hours at a time. She has three close literary friends and together they form a tightly knit circle, encouraging each other and talking incessantly about literature. She is also a voluminous letter and postcard writer, a task she feels obligated to undertake before getting down to her serious writing.

When the time comes to collect her complete correspondence, as

far flung as it is, it may be difficult; it will be a much easier task
for scholars to deal with the manuscripts of her serious writing.
Ozick reveals that the first draft of her writing—excluding the
typescript—is also her last draft, because she never goes on to a
second sentence until she has perfected the first. This quirk will
have aesthetic consequences in "Puttermesser and Xanthippe," as
will be seen later on in this study. When she writes, she finds that
she has entered, trancelike, into the world of language, where she
lives a life that belongs exclusively to the page, without the "im-
pediments of externality. Bodyless. Peopleless." It would not be an
exaggeration to suggest that it is this complete seizure by language
that has made Cynthia Ozick a writer of stature.

Indeed, given Ozick's stature, it would be only a slight exaggeration to suggest that, in the admittedly narrow world of fine
literature, the 1970s and 1980s seem to constitute a miniature "Age
of Ozick." Five of her stories have been chosen for republication in
the yearly anthologies of *Best American Short Stories.* Three of her
stories have won first prize in the O. Henry Prize Stories competition. The editor of the 1984 volume called her one of the three
greatest American writers of stories living today. She was nominated
for the National Book Award and the PEN/Faulkner Award. She
has won outright half a dozen coveted awards and grants, including
both a Guggenheim and a National Endowment for the Arts Fellowship. She was also given that precious commodity—time—in
the form of the American Academy and Institute of Arts and Letters
Mildred and Harold Strauss Living Award, which provided her with
an annual grant of $35,000, tax-free, for five years to pursue her
craft. She has received several honorary doctorates and was invited
to deliver the Phi Beta Kappa Oration at Harvard University.

Papers on her work are delivered at the convention of the Modern
Language Association. Her novels and stories are taught in college
courses, both in America and abroad. Harold Bloom, the eminent
literary critic at Yale, has edited a volume of criticism on her work.
She is the subject of several books. Ruth Wisse, a respected literary
essayist for *Commentary,* has called her the leader of a Movement,
an admittedly nonexistent movement, of Jewish writers whose fiction draws extensively from the Jewish textual tradition. When Bill
Moyers needed an American Jewish cultural hero to interview for
his "Heritage Conversations" series on public television, he turned
to Cynthia Ozick. Her public appearances regularly draw large au-

diences, although it appears to her that more people come to see her than sit at home to read her. A crowd of 2,500 people showed up at Lincoln Center in June 1984 when she was interviewed for the Dialogue Forum Series.

Knopf publishes her novels as they come off her pen and also collections of her previously published essays and short stories. Paperbacks follow regularly, and she has been translated into eleven languages, including French, Hebrew, and even Finnish. She has ready entrée into the *New Yorker,* where Robert Gottlieb, her publisher at Knopf, is now editor. For a while in 1987, she wrote a monthly column for the *New York Times Book Review.*

And yet, says Cynthia Ozick, she still feels like a beginner. Perhaps for some reason she needs to feel like a beginner. She tells how, as recently as 1982, "Puttermesser and Xanthippe"—one of her best stories—was rejected by several magazines, among them the *New Yorker, Atlantic, Harper's* and *Playboy,* before it was accepted by *Salmagundi.* "*Atlantic* and *Harper's,*" she says, "have consistently sent back everything, in whatever form (verse, fiction, non-fiction), I have ever submitted, and this has been going on for twenty-five years. In certain ways I am still a hopeful tyro; my psyche is still fixed in that attitude, I believe. I have never recovered from early neglect. Who does?"[9] Since the interview in which these remarks were made, *Harper's* has published the essay by Ozick about her first day at New York University. The *New Yorker*'s rejection of "Puttermesser and Xanthippe" came about, it appears, as a result of the settlement of a threatened lawsuit by a day school headmaster who had read himself, justifiably or not, into an Ozick story, "The Laughter of Akiva," which had appeared in the *New Yorker* in 1980, and which subsequently had to be transformed—good luck arising from bad—into Ozick's second novel, *The Cannibal Galaxy.* For a while, however, it appeared to Ozick that her publishing career was doomed, for the *New Yorker* had cancelled for a year the reading agreement the magazine had with Ozick. She suffered terribly from that episode, she says, as she had suffered ten years earlier, to a different degree, when the Yiddish poet Jacob Glatstein saw himself in "Envy," and bore Ozick a grudge until his dying day.

Ozick's problem with real people in her fiction stems perhaps from the distinction she makes—only a membrane's thickness worth of distinction—between herself as a writer and herself as a citizen. A good writer, Ozick asserts, is necessarily a bad citizen. When on the job, fiction writers are programmed "not to polish [ego] up for public relations," but to make ego serve rapture, "the rapture of language and drama, and also the rapture of deceit."[10] Ozick maintains that there is a compact between the novelist and the reader that the novelist will lie and that the reader of the lie will accept it as such. She is hurt when the reader takes her lying literally.

No such compact exists, of course, for the writer of essays, although it is not always clear when an Ozick essay becomes a fiction. In an essay the writer promises to tell the truth, or at least what is really on her mind. As an essayist Cynthia Ozick is not the wounded sparrow she sometimes appears as a writer of fiction. She has never refrained from expressing her opinions forcefully, nor has she had difficulty getting them into the public arena. Cynthia Ozick has made some harsh declarations as a polemicist—modeling herself to some extent on Maurice Samuel, a curmudgeonly essayist and lecturer famous for his bluntness, whom she admired—and she has never been taken to task for them the way she has been taken to task for her fiction. On the contrary, her straightforwardness has earned her almost universal respect.

Ozick is especially forceful and intense about conveying a greater understanding of the role Judaism has played—and continues to play—in the development of Western civilization. Nothing wounds her more, nothing angers her more, she told interviewer William Berkowitz at Lincoln Center, than the charge that Jewish writers are parochial. First of all, she says accusingly, it is a charge made essentially only against Jewish writers, mainly due to an absence of goodwill, to obtuseness. Second, she asserts, the charge is not true. "The entire planet," she proclaims, "is founded on Jewish literature, on Torah." And she calls for an assimilation of a new type, one that reverses the normal direction. "The world ought to be reassimilated into the Jewish tradition. I want gentiles in our community to say *Shavuot* and to learn what it means."[11]

Ozick also has a wish for the Jews. She wants Jews to be particular, but not separate. She wants Jews to see that "to be a Jew," as she told Bill Moyers, "is quite the opposite of the parochial; to be a Jew is the expression of universalism."

These ideas of Ozick the citizen necessarily find their echo in Cynthia Ozick's fiction of the 1970s and 1980s, in her short stories and novellas, collected in three volumes, and in *The Cannibal Galaxy* (1983) and *The Messiah of Stockholm* (1987), Ozick's latest novels.

In her fiction, Ozick's opinions will be nuanced, muted, often contradicted, transformed into something else. That something else is Ozick's art. For, in the end, in her fiction, Ozick is an artist. To get an idea of the complexities and beauties of that art, the reader is invited to read on, to enter, on a dusky winter evening, by way of a reflecting mirror, into the drugstore of the following pages. The mirrors in that drugstore reflect the sky and the street, and, in ways that history may one day make clear, our times.

Chapter Two

A Poet Is Born and Unmade: "A Riddle" and "Envy; or Yiddish in America"

Poems composed by Cynthia Ozick have appeared in such prestigious literary journals as the *Literary Review* and the *Virginia Quarterly Review*. Her verse has been disseminated as well in important Jewish periodicals, including *Commentary, Midstream,* and *Judaism.* Some of her "Jewish" pieces have been anthologized in *Voices within the Ark: The Modern Jewish Poets.* Ozick is also a premier translator of Yiddish poetry; her translations have been published in *A Treasury of Yiddish Poetry* (1969) and in the 1987 *Penguin Book of Modern Yiddish Verse.*

And yet, when it was suggested to Ozick not long ago that she permit her poems and poetry translations to be collected in a single volume, she demurred. Her scruples, she intimated, stemmed from her "overwhelming sense that I'm not a poet and shouldn't masquerade as one." She did not deny that her verse may be of sufficiently high quality to merit being collected between the covers of a book of their own. It was a matter, rather, of "the market" for such a book on the one hand, and of her current literary preoccupation with prose on the other.

Ozick admits, however, that she "was once obsessed and possessed by poetry," but that the furnace of poetry has cooled down considerably. She says, further, that since she has not written a poem—except for Yiddish translations—in more than twenty years, she would be embarrassed to be looked on as a poet. After all, she says, "T. S. Eliot, or someone else equally authoritative on the subject, once said that all writers are poets until the age of thirty-five, but only poets are poets forever, until death."[1]

Ozick is being neither disingenuous nor coy on "the subject" of her poetry. And yet, although it might embarrass Ozick to be called a poet, she is, nevertheless, unabashedly a writer who has composed poems of serious content and to which a great deal of stylistic attention has been paid. These poems, therefore, deserve attention for the role they play in Ozick's oeuvre, both for their intrinsic qualities and for the light they shed on her more mature work.

In talking about her early novel *Trust,* a novel written at the age when the poet becomes a "writer"—and is no longer a poet—Ozick once averred that that book was written with the meticulous care usually reserved for poetry. In fact, she said, one might go so far as, metaphorically, to call every paragraph of that novel a poem. More than one critic of Ozick's prose has complained that she tends to "overwrite," and that her prose style is too exquisite for narrative. If this characterization of her prose is true, then it may indeed derive from Ozick's early seizure by the muse of poetry.

An initial reading of Ozick's body of poems reveals the first blossoming of many themes that would subsequently flower in her later prose fiction.

It would also reveal Ozick's willingness to take risks in matters of poetic form and diction. Ozick is at times audacious, and there is even a sort of stylistic consistency in the audaciousness of her prosody. She has quatrains in which only the second and fourth lines rhyme, as in "Apocalypse," "The Engineers," and "Stile." Often her poems will resist closure, creating a feeling not necessarily of open-endedness but of circularity. The closing lines of "To My Uncle, a Craftsman," "The Artist, Ha, Ha," and "Footnote to Lord Action" turn the poem back onto itself and in doing so turn the poem into a parable. One of her poems, appropriately entitled "The Seventeen Questions of Rabbi Zusya," is literally a series of seventeen questions. Another poem, "When That With Tragic Rapture Moses Stood," contains within it a nine-word alliteration, describing Moses the lawgiver as "he whose head history has hammered holy, hoary, heavy." Many of Ozick's poems read like rabbinical commentaries, even if they are not all commentaries of biblical texts. Three of these, "The Engineers," "The Wonder-Teacher," and "Urn-Burial," are commentaries, variously, on an article in the *New York Times,* a passage from Martin Buber, and a poem by Sir Thomas Browne, all quoted as epigraphs to the poems. "Yom Kippur, 5726," about the holiest day in the Jewish calendar, a day of fasting, is a poem in which the meaning of the expressions for eating and for abstaining from eating are redirected into expressions of theological doubt. Thus, for example, the poet both abstains from the congregation and does not take the meal of Torah. Because history has fed on too much Jew, the poet requires that God, on this Day of Atonement, atone for His absence.

The poem "The Arrest," about the Messiah who demands the freezing of time before he will come, is a tour de force of technical virtuosity. That poem is divided into five stanzas, including three six-line stanzas urging the reader to "wait," "withhold," and "depose," in order to make room for the conquering general that is the Messiah. The pyrotechnics of the poems can be traced, foremostly, to the rhyme-scheme of these stanzas. Taking interior rhyme to its furthest limits, the first and second words of each sestet are, first, repetitions of the same word; they are then made to rhyme with the last word of the second verse of each sestet. In a feat of stanzaic acrobatics, the third and fourth lines of each stanza are made to rhyme with the third and fourth lines of each of the other two stanzas, while the fifth and sixth lines of each stanza end in the same words as the other two. The effect of this accumulation of repetition is to mesmerize the reader and, indeed, to cause the reader to wait, if not for the coming of the Messiah, then at least for the effect of the poem to wear off. The mesmerizing power of the two terminal verses of each stanza comes not only from the rhyme but also from their persistent rhythm. "Do not oblige life by too much living it" is followed by "Do not entice trust by too much giving it." This line is in turn mirrored by "Do not insult the Red Sea by too much cleaving it." These three lines, taken together, create the same effect of deadening monotony as the sound of primitive drumming. The three lines are also evocative of Ozick's later fiction. The enigmatic nature of the poem—causing the reader to puzzle over its meaning, not necessarily always successfully—can be traced to the reinforcement provided by the hammering quality of the sixth and last lines of each of the stanzas in question: "I have had several flats but I am on the way"; "I have lied several times but I am on the way"; "I have been delivered of several hallucinations but I am on the way."

The riddle of a Messiah having several flats, because he is riding not on a white mule but in a khaki army truck can be approached by reference to the characterization by Moses Maimonides, the twelfth-century Jewish philosopher, of the Messiah as a general who returns political sovereignty to the Jewish people. The lying and the hallucinations of the Messiah may refer to the many false messiahs, like Jacob Frank and Sabbatai Zevi, who have plagued the

Jewish people with their false claims. The poem is problematic because it is not clear to what extent Ozick identifies with the speaker in the poem, demanding so much passivity, however ironically. But Ozick's poem is dazzling not because the reader is able to decipher all of its riddles but rather because of the intricacy of the way meaning in the poem is strived for.

"A Riddle"

Many of Ozick's poems, symbolic and arcane, are presented, playfully, as riddles, and as invitations to the reader to struggle for meaning. A case in point is the poem called, and presented in the form of, "A Riddle," complete with an answer to the riddle supplied as the poem's ending. This poem, as becomes clear from a close reading of it, requires detailed analysis, for it is illustrative of the artist's creative imagination. It is also written against the background of Ozick's lifelong philosophical, theological, and artistic concern with what she has termed the "Jewish idea." This is the idea, found in the antipagan religion knows as Judaism, but not by any means tantamount to Judaism, which says that the artifacts of a culture, for that culture to be considered Jewish, must help us to interpret and judge the world—both God's world and man's:

A Riddle

I walk on two legs.
The right wears a tough boot and is steadfast.
The other is got up in a Babylonish slipper of purple laces,
and hops, hops.
All day they are lacing and unlacing the ties,
the little one in his first cap and the old one in his last shawl,
in, out,
digressing through the eyelets
as past a chain of windows the turn of one bird
grows four birds, their four bills painted
with fleet phantasmal jokes.

My dancer foot is honeyed,
and its way is where it wills.

My stronger foot is sternly shod and treads behind a hedge.
The toe is the pointer, the heel in logic follows,

and mediating is the arch exegetical,
latching the former to the latter, the rear to the forward,
and the last to the first.
Its laces rein, its print governs.
The prime one in his prime runs to keep pace.

My stepping shoe is hard,
but the way has not worn it.

I have walked time thin
to bring Messiah in.
My dancer foot can kick,
my binding step may prick,
but my slipper and my boot
shall stamp my exile out.

Know how I comment,
solve my name in a moment.

Answer:
> *Talmud, with its two elements:*
> *Aggadah (legend, tale, and lore) and*
> *Halachah (law and code)*[2]

In this poem Cynthia Ozick uses the fact that humans walk on
two feet as a metaphor to designate the bipolarity of the Jewish
textual and cultural tradition. The poem says nothing directly about
the *Western* cultural and textual tradition and yet, by using footwear
as a further organizing metaphor, Ozick's poem seems to allude to
the "buskin," or "cothurnus," a thick-soled boot, laced halfway to
the knee, worn by actors in Greek and Roman tragedy. A buskin
is not only a shoe, but also, by metonymy, a tragedy itself. By
extension as well, something dignified, somewhat stilted, and yet
tragic, may be said to be "cothurnal."

In "A Riddle" Ozick shows how the classic textbook of the Jewish
tradition, the Talmud, is different from the quintessential Western
text, the tragedy. A tragedy may be said to travel on its cothurnus.
The Talmud, by contrast, walks on two legs, one leg wearing a
"tough boot," the other wearing a "slipper of purple laces." One
shoe is stern and sober, "steadfast." The other spends its time
dancing and hopping. The end of the riddle explains that the Talmud

has two major types of discourse. One of these, the stern and steadfast one, is used for the discussion of the Law. The Talmud has another side as well, less severe, in which tales are told in order to illustrate the Law. These two types of discourse are known as Halachah, law (literally, "the going"), and Aggadah, legend (literally, "the telling").

To solve the riddle of what walks on two such disparate legs, the poem divides itself into four parts. After a four-line introduction to the Talmud's two legs, and the fact that its shoes come from the Babylonian exile of the Jews, there follow a nine-line description of the playful foot and a nine-line description of the stern foot. These two stanzas are perfectly balanced, each one further divided into a seven-line description and a two-line discussion.

The Aggadic activity is an all-day affair, indeed it is carried on at both extremes of a person's lifetime, from the time the little boy dons his first cap (the covering of the head is a religious injunction dating only from the time of the Talmud) to the time the old man is laid to eternal rest, wrapped in his prayer shawl. This section reminds us that the Talmud is full of disgressions, a main story interrupted by a subsidiary story, which for the moment takes on the dimensions of a main story and turns the story into which it has been embedded into a frame, or a series of frames.

The chain of four window frames, in the simile beginning in the ninth line of the poem, provides the limits of the artistic text. Through these artistic frames, the magic of perception transforms one bird into four, and reality into playful fantasy. The stanza concludes with information about the dancing foot. Jewish custom has insisted that initiation into learning be a sweet process. There is even a custom to put a dab of honey on a child's first alphabet book, so that the child will associate learning with sweetness. The Aggadic component of the Talmud is similarly pedagogical. It speaks of the fancy that derives from fantasy and of desire and the freedom to fulfill desire. To say, as the poem does, that Aggadah's "way is where it wills" is to imply that Aggadah has no way at all. The "way" is reserved for the next stanza, the stanza that deals with that part of the Talmud that discusses the Law.

One of the functions of the Talmud, in addition to its role as exegesis of the Torah, is to create a "hedge" about the Law. The legal part of the Talmud is so careful that laws not be trespassed that it creates new laws—hedges—whose observance will prevent the observer from transgressing the biblical laws. The legal aspect of the Talmud may be stern but it is logical, consistent, the heel always following the toe. (Indeed, the Hebrew word for "consistent" derives from the same root as the Hebrew word for "heel.") Whereas the previous stanza used the words first and last to trace the human life cycle, and did so sentimentally, using the verb "to lace," the current stanza picks up the words "last" and "first" and, in a series of expressions that imply earliness and lateness, insists, by using the verb "to latch" in place of "to lace," on the necessary connection, hard and fast, between the stages of the human life cycle.

The legal component of the Talmud has no patience with frivolous lacing; it speaks only of organic latching. The laces of Halachah do not meander; they rein, that is to say, they prevent fanciful soaring. They function like the hedge of the stanza's first line, because the printed word is meant not for stories but for governing the world. The meaning of the seventh line of this part of the poem is enigmatic. Who is "the prime one"? A hint is provided by the use of the expression "in his prime" immediately following. This describes the stage in Talmud study that is midway between that of "the little one in his first cap" and "the old one in his last shawl." The "prime of life" is apparently the stage suited for the study of the legal aspect of the Talmud; that is the age of leadership and mastery and bespeaks as well the seeming primacy of the halachic mode. The Aggadist— the youth or the old man—dances. The Halachist, as the final two lines of this stanza have it, does not have a "dancer foot," but has, rather, a "stepping shoe." Compared to the flexibility of the Babylonish slipper of purple laces, the stepping shoe is hard. Somehow, however, it does not wear down, perhaps because it has a way that is indeed a way.

Lest we be led to believe that the legal aspect of the Talmud is preeminent, the poem provides a fourth part, made up of four rhyming couplets. (This, by the way, is the only part of the poem to use rhyme at all.) These rhyming couplets hint at the necessary bond between Halachah and Aggadah, the one leading to the other. The goal of the Talmud is neither Halachah nor Aggadah; these are but means for the bringing of the Messiah. Both are necessary for the achievement of this goal in history.

The way a goldsmith beats gold to a fine thinness, so the Talmud, which is a testimony to the historicity of the Jewish people, has wrought time to an exquisite gossamer. The free kicking of the dancing slipper and the restrained pricking of the stepping boot

work in harmony to achieve one goal—to "stamp out . . . exile."
The poem concludes with a final couplet, this time a rhyme for the
eye and not for the ear. This couplet implies that it is not enough
to know that the Talmud is a commentary on the Bible. One must
know *how* the Talmud comments. By using both the law and the
lore, the Talmud strives to solve the riddle of the Jewish idea.

This poem is central to Cynthia Ozick's writing activity. It is
curious that Ozick, a master of prose fiction, uses poetry to describe
the essence of the Jewish cultural tradition. Throughout her career
Ozick has represented the Jewish tradition as the arch enemy of
poetry. In "Toward a New Yiddish," Ozick asserts that a poem is
the equivalent of an idol. "An idol is a-thing-that-subsists-for-its-
own-sake-without-a-history; significantly that is also what a poem
is."[3] In this essay, delivered as a lecture in 1970, Ozick calls for a
new type of literature, a literature that derives from what Alvin
Rosenfeld, writing about Ozick, has called "classically Jewish con-
ceptions of culture, especially as these relate to art and insist on the
imperatives of art to understand, interpret, and judge human action."[4]

Hebraism and Hellenism

In "Toward a New Yiddish" Cynthia Ozick calls for a literature
that is similar not only to her own prose but also to her own poetry.
In that essay she calls for a "liturgical literature—not necessarily
prayer, but a "literature that includes history." Again, Rosenfeld
explains that, for Ozick, Hebraism, the polar opposite of Hellenism

has its own presiding presence, the God of History, in whose service
human conduct is bound to commandment and feeling is channeled into
deed. Between these two irreconcilables—Hellenism and Hebraism, the
gods of Nature and the God of History, Pan and Moses, ecstasy and
prophecy—there is an eternal quarrel, one whose tensions have long pulled
at Cynthia Ozick's imagination, acting as the driving energy of much of
her work.[5]

In another of her essays, "Bialik's Hint" (1983), Ozick makes a
vast stride toward solving the quarrel between Hebraism and Hellenism of which Rosenfeld speaks. Hayyim Nahman Bialik, the
Jewish national poet, wrote an essay in 1915 called "Aggadah and
Halakha," in which he, like Ozick in "A Riddle," confronts the
two strands of talmudic thought, its law and its lore. Writing

against the notion of art for art's sake, Bialik notes that Aggadah and Halacha are neither separate nor separable entities but that Aggadah, the story-telling half of the Talmud, its free, soaring imagination, always leads to Halacha, Jewish moral seriousness, obligation, duty. In her essay, Ozick sees, in the duality of the Talmud's structure, the hint of a message for modern times. For Ozick, "to be a Jew is to be old in history." Ozick claims that throughout Jewish history, not only in Golden Age Spain, Renaissance Italy, and Enlightenment Europe, but also in the time of the Talmud, Jewish culture mingled with other cultures and was enriched by them. Ozick asserts further that the rabbinic ideal of Jewish study-centeredness stems not from Scripture but from Hellenism itself. Socrates, and not Moses, she maintains, was specifically a teacher of students. The Talmud, therefore, the richest expression of purely Jewish culture, owes much to the freedom of thought and imagination proposed by gentile culture. "As with Greece," concludes Ozick, "so with the Enlightenment." Ozick proposes in 1983, using the same bipolarity of Halacha and Aggadah, what she had already accomplished in her 1965 poem, the expression of a Jewish idea in poetry. Poetry—indeed all literature, including fiction—need not lead to idolatry. Poetry, even in the twentieth century, may also be used in the service of prophecy and may use its own ways and means to bring redemption to the world.

That the world is in need of redemption by a work of literature we see in many of Cynthia Ozick's works, including not only her latest novel, *The Messiah of Stockholm,* but also in her story about the dilemma of Yiddish poets and novelists in America.

Yiddish Culture in America

The word "or" in the title of "Envy; or Yiddish in America" sends to the reader the message that the story is to be read as though it had been written in an alternating current. The work of fiction would therefore be a double one, simultaneously telling two stories. The other words of the title suggest that readers will be required to alternate their perspective, as they read, between the story of an individual's pathos and the epic of a people's history.

On its deeper level, the tale is about "Yiddish in America," that is, about the confrontation of a thousand-year-old Jewish culture that flourished in Eastern Europe with the modernity of that most modern of modern states, America. It is about the struggle of this liturgical culture to survive in its new secular setting. Given that setting's apparent disinterest in things historical, Yiddish culture's struggle seems tragic, doomed to failure. The other half of the story, about "Envy," is a *conte à clef*. It concerns the jealousy of an un-translated Yiddish poet, roughly modeled on Jacob Glatstein, for the worldly success of an Americanized Yiddish novelist and short story writer, patterned after Nobel laureate Isaac Bashevis Singer. This latter character's success, if not Singer's, is directly traceable to the fact that his work has been blessed with translations that have made his work accessible to American readers.

Of course, it is not true, as the story asserts, that Yiddish poets in this century in America have not been translated into English. Witness Irving Howe's *Treasury of Yiddish Poetry*, which by any criteria must be considered a popular publishing success. This anthology contains selections not only from the work of such poets as H. Leivick, Moshe Leib Halpern, and Chaim Grade, but also several poems from the oeuvre of Jacob Glatstein.

One of the poems in the collection, David Einhorn's "The Last to Sing," was translated by Cynthia Ozick and gave birth to an essay by her on the art of translation from the Yiddish. In the essay, entitled "Prayer Leader," named after the rejected English trans-lation for the Yiddish expression *bal-tfile*, Ozick makes several points that are germane to the issues being discussed here. The first is that, almost despite itself, Yiddish poetry has a "liturgical impulse" and seems in some ways to be a "continuation" of Scripture.[6] Ozick is bothered here, as she was in "Toward a New Yiddish," by the language question. To translate from Yiddish into English is to try to render a Jewish idea in a Christian medium. How can one translate *bal-tfile*, who is an "underpaid secondary cantor," into an English expression like "Prayer Leader" without at the same time turning this Jewish religious functionary into a Quaker?

Ozick tells in this essay how she learned several lessons from her early experience as a translator. Not the least of these lessons is that to translate a poem well one is required to turn it not into a trans-lation but into a poem, into the poem itself, into a poem equal in authority to the original, and, therefore, into an original poem. Time and again, in her fiction, Ozick will perform this transforming activity, rewriting other people's poems and stories into works of art of her own, and arrogating to herself the artistic right to do so.

She will do this twice with Jacob Glatstein, once in "Envy," and once in the *Penguin Book of Modern Yiddish Verse,* where she has translated no fewer than ten of Glatstein's poems.

One of Glatstein's poems translated by Ozick has particular resonance for a chapter centered on the conflict between Jewish particularity and universality. Glatstein-Ozick's "Genesis" is a liturgical poem in which the poetic speaker addresses himself, and, in this case, herself, to God and notes that "the Jewish success in spreading the idea of a universal God, first through Christianity and Islam, then through secular messianism of modern political movements, benefited neither the Jews nor the God whose messengers they presumed to be."[7] The poem suggests to God that He begin His world anew—hence the title "Genesis"—scaling down his message to a smaller audience. "Why don't we both go home and start over,/ from the very beginning,/ out of our littleness? . . . We'll both be provincial,/God and His poet . . . No one beyond our borders will hear my name,/ or Yours." Glatstein in this poem is far from Edelshtein, the poet in "Envy," who seeks nothing more fervently than to break out beyond the borders of the Jewish people.

It cannot be overly emphasized that the poem "Genesis" is not Glatstein's alone. It also belongs, by way of translation, to Ozick. Ozick views her translation from the Yiddish as a holy task, as a work of memorialization, as a way of saving Yiddish from the ashes of the Holocaust. "How strange," she writes, "to live in a time when murdered Yiddish begins to take on some of the holiness of liturgy and hallowed Hebrew becomes workaday *mamaloshn.* —In any case I feel the Shekhine comes to rest on the pen struggling to translate from the Yiddish memorializing text."[8]

Ozick's story "Envy," we may be sure, was written in the same memorializing spirit as her translations from the Yiddish. Unfortunately, that is not the way "Envy" was taken by the Yiddish literary community. In a speech given in 1972 on the occasion of her reception of the B'nai B'rith Book Award for the book of stories in which "Envy" found its permanent home, Ozick tries to heal the wound caused to Jacob Glatstein by her story. She explains that, having, as a young adult, abandoned her Yiddish family background for the world of English and American literature, she was given the opportunity to "return" to her roots by Irving Howe and Eliezer Greenberg, the editors of the anthology, who invited her to try her hand as a translator for their book of Yiddish poetry. Her "return" turned out to be a complete transformation, because, as she asserts, she became the poet who had written the poem she was translating. "And then," she goes on, "because all this had happened, I wrote a story called 'Yiddish in America.' I wrote it as an elegy, a lamentation, a celebration."[9] She wrote the story, she says, because she felt that "translation would never, never engender the splendor and richness and dearness and idiosyncrasy of Yiddish." But that is not the way the story was taken. "I found myself and the magazine which had published my story branded as enemies of Yiddish and Yiddishkayt. One writer compared me with Goebbels and with Moscow. . . . To my grief, Jacob Glatstein was among those who misunderstood, who took sorrowing love for hatred and mourning for self-hatred."[10] Ozick wrote her *bintel brief*—a Yiddish phrase for a letter to the editor of a Yiddish newspaper asking for advice with interpersonal problems—in an effort to seek reconcilement with the shade of Jacob Glatstein, who at the time of the speech was already dead. Jacob Glatstein the artist, and moreover the devotee of true art, had he been able to divorce *himself* from the story, would have been the first to admit—indeed, to proclaim—that what Cynthia Ozick has written about Yiddish culture in America, from both the microcosmic and the macrocosmic perspectives, has the ring of truth.

Glatstein himself had no less a critical eye than Ozick and was even more critical of Isaac Bashevis Singer than the fictional poet Edelshtein is of the fictional novelist Ostrover. In fact, Glatstein wrote an essay on Singer that may have served, no less than the story of the translation of his poetry, as the impetus for Ozick's story. In this essay, Glatstein takes Singer severely to task for his "unpleasant stories, . . . tales of horror and eroticism," filled with "all kinds of spiritual and physical depravity."[11] Singer's heroes are, according to Glatstein, dehumanized, committing ugly deeds of "villainy, brutality and cynicism at every turn." It does not surprise Glatstein, however, that Singer is popular among American readers who have no Jewish background, including, especially, young American readers of fiction. Glatstein even goes so far as to imply that Singer is not a Jewish writer at all. "A Bashevis story has a Jewish façade," writes Glatstein, "but paradoxically it reads better and pleasanter in English than in the original Yiddish. His stories are more attuned to the non-Jewish than to the Jewish reader, to whom Bashevis' themes are a distasteful blend of superstition and shoddy mysticism."[12] Given his judgment of his colleague's literary worth, Glatstein is perplexed that Singer should have gained status as a world literary figure. It is on the skeleton of Glatstein's article, in an effort to account for the tension displayed by the Yiddish poet, that Ozick builds the edifice of her story, "Envy; or Yiddish in America."

The story of Hershele Edelshtein, Yiddish poet, is among the most poignant in Cynthia Ozick's oeuvre, rivaled only by "Rosa" for first place in this category. Sixty-seven years old, a widower, childless, he earns his living by giving lectures on the death of Yiddish at synagogues and community centers. He is the author of four volumes of Yiddish verse himself, much of it acknowledged among the cognoscenti to have attained a high standard of excellence. But, untranslated into English, and, therefore, unknown, Hershele struggles against his present degradation by living in the past and for the future. He remembers particularly—and embellishes touchingly—one scene from his childhood, a scene he is able to call to mind at will by staring fixedly at almost any object, such as a garbage can lid or a street light. His father had been a *melamed*, an itinerant teacher, who once took Hershele with him from their hometown of Minsk to Kiev. His job was to teach Jewish Scripture to the son of a semi-assimilated rich Jew who had changed his name from Katz to Kirilov and who insisted that his son Avremeleh (a Yiddish diminutive for the name Abraham) be called Alexei.

Edelshtein remembers from that sojourn the opulence of the Kirilov home, the little boy's collection of mechanical toys, and Avremeleh's ability to absorb learning. Edelshtein fantasizes an adult life for the Kirilov boy, sometimes making him into an engineer for today's Soviet Union, sometimes imagining him murdered by the Nazis at Babi Yar. Edelshtein also has another fantasy about his relations with Alexei, a fantasy bordering on the lewd and licentious, a fantasy worthy of the imagination of the man toward whom Edelshtein directs much of his animosity, Yiddish novelist and storywriter Yankel Ostrover.

Edelshtein has for years belonged to a circle of Yiddish writers and intellectuals. Edelshtein's best "friend" is Ben Baumzweig. Baumzweig, as the editor of *Bitterer Yam* (Bitter Sea), periodically publishes his friend's poetry and patronizes him for the fact that he cannot get published in a magazine with greater diffusion. Paula, Ben's wife, sarcastically calls the low-circulation magazine "Invisible Ink" and patronizes Edelshtein in her own way for the fact that

Edelshtein's late wife, Mireleh, had had seven miscarriages without bringing one pregnancy to term.

The glue that holds the friendship between Edelshtein and Baumzweig together is their common hatred for Yankel Ostrover. Ostrover is the feted and touted darling of the American literary establishment, a celebrity novelist. He gives his public what they crave, un-Jewish lewdness thinly veiled by a Jewish gauze. His charm stems from the fact that his public can never tell what they are getting, a Jewish Jew playing at being a Gentile, or a Jewish Gentile playing at being a Jew. Ostrover's essential quality, as can be seen from both his stories and his disdainful answers to questions posed to him after public readings, is his exaggerated playfulness, his lack of moral or artistic seriousness. Edelshtein is enraged at Ostrover's fame, both because it misrepresents Yiddish culture and because Edelshtein craves Ostrover's recognition.

Pathetically, Edelshtein believes that translation is the answer to his dilemma. Is that not how Ostrover became famous, he asks? He goes in search of someone to help him "reach" out, beyond the Yiddish-reading public, first, to Ostrover's publisher, then to one of Ostrover's translators, a European-born, American-educated former poet. She refuses Edelshtein's approach because she would gain neither money nor prestige—gauged by entrée into the gentile literary world—by translating the Yiddish poetry of an unknown. Edelshtein then goes to court Hannah, the niece of another of Ostrover's translators, the mad mathematician Vorovsky. American-born Hannah reads Yiddish fluently and even knows some of Edelshtein's poetry by heart. She is, however, enamored of Ostrover's Yiddish prose and despite Edelshtein's repeated entreaties, she refuses his offers. "You don't interest me," she says coldly. "I would have to be interested."[13]

Edelshtein, defeated, forlorn, in need of consolation, steps into a telephone booth and dials the number of a Christian missionary who advertises on the walls of telephone booths. In place of consolation Edelshtein receives a sermon on the outdatedness of Judaic exclusivity and on Judaism's universalization by Christianity. Responding that he is unwilling to accept Jesus, Edelshtein is abused by a blast of anti-Semitic vituperation, containing all the clichés of the genre. The story ends on a plangent note, with Edelshtein shouting back into the telephone, "Nazi! . . . On account of you I have no translator!" (100). Is Edelshtein as pathetic as he appears?

A reading of the alternate face of the story, about "Yiddish in America," reveals in Edelshtein an important spokesman for the Jewish idea.

Ozick refuses all temptation to make Edelshtein into a hero at the end of the story. For her, and for us, he is what he is. And yet, if one is correct to say that Edelshtein is an ordinary man, petty, mean, self-serving, one is no less correct to observe that he is a Jew who lives enthusiastically within his history, the bearer of an extraordinary tradition.

Edelshtein shares this duality with Vorovsky's niece, but his is the obverse of Hannah's coin. She is one of several bright, intellectual, twenty-three-year-old women who populate Ozick's tales. Like Una Meyer in "An Education" and Allegra's daughter in *Trust,* Hannah has found someone—in this case the writer Ostrover— whom she might consider her literary master. "Envy" does not deal with the misplacement of Hannah's trust but rather presents Hannah as an ambiguous character, one who is educated in Yiddish culture but who nevertheless disdains the historical foundation on which it rests.

Hannah's error is to take the content without the form, the text without the context. Edelshtein, when he first meets Hannah, has no suspicion of Hannah's quirk and misreads *her* text. When he learns that she speaks Yiddish and is able to read Ostrover in the original, and moreover, knows an Edelshtein poem by heart, he mistakes her for a goddess Futura, the hope for the next generation. But Hannah is not an abstraction for the future. On the contrary, she is America, an abstraction of the worship of the present. History, she says, is "a waste" (92), and she can, therefore, easily, despite her Yiddish, remove herself from the Jewish community. Like the Wicked Son of the Passover Haggadah, she says "You Jews" to Edelshtein and his ilk. Furthermore, Hannah may be compared to a concrete mythical hero of the Western tradition, Don Juan, whose obsession with the seduction of women is only a symptom of a greater malaise, a lack of feeling for continuity. Like Molière's Don Juan, for example, she wishes to be rid of the parental generation. "Die now, all you old men, what are you waiting for? Hanging on to my neck, . . . the whole bunch of you, parasites, hurry up and die. . . . You eat people up with your disgusting old age—cannibals, all you care about is your own youth, you're finished, give somebody else a turn!" (97–98). Hannah, it is obvious, has no use for Edelshtein's wisdom; she wants his place. Paradoxically, Hannah finds that she can live alongside Ostrover, who, though of Edelshtein's generation, is a spokesman for youth. For Hannah, Ostrover is "a contemporary. He speaks for everybody. . . . Humanity" (95).

Ostrover has succeeded in bursting out from the confinements of Jewishness, not only into modernism, but also into what he calls (to distinguish it from Jewishness) "the world of reality." There is a hidden implication here that true Yiddish writing takes place in another world, the world of fantasy. True to some extent, this is a charge that Edelshtein will have to deal with. He begins by attacking Ostrover both as "a pantheist, a pagan, a goy" (95) and as a poor writer.

The catalog of criticism of Ostrover's style presented here is more than faintly reminiscent of Jacob Glatstein's diatribe against Bashevis Singer. "His Yiddish was impure, his sentences lacked grace and sweep, his paragraph transitions were amateur, vile. . . . His subject matter . . . was insanely sexual, pornographic, paranoid, freakish—men who embraced men, women who caressed women, sodomists of every variety" (47). Edelshtein's greatest criticism of Ostrover, the popularizer and vulgarian, is that he is "a panderer to people who," like Hannah, "have lost the memory of peoplehood" (79).

This criticism of Ostrover seems to go one step further than Edelshtein's criticism of American Jewish literature in general. He takes to task the writers of "Jewish extraction" who are considered, therefore, Jewish writers but who are ignorant of the Jewish textual tradition. "What do they *know*," he asks, "I mean of *knowledge?*" (79). These novelists claim to satirize Jewish life, but they are completely ignorant of the culture they aim to satirize. In Yiddish, "they know ten words for, excuse me, penis, and when it comes to a word for learning they're impotent!" (80). Yiddish, Edelshtein reminds us, was once an instrument for Jewish learning, a liturgical language that "squeaked up to God with a littleness, a familiarity, an elbow-poke" (51), as in Glatstein's poem "Genesis."

Edelshtein recognizes that Yiddish was murdered during the Holocaust and that, today, "whoever uses Yiddish to keep himself alive is already dead" (67). But he also recognizes that the world has a need for Yiddish and the role it played. English cannot take Yiddish's place. "When a goy from Columbus, Ohio, says 'Elijah the Prophet' he's not talking about *Eliohu Hanovi*. Eliohu is one of us, a *folksmensh*, running around in second-hand clothes. . . . The same biblical figure, with exactly the same history, once he puts on a name from King James, COMES OUT A DIFFERENT PERSON" (82).

Ostrover advises Edelshtein to "stop believing in Yiddish" (68). Edelshtein's problem is that for him Yiddish is holy. Ostrover, the realist, admonishes Edelshtein that "holiness is for make-believe" (69). Edelshtein can only retort that "whoever forgets Yiddish courts amnesia of history" (74). But Edelshtein is caught on the horns of a tragic dilemma. He knows that there is no possibility of redeeming Yiddish. The only way to succeed in preserving Yiddish culture is to translate it, and thereby to doom that culture to extinction. In a moment of high drama in the story, reaching for the tragic, Edelshtein personifies Yiddish and addresses to Yiddish a challenge: "Yiddish I call on you to choose! Yiddish! Choose death or death. Which is to say death through forgetting or death through translation. Who will redeem you? What act of salvation will restore you? All you can hope for, you tattered, you withered, is translation in America!" (74–75).

A tragic dilemma like the one so lucidly presented by Edelshtein can lead only to despair. But Edelshtein lacks the tragic dimension of Vorovsky. Vorovsky had also tried to "reach out" with his mathematical dictionary but he soon found out that "reaching is impossible." He learned that "when you get to where you wanted to reach to, that's when you realize that's not what you want to reach to" (65). And so Vorovsky goes mad. But he plays two roles. He exemplifies to Edelshtein real despair—and demonstrates to him that the latter requires further schooling in this matter—and he also brings, albeit inadvertently, the hope of redemption, in the form of his niece Hannah.

In the final analysis, it is Edelshtein who confers on Hannah messianic qualities. In his pathetic effort to convince her to become his translator, he says to her by way of argument, "You'll save Yiddish . . . you'll be like a Messiah to a whole generation" (93). But of course what he wants from Hannah is that she serve as an instrument for his own aspirations, that she be, not a Messiah, but a golem.

Edelshtein himself is the one with messianic pretensions, if not indeed messianic attributes, in this tale. By seeking to save Yiddish, it is he who—despite the egotistical aspect of his wish to be translated—seeks to retrieve the past, and redeem it. He quotes a passage

from the Talmud about the sanctity of human life and makes a leap
from human life to language. "In Talmud if you save a single life
it's as if you saved the world. And if you save a language? Worlds
maybe. Galaxies. The whole universe" (83). Edelshtein's faith in
language is extraordinary. One gets the impression that he actually
prefers the language to the literature written in that language. For,
were it not possible to recover the liturgical literature written in
Yiddish, however holy, Edelshtein would be satisfied to let the
language survive. He sets his willingness to compromise with history
in an intimate theological context.

That baby should follow baby is God's trick on us, but surely we too can
have a trick on God? If we fabricate with our syllables an immortality
passed from the spines of the old to the shoulders of the young, even God
cannot spite it. If the prayer-load that spilled upward from the mass graves
should somehow survive! If not the thicket of lamentation itself, then the
language on which it rode. (74)

So fervently does Edelshtein love the Yiddish language that for
a brief moment he appears to be, not its Messiah, but rather its
public relations director. Thus, he takes Ostrover's publishers to
task for their exclusive concentration on Ostrover. "Esteemed
Gentlemen," he writes, "you publish only one Yiddish writer, not
even a Poet, only a Story-writer. I humbly submit you give serious
wrong impressions" (52–53). But of course Edelshtein is not merely
the crank he seems. He is indeed a prophet. He knows that the
frame in which a message is placed is part of the message itself.
Yiddish is the language of a self-liberated people, he proclaims, a
language of justice. Yiddish, finally, is a language that "works under
the laws of purity, dividing the Commanded from the Profane"
(86).

And thus we arrive, as we always arrive in Ozick's work, at the
Jewish idea, the idea that warns against making idols out of artifacts
and teaches one to seek after distinctions between the two. Despite
Edelshtein's inability to reach out, he can console himself with the
belief that in his lifetime he has acquired essential wisdom. His
statement to Hannah that "at least I had a life" is equivalent for
Edelshtein to saying "at least I understood something" (97). That
something is the ability to make a crucial distinction between the
inside and the outside. Edelshtein has a vision, an illumination:

He saw everything in miraculous reversal, blessed—everything plain, distinct, understandable, true. What he understood was this: that the ghetto was the real world, and the outside world only a ghetto. Because in actuality who was shut off? Who then was really buried, removed, inhabited by darkness? To whom, in what little space, did God offer Sinai? Who kept Terach and who followed Abraham? Talmud explains that when the Jews went into Exile, God went into Exile also. Babi Yar is maybe the real world, and Kiev with its German toys, New York with all its terrible intelligence, all fictions, fantasies. Unreality. (96)

For Edelshtein, it is not true, as Ostrover claims, that Western civilization is the only reality. Perhaps it is Jewish history, vast and eternal, like poetry, that is real. In a prosopopoeia to Alexei, in which Edelshtein calls the dead Avremeleh back to life and addresses him, Edelshtein cries out, "Avremeleh, when you fell from the ledge over the ravine into your grave, for the first time you fell into reality" (96). Curiously, this martyrdom does not cause Edelshtein to despair, like Vorovsky the master of failure. Edelshtein has his art, an art with which he can redeem the dead.

"Envy; or Yiddish in America" is exemplary of the art of Cynthia Ozick because it demonstrates how this art is used. The forms of the story seem to contain its essential message. In writing the story Ozick has recourse to several means of communication, both oral and written, both ancient and modern. Embedded in the story are several poems, in both Yiddish and English. The story is also, to an extent, epistolary fiction, like the great epistolary novels of the eighteenth century, but here containing letters written in immigrant's English, imitating Yiddish diction, and letters translated into English from Yiddish. There are letters of special pleading and letters of literary criticism. There is even one case where Edelshtein writes a letter to Hannah in Yiddish. Although the letter is imbricated into the text in English, the reader is expected to suspend disbelief and to act as though he is reading that letter in Yiddish.[14] The Yiddish letter to Hannah is never sent, and need not be sent to have its message "reach out." In reality, it is a *bouteille à la mer,* an open letter to posterity about the real and the unreal.

The story ends with a curious communication, which is not so much a telephone call as it is a debate, one more time, in a modern setting, between *ecclesia* and *synagoga,* in which reasoned discourse on the pre-excellence, respectively, of Christianity and Judaism, gives way too soon to the venomous hatred caused by anti-Semitism.

The story is theatrical as well, and not only because it presents the tragedy of Yiddish. The narrative describes Ostrover's performance at the Y during which he reads one of his stories; it includes verbatim his clowning vaudeville performance in the routine known as the "Question Period." Reference is also made to the dramatic presentation of herself that Mireleh, Edelshtein's wife, makes. "Mireleh was a tragedian. She carried herself according to her impression of how a barren woman should sit, squat, stand, eat and sleep" (48). Mireleh is a character out of Yiddish melodrama, perhaps, but the real drama of this story takes place not on stage but in the wings, where Edelshtein tries to come to terms with Ostrover's success among the young.

Indeed, one might conclude that the essence of the story can be found not in the story itself but in two other stories that are nested within the larger text. In one of these, daringly given in toto, Ostrover tells a supernatural tale of a bad poet who sells his soul to the devil in exchange for the ability to write in several languages. However, no matter in what language the bad poet writes—be it Zwrdlish (Ostrover's Yiddish), French, Italian, Swahili, or Armenian—he cannot get published. Obviously, then, he's a bad poet. He is enjoined by Satan to accompany him down to hell. There, he is condemned to write his poetry into eternity, and, into the flames of eternity, to throw each and every stanza as it comes off his pen. The lesson is clear: Hell is not getting published.

Edelshtein retaliates by telling another fantastic story, a parable about Ostrover, a man who leaves no sign of himself—no blood when he cuts himself shaving, no reflection when he stands before a mirror, no sound when he tries to cry out. Edelshtein is confident that, over the long haul of history, his poetry, a matter of both substance and form, will win out over Ostrover's facile prose. Edelshtein, the born poet, appears to have been unmade by the forces of history over which he has no control. His belief is that, in that part of history known as the future, his poetry and his message will be reborn and redeemed.

Should Cynthia Ozick permit her own poetry to be collected in a volume? That is a question only the history of the future can answer.

Chapter Three
The Education of a Master: *Trust*

The scene is a studio at WNET/Thirteen, a public television affiliate station in New York City. Bill Moyers, interviewer extraordinaire, is engaging Cynthia Ozick in a "Heritage Conversation," designed to introduce the station's series for public television, "Heritage: Civilization and the Jews," to its viewers nationwide. The series itself is meant to demonstrate the symbiotic relationship that Jewish and Western civilizations have enjoyed through the ages. The subject turns to Cynthia Ozick's first novel, *Trust,* and to its inherent duality.

> *Moyers:* When you published *Trust,* your novel, you acknowledged that you began writing as an American writer, and ended as a Jewish writer.
>
> *Ozick:* Yes. That's when I began my education so to speak, my adult education, and I began to read very deeply in Jewish history. . . . I have such a sense of interest in this history and these ideas that it seems to me [that] had I been born outside of this tradition, I would have gravitated toward it anyway. . . . I was immensely influenced by an essay by Leo Baeck called "Romantic Religion," which I read at the age of 25 [and] which seemed to decode the universe for me.[1]

The parallels to the novel are striking. On the one hand, the narrator of *Trust* was not born a Jew and yet gravitated toward Jewish ideas and history. On the other hand, the hero of *Trust* is a decoder of the universe.

Cynthia Ozick herself was born into both the Jewish and Western traditions, and, as her biography attests, she approaches both of her traditions with an impressive set of credentials. Nevertheless, the beginning novelist is deeply aware that she is in need of an "education," both as a novelist and as a Jew.

This is not to say in any way that *Trust* is to be dismissed as a five-finger exercise written by an unripe tyro. On the contrary, Victor Strandberg, in a fine literary analysis of the novel, marred only by the fact that it chooses to ignore both the duality of the novel and the evolutionary process discerned by Moyers, has gone so far as to call *Trust* Ozick's "masterpiece."[2]

Trust is, to be sure, exquisitely artful. At times, the novel's superabundance of language, especially when it turns to play, as it does often, takes on the characteristics of a luxury, and like a fine champagne imbibed in doses too large by someone not accustomed to it, it can cause a relentlessly painful sensation.

Ozick herself acknowledges that the book, which took almost seven years to write, attempts to crowd dense poetic diction into an expansive prose work. "That novel," she writes of *Trust,* "the product of my education both as student and autodidact in the forties and fifties, cared about High Art and its issues, it was conceived in a style both 'mandarin' and 'lapidary,' every paragraph a poem."[3]

How is one to approach a long novel in which every paragraph is intended to be a poem? Ozick herself supplies a clue to the decoding of her literary universe as she distinguishes between the short and long forms of fiction. "The novel is long," she avers, "because it commences green and innocent. The novel is long because it is a process, like chewing the apple of the Tree of Knowledge: it takes the novel a while before it discovers its human nakedness."[4] Like the novel, the main characters of *Trust* also begin green and ignorant. (One character is named Adam Gruenhorn, as green and innocent as one can get.) It is also no coincidence that the theme of the Tree of Knowledge and the discovery process to which Ozick alludes are central to her novel's plot. Another word for the process is "education," including not only Ozick's education as a budding novelist and her Jewish education, but also the suggestion that the novel, as a genre, provides an education in which the text is seen as both a quest for knowledge of the world and as a tool for its decoding.

The Plot

The novel begins in 1957, during the Eisenhower years in America. The narrator, an unnamed woman of twenty-two whose identity must be searched for by herself and the reader, has just been graduated from college. Although it is clear that, intelligent and bookish, she has had a fine classical education, it is no less certain that her formal schooling has been for her a moratorium and that, now that schooling is over, the time of her real education has arrived. The novel then will present itself as a bildungsroman, in which the protagonist enters on a quest, a search for the moral knowledge that will make her independent.

Trust is indeed a process; in four parts it takes us from America in 1957, to war-ravaged Europe in 1946, to a cottage in Brighton Beach (England) in 1935, and finally, returning to 1957, to an abandoned mansion-supposed-to-become-museum in Duneacres, an island estate in Westchester County, New York, where the narrator receives her revelation. Temporally, the novel is a framed text, whose end takes us back to its beginning. It meanders in and out of history, both personal and social, and in doing so it describes a mental process, and a narrative strategy that might be called *plotting*. The story itself, the plot, is straightforward, however, and its events may profitably be narrated in that manner.

It begins in the 1930s in America, a time of social ferment and experimentation. American intellectuals are taking seriously the new political idealogy being tried out in Russia. Even some members of America's privileged classes, always attuned to fashion, are flirting with socialist ideas. Nevertheless, "Families" are still promoting family and proper marriages in good society still take place. It is against this background that young Allegra is married to William. Allegra is a product of Miss Jewett's school, distinguished for producing very few college entrants but rather for preparing its nubile graduates, through the cultivation of team sports, to be wives and mothers. She is a daughter of wealth and privilege, and a bit of a rebel. William, from the same class, a bit older, a lawyer, devoted to capitalism, has made both an appropriate and a good match, for Allegra is heir to a substantial fortune. Trustworthy William is named trustee of his wife's father's estate.

Allegra, however, is a romantic; she needs to "feel," she needs enthusiasms, like those she experienced on the playing fields of Miss Jewett's. William, in her young eyes something of a prig, is incapable of supplying these. So Allegra, a modern Emma Bovary or Anna Karenina, rebels against her married state. She convinces William to permit her to use her father's estate at Duneacres, which had been destined by him as a maritime museum, as a compound for a budding proletarian youth movement. There she comes under the influence of two young men. Enoch Vand, a young Jew intent on realizing prophetic pronouncements of social justice, is the youth leader, the political and philosophical mentor of the group. Gustave Nicholas Tilbeck ("Nick"), a seventeen-year-old-youth of unbridled sexual drives, takes it upon himself to initiate Allegra into the secrets of sexual play. Tilbeck, of Greek-Swedish extraction, is attracted to the playful cultivation of the arts. He even encourages Allegra to complete a novel, *Marianna Harlow,* ostensibly about social justice, but, under his tutelage, essentially a tract on sexual fulfillment. Allegra thus has two mentors, two masters, one of whose influence is decisive.

At the close of their extended season at Duneacres, distinguished only by the suicide of the young architect who had been engaged by William to design the museum, but who could not begin work because of the movement's occupation of the estate, Allegra and Tilbeck run off to England, accompanied by Enoch Vand. There, on Brighton Beach, they live an idyllic existence. With Nick as her muse, Allegra completes her novel. The couple also frolic, a faun and his nymph, in nature. And one frolic leading to another, Allegra becomes pregnant. Upon the birth of the baby girl, Nick abandons the hearth.

William, meanwhile, whose sense of family honor cannot sustain the stain brought on by his wife's misbehavior, divorces Allegra. Since there are rumblings of imminent war in Europe, Allegra and her daughter return to America and to her trust fund, still administered by William, who has remained her lawyer. She is followed to America by Enoch, who is determined to become Allegra's husband, but who resists all suggestions that he "refather" the baby.

It is now ten years later. The war is over, having wrought destruction, on Europe, on Europe's Jews, and on Enoch's belief in God and the perfectibility of man. Enoch has by now married Allegra and his career is on the ascent. He has been appointed to a postwar bureaucratic position, in which he is to account for the Jews murdered in the Nazi death camps. He takes his wife and stepchild, accompanied by a young Dutch governess, Anneke, to live in a village in the provinces of France. Confronted with the evidence of horror he sees, Enoch, who was presented earlier, in his prewar stage, as prophetic and messianic, is now finding it even more

difficult to wrestle with the concept of a benevolent God. The
political master, the prophet of social justice, undergoes a painful
education. The wisdom he acquires he sets down in a series of
aphorisms, pithy texts that read much like Pascal's *Pensées* or La
Rochefoucauld's *Maximes*. The only "events" to occur in this episode
of the aftermath of The Event are a scandalous automobile accident
caused by reckless Allegra in Paris and the arrival on the scene of
Gustave Nicholas Tilbeck. The latter has gained information about
Mr. and Mrs. Vand from Anneke, whom he has seduced. He arrives
one day on a beat-up blue bicycle flying an American flag to ask
Allegra, not for his daughter to whom he is indifferent, but for
money on which to live.

The ten-year-old girl has been sheltered from knowledge of her
biological father by a mother determined to bring her up under the
illusion of freedom. The young girl is locked in her room, but,
thirsting for self-knowledge, she intuits that she is somehow related
to the seductively mysterious visitor of her parents. Although Enoch's embassy is not yet finished, mother and daughter return once
more to America, having avoided the ill-starred encounter.

Twelve more years have passed. It is now 1957, the present of
the narrative. Allegra's daughter has been graduated from college
and is now being sent by her mother on the de rigueur romantic-
educational tour of Europe. William, in the meanwhile, had re-
married and fathered several children, among them a son,
approximately the narrator's age, who is bent on following in his
father's footsteps. The relationship between Allegra's daughter and
William's son is an ambiguous one. Almost brother and sister, but
not quite, they are always on the verge of falling in love. One gets
the feeling that for the narrator a marriage with William's son would
be a consummation devoutly to be wished. William's son has other
ideas, however. Like his father he will marry, appropriately, a graduate of Miss Jewett's, one Stefanie Pettigrew. Furthermore, William's son learns a lesson about "trust" when he comes across Allegra's
file in his father's office. He will blame his father for the betrayal
of the young architect who killed himself in despair at not being
able to provide a livelihood for his betrothed.

As for Enoch, his diplomatic career has progressed geometrically.
He has been appointed ambassador by the president and is merely
awaiting senate confirmation to take up his duties. Allegra is ecstatic
at this turn of events. In democratic America royalty exists only in

America's far-flung embassies, "palaces" in her eyes. For her, the
wife of an ambassador is nothing less than a queen. There is, unfortunately, an obstacle. Allegra and Enoch have received word from
Tilbeck, who finds it urgent, just at the time of the senate confirmation hearings, to ask for his "daughter." Obviously not moved
by paternal emotions, he can only be using his daughter as a pretext
to blackmail the would-be ambassador and his wealthy wife. As
they did earlier in Europe, Allegra and Enoch give in to Nick's
demand. The narrator's trip to Europe is postponed, and she is sent
to confront the father whose "illegitimate issue," as William the
lawyer has put it, she is.

Tilbeck has set himself up at Duneacres, the family manse now
in ruin. To Duneacres, Tilbeck, a generous lord of the manor, has
invited a family of Quakers, Mr. and Mrs. Purse and their seven
children. The Purses are distinguished by three characteristics: the
father's stinginess, the children's names (called after the likes of
Henry David Thoreau and Harriet Beecher Stowe, "for inspiration"),
and the mother's excessive wit. She believes it her duty to make
puns, dozens and dozens of puns, on her husband's name. Mrs.
Purse treats her husband comically in another manner as well, taking
advantage of the surroundings and the situation to sleep with Nick
every night of their brief stay at Duneacres, thus betraying her
husband's trust in her with the same man Allegra betrayed William's
trust.

To this magical island the narrator is brought, a Miranda come
to observe what is for her a "brave new world," complete with
Caliban. The narrator has already learned that she is "illegitimate
issue." Confronted with the playfulness she observes, she realizes
that a boy, a boy of seventeen, had made her. Her father is supremely
egotistical and his behavior knows no bounds. His daughter, in
search of knowledge, is especially vulnerable to her father's seductiveness. Incest is touched on briefly here as Tilbeck connives to
give his daughter a kiss on the lips, going so far as to insert his
tongue inside his daughter's mouth. The daughter is momentarily
mesmerized. She enjoys the moment and freezes it in her mind.
Like the young girl on the Grecian urn, however, she flees. She
does not let the action proceed further. If she is to gain knowledge
of what her mother knew, it will not be via an irreversible act, but
rather from observation.

At this moment, two new actors arrive on Shakespeare's stage,

William's son and Stefanie. Ignorant that the island was momentarily populated, they have come to try out a little premarital sex.
Tilbeck is immediately attracted to zestful Stefanie and turns his
attention exclusively to her. He will re-enact his earlier betrayal of
William with Allegra by making love to William's son's fiancée.
Stefanie, also a product of Miss Jewett's, is apparently more like
Allegra than Allegra's own daughter. Flouting all social conventions,
she will have sexual intercourse with Tilbeck under her fiancé's nose.

   The act also takes place in front of the narrator's eyes, who,
voyeuristically, observes the sex-act in its pure form, devoid of love.
She now knows what her mother knew. She learns more the next
day when, Nick and Stefanie having decided to row to the mainland,
the satyr falls into the water and drowns. A coroner's inquest reveals
that Tilbeck's hair was merely dyed blond; he has been a fraud from
beginning to end.

   Allegra does not even begin to mourn her former lover's death.
She is much too busy mourning the effects of world politics. Two
hours after Enoch's confirmation by the senate, a coup in his appointed country has put into power a regime hostile to America.
Enoch's diplomatic career is in ruins, irretrievably crushed by mockery. Allegra's dream of royalty evaporates into thin air. Enoch,
however, recovers from the blow and he will set out to complete
his education: he will study Jewish texts, Bible, the Ethics of the
Fathers, the Talmud. The narrator's education is also not complete.
She will "go to weddings," that is to say she will write novels, and
her novels will be a commentary both on the world she observes
and the texts Enoch studies.

The Characters

   In *Trust,* as may be deduced from the foregoing summary of its
plot, there are, broadly, two classes of characters, the "youths" and
the "heroes."[5] The youths include Allegra in the 1930s, Allegra's
daughter, William's son, and Stefanie. The group of heroes is comprised of Nick, Enoch, and William. Allegra, the author of a book,
might have been a hero to her daughter but is not. She was once a
youth and still remains one, an older but more complicated Stefanie.
"Compare if you will," says the narrator imagining her mother at
fifteen, "Stefanie Pettigrew, a rougher sketch of the model, an
artist's poor copy of the hanging masterpiece, daringly embellished

with up-to-date technique. . . . Allegra is subtler than Stefanie perhaps. (We are, you see, laying a swathe through the generations, and setting all forms of youth side by side, as if they were for the moment immortal. And what a charm it is which allows us to think of Stefanie and Allegra as contemporaries!)"[6]

Synchrony allows for further overlaps. Nick, for example, acts as if he were still a youth, but he is not. His pretension to abiding youthfulness in the end is what will cost him any claim he may have to hero worship. William's son, disappointed by a father in whom he can no longer trust, quickly becomes his father's double and, just as his father is no longer a hero, he is no longer a youth. This leaves the narrator as a youth in search of a hero in whom she may trust, and Enoch, whose very experiences in the world and outlook on life place him in a pre-eminent position to serve as a hero for his wife's daughter.

Allegra

Allegra might have been a figure to be emulated by her bookish, literary daughter. After all, she does patronize a review of poetry, *Bushelbasket;* after all, she did succeed in writing and publishing a novel, and her conversation constantly alludes to literary classics, especially Tolstoy's *Anna Karenina.* She is, further, enamored of European culture. Allegra's initial attraction to young Nick Tilbeck was that he represented for her the incarnation of sacred beauty. But even Nick recognizes the hollowness of *Marianna Harlow,* the novel whose muse he was. He calls it "The Girls' Own Das Kapital. Or the Double -x: se- and Mar-" (519). Allegra's first husband, William, concurs, calling the novel "a puerile outrage" (298). The narrator's criticisms of her mother's literary talents are more general. She notes that Allegra's biggest failing as a writer is that she does not love language enough.

Not only does Allegra write fiction; she is also a compulsive liar. Allegra rarely tells the truth because truth is too commonplace for her. "She needed the gorgeous gesture, the sign of recklessness; she had to declare that she was not responsible" (18). Allegra is not only a romantic who needs outsized gestures, she also needs scandal. "She was as exhilarated after scandal as an arsonist after some great . . . conflagration; she had had her burning" (108). When confronted with a scandal she had caused in Paris after the war, in which she had almost killed her chauffeur, Allegra dismisses the issue abruptly, asserting that near misses do not count. Allegra cannot be bothered by mere detail. Even her ignorance does not deter her. An American Mrs. Malaprop, she can use the French word *écart* when she means *éclat*. She can place Venice's Bridge of Sighs in Cambridge, England. She can translate the Italian proverb *"Ogni medaglia ha il suo rovescio"* ("Every coin has its reverse") as "A nicely arched posterior deserves a medal," because by the time her listener has caught on to the enormity of her assertion she has moved on to a completely different topic.

Allegra is constantly in motion. She sees herself moreover as a huntress out to conquer the world, and the world as a bird to be hunted. "My mother really thought the world was a bird to be pursued with audacity and pleasure, and she deemed herself a huntress. . . . She fashioned immense and brilliant scenes over which she ruled poignantly and without justice, . . . fabricating event, dining on the heart and bowels of this wild splendid bird which was the world" (109). Tilbeck is perhaps more accurate when he calls his mistress, the queen who rules without justice, not a huntress but a pagan, one who is against history, has no concern with the past, and lives in an eternal present. For example, the reason Allegra never speaks to her daughter of the latter's biological father is that she herself no longer thinks of him. He is in the past; he no longer exists. The narrator explains her mother's attitude in this manner:

My mother had no concern with the past, which she considered eccentric, because it differed from the present. Everything old struck her as grotesque, like costumes in photographs or dead aunts. She did not believe in old obligations or old loves; she was wholly without sentimentality. . . . She considered that everything wore out extrinsically by virtue of her own advancement, no matter if it were as good as new. I began to see that her indifference was not for the thing itself, but rather for her former judgment of it: it was her old self she discarded. (24–25)

This attitude leads to drastic consequences. In 1946 it leads to a complete dismissal of the Holocaust. If, as she screams, "The concentration camps are all over!," then there is no need any longer to concern oneself with them, and Enoch's embassy lacks all meaning. Allegra does not see Europe as a place where history has happened.

Europe is, for her, a stage where pageants are performed. She is devoted to a Europe "of spectacle, dominion, energy and honor, a Europe misted by fame and awe" (99). Even though she sees Enoch as the incarnation of Europe, she misreads him by thinking he is devoted to the same Europe as she is.

Allegra is a fabulous misreader. She misreads both Tolstoy and the Jewish condition. She waxes ecstatic over the haying scene in *Anna Karenina,* to be sure, but seeing a bit of herself in the heroine of *Anna Karenina,* she does not understand how Vronsky could have tired of such a bright woman. She would, of course, have rewritten the ending of the novel, depriving it of its tragic dimension by having Anna take a new lover instead of committing suicide. She is capable of rewriting Tolstoy because she is not at all a European; she is thoroughly American and therefore can easily conceive of a heroine who lives one day at a time.

Allegra's romanticism—in Leo Baeck's terms—can best be seen in her attitude toward the Jews and the Jewish religion. Although she finally married a Jew and even consents to have her name put on pro-Israel letterheads, Allegra is an anti-Semite. She blames the Jews for not accepting that the Messiah has already come. She wants and sees everything complete and so wants the Messiah that way. She does not understand that the Jewish idea of the Messiah is one of continuing repair. Not only does Allegra blame the Jews; she hates Jews as a people. She explains to her daughter why she and Enoch were not married in a Jewish ceremony: "Would you have expected your poor mother to join him under a greasy Oriental canopy to be jabbered over by a little whiskered Shylock of a rabbi?" (431). She insists further that she does not like Jews when they are grateful and does not like them when they are ungrateful. "Well, look, you're not going to tell me they're *all* like King Solomon or King David or somebody" (414). Most damningly of all, she accuses her daughter, at the end of the latter's quest, of having become "a Goddamn little Jew" (623). While Allegra's language is vehement, her insight is most compelling. The woman who had misread Tolstoy and mistaken her husband Enoch reads her daughter's end, as we shall see, correctly.

Although one may easily become impatient with her, Allegra is in many ways a sympathetic character. Even her daughter likes her. She is attractive, like her mentor, but she is much less dangerous than he.

Tilbeck

According to Victor Strandberg's reading of *Trust*, Gustave Nicholas Tilbeck is not only Allegra's mentor; he is also the role model
for Allegra's daughter, the character in the novel who "engages her
allegiance." Strandberg's reading of the text derives from his refusal
to accept Ozick's assertion in the novel, basic to its composition,
that environment is a more important factor in human development
than heredity. Strandberg insists on seeing Allegra's daughter as
truly her mother's daughter, fated, for reasons of genetic imprinting,
perhaps, to recapitulate her mother's past. He ignores the simple
evidence that what Allegra did with Tilbeck twenty-two years earlier, however seductive, is performed, not by her biological daughter, but by Stefanie, Allegra's real double, a product of Allegra's
environment.

Strandberg is perhaps correct in his assertion that the Hellenism
that produced the pagan gods "has posed so magnetic an attraction
as to nearly tear [Ozick] loose from her Jewish moorings, as she
attests in books like *Trust* and *The Pagan Rabbi*."[7] Of course the
point of many of Ozick's narratives is that Hellenism, however
seductive (and seductive it is), did not succeed in tearing her loose.

Strandberg insists on seeing Nick as the hero of the novel. "Tilbeck, in sum," says Strandberg, "is a singular example of Europe
at its best, made all the more attractive by the book's otherwise
ruinous expanse of cultural negations."[8]

First of all, there is no "Europe at its best" in this novel. Allegra's
vision of Europe as a kingdom misted over with honor is an illusion.
True, Tilbeck is a charismatic figure whose attractiveness is beyond
dispute. It is for this reason precisely that Ozick delays his entry
onto the stage of the novel until the fourth and final part. The brief
appearance made by Tilbeck in part 2 of the novel, arriving on a
blue bicycle zanily displaying an American flag, makes of him an
intriguing figure for the ten-year-old girl who had followed her
parents to war-devastated Europe in 1946. This brief glimpse of
Tilbeck is countered throughout the novel by an effort on the part
of the narrator to attribute to Tilbeck negative qualities. Thus,
toward the beginning of the novel Tilbeck is yoked with Ed
McGovern, the parasitic editor of Allegra's poetry review. McGovern
and Tilbeck are "two birds of the same species perched upon my

mother's shoulders talon-deep, . . . two terrible hawks" (58). Preparing the terrain for a later narrative development, the narrator comments on the museum figuratively curated by Tilbeck. "The cost of the exhibit was too high, and the admission price was ferocious. What you paid was yourself. In order to get in you had to join the bad and dirty things on display: you had to change and be one of them" (74).

The narrator recognizes early on in the novel that the values she chooses to live by are threatened by Tilbeck's proximity. It is as though he represents some sort of moral pollution. Throughout the novel negative epithets are applied to him. He's an "opportunist" (119), a "terrible Beast" (210), an "evil genius" (220), "slime" (220), the "devil" (239), a "cheat" (372), an "all-around charlatan" (497), a "pagan," one who "doesn't have a sense of justice" (601), a "blackmailer" (609), and, most damning of all, "a boy," (609), who cannot hope to compete with either William or Enoch who, because they are "men," are at least available as heroes.

It is Allegra, unreconstructed adolescent that she is, who tries to make Tilbeck "juicy" by comparison to Enoch. But the narrator, even before she meets Tilbeck, is not fooled by her mother's portrait. "All the same he did not emerge as juicy: Posterity, being better read than Allegra, would tick off all the influences, it would label Nick 'derivative' and toss him off as a husk. . . . All the effects were staged" (421). Not only is Nick not original, he is pathetic. At the end of the novel, when his body is fished out of the water, the medical examiner notes that his hair had been dyed blond. He is an imposter of the first water, tawdry: "To hope to bring to life one of those boys on an amphora, bright-haired, goat-legged, with a little tibia pipe poised and halted for laughter, among those love-exalted girls? A dye! Aha, my mother's fantastic lover, potter, Muse, charlatan, insincere blackmailer—somewhere and sometime he had to bend, grimace, crouch . . ., dip his whole head into a vat of fake youth" (609).

The confirmation, at the end, of Nick's pathetic imposture calls into doubt, at least as far as the narrator is concerned, all of his ostensibly attractive features. True, he served as Allegra's muse; but he was a muse for a second-rate novel. His claim to have no desires and his protestation of his freedom are also mere wind. Whatever else one may think of him, he is to be rejected as a possible hero-figure and role model for the narrator in search of an identity. If anyone is able to play the role of hero in this novel, it is Enoch Vand.

Enoch Vand

Who is this Enoch Vand whose presence looms so large in *Trust?* His influence is felt to such a degree that he has two names in the novel—Enoch Vand and Adam Gruenhorn—and several identifying epithets. His judgments of the world weigh so heavily in the novel's scales that there is even a complete chapter dedicated to his aphorisms, forming a "Book of the Secrets of Enoch" within the novel. One of these aphorisms is even extracted from the novel and placed in its frame, as an epigraph. As Adam Gruenhorn, he is the original man, Adam, an innocent, a "greenhorn." As Enoch, he recalls the biblical figure of Enoch, a righteous man, one "who walked with God," a man associated with knowledge and at the root of whose Hebrew name, Hanoch, is the notion of education.[9] Enoch Vand is a master of knowledge who will dedicate himself to his own education. Through him, both the narrator and the reader—and perhaps the author—will also go through an educational process.

Twice during the novel, Allegra equates Enoch with Europe. It is not at all clear whether she means the romantic Europe of her dreams, the one that no longer exists, because it never did, or the all-too-real Europe of the present, the Europe of destruction, which both scattered its Jews as ashes to the wind and disgorged its remaining Jews out to the four corners of the world. Allegra is also fond of calling her husband "Disraeli in the mornings, and in the evenings Moses" (69). Whatever Allegra may have meant by her characterization of her husband, Enoch is certainly a "surviving Jew" and at the same time one who inscribes himself in the history of the world.

Enoch is presented at polar opposites to Tilbeck. If Nick is a symbol for sacred beauty and ancient Greece, Enoch is devoted, like the Hebrew prophets, to social justice. A debate between the two sums up the polarity nicely. It also provides an example of the "richness" of Ozick's language. Enoch accuses Nick of lacking lofty ideals and even indulges in a bit of name-calling, launching at him an epithet associated with the biblical Esau, Israel's brotherly enemy. "Mess of pottage," Enoch calls Tilbeck. Not to be outdone, Nick turns Enoch's accusation around, calling him a "pot of message" (399). Only by Nick is this appellation to be taken pejoratively. Enoch will wear it as a badge of honor, the way he counters Nick's boast of his complete and absolute freedom with his own boast that he, Enoch, was a slave in the land of Egypt, thus identifying himself, by communal memory, with the ancient Israelites.

Throughout the novel Enoch is referred to as prophetic and messianic, as though he will either announce the savior or bring redemption himself. Enoch, however, is a bit more complicated than that. First of all, it must be stated clearly that for Enoch the Messiah has not come. Enoch is, moreover, anti-Christian and anti-Christ. Enoch believes that Christianity is synonymous with heathenism because like most successful religions, it "tells lies in the most picturesque way" (397). He explains that there are more Christians than Jews because Christians know how to put on a good show. Like Nick, Christianity is attractive. Enoch chastises Christ, however, for a different reason. He blames Christ for removing the Kingdom of Heaven to heaven:

He chose Christ for enemy not merely for his cruelty in inventing and enforcing a policy of damnation, but more significantly for his removal of the Kingdom of Heaven to heaven, where, according to Enoch, it had no business being allowed to remain, by the Saviour or anyone else, and ought instead to be brought down again as rapidly as possible by the concerted aspiration and fraternal sweat of the immediate generation. (427)

Enoch is messianic to be sure, but he has no calling to be a messiah. He does not even admit that he is awaiting the Messiah. With a twinkle in his eye, he asserts that both he and the Messiah wait together for the redemption, which Enoch sees as a form of revenge on Europe.

The notion of vengeance is crucial here. It relates to the central idea of Enoch's philosophy, which is probably the central idea of the novel, and quite possibly of all of Ozick's later writings. Enoch is looking for a sign, "something to show that Creation was a covenant and not a betrayal" (227). His pessimistic view of creation stems from his reaction to his posting in Europe after the war, during which it was his assignment to account for the dead. The record is kept in a ledger, but it is more than a list in a book. In Ozick's hands, this mournful duty of naming names takes on a liturgical quality and becomes a sort of prayer for the dead. In a very moving passage, one of Enoch's two assistants reads the name of a deceased Jew. The other reads the name of the death camp where the Jew perished. The reading becomes a litany. The narrator, moved to comment, states that "it was like what I imagined prayer to be, full of attack and ebb, flow and useless drain, foolish because clearly nobody heard, neither deaf heaven nor the dry-lipped deafer communicants; it was in short a sad redundant madrigal, droned out for its own sad sake" (95–96). But the narrator does not yet understand. It is even more than prayer. The ledger in which Enoch records the names of the dead is like a Tablet of the Law, a Priestly Breastplate. His ledger "shone on his breast like plates of armor, and he clung to it in the fancy that it had powers still untried . . . and he wore on his body that book of woe as he might have worn Urim and Thummim" (124). It is through the prism of this ex- perience that Enoch, who had previously been an optimistic "youth leader," believing that political ideology might redeem mankind, turns his attention now to vengeance, looking for anything that will prove that creation was, as he says, "a covenant and not a betrayal." Vengeance, Enoch says after the experience of the Shoah, [10] is too enormous, not only for man but even for God himself. There is a new force now. "It's history that's the force!" says Enoch. "It's history that avenges and repays! It's history that raises the dead! And when we talk of redemption, it's history we mean!" (231).

We may get an inkling of what Enoch means by history by looking at his way of viewing literature. Tolstoy's *Anna Karenina* races throughout the pages of Ozick's novel and is commented on and alluded to by a significant number of the characters. It is sort of a document common to the culture of the novel. Enoch also has his say about it. He claims that Tolstoy, like all great writers, knew nothing about literature. "All they know," he says, "is life." What writers do is to comment on life, to judge life and the world.

In Enoch's cosmos, that is precisely what history does. "History?" he asks. "You want to know what it is? It isn't what you think. It isn't simply what has happened. It's a judgment on what has hap- pened!" (229). If that is an acceptable task for history then Enoch himself is the historian par excellence. For, as he explains to the narrator (who has by now become his disciple), one must not shirk from judging God's creation. He had made a covenant with God, he explains in an *apologia pro vita sua,* to be just. But he realized very soon that he had been a greenhorn. He may have passed for a master, but in reality he was a student, someone in dire need of an education. This is precisely what he teaches to the narrator—herself thirsting for wisdom—in the following lecture:

> I was born, and found the world the way it is, and myself a Jew, and God the God of unredeemed monstrosity. . . . In my simplicity I thought that whatever you come upon that seems unredeemed exists in this state for the sake of permitting you the sacred opportunity to redeem it. I used to have a crooked idea that man finds the world unwell in order to heal it. I had the presumptuousness of thinking myself one of the miracle rabbis. . . . But afterward I became wise, and learned how the world isn't merely unredeemed: worse worse worse, it's unredeemable. (451)

Enoch, unable to accept God's justice, places himself outside of God's creation, makes of himself an adversary. His judgment of God's creation is closely linked with his judgment of God's texts. He has difficulties with the biblical text in the Book of Genesis, for example, in which the Binding of Isaac is narrated. "The ram demands to know why he, also God's own creature, is less worthy than Isaac. Everybody worries over Isaac, and then the ram substitutes under the knife and nobody cares. A subject the Commentaries leave unexplored" (464). In the face of such seeming injustice, Enoch becomes what he calls "a disappointed religious" (450).

It is because of his disappointment with God that Enoch turns to history for his salvation. History, he believes with a fervent belief, finally does provide justice. In the end, history brings redemption:

> In the long, long, long, long memory of history . . . the dead are at last resurrected: even at the price of sublime civilization. It is the exactly balanced irony of vengeance that only the wronged survive. Where now is Assyria? Who sleeps under the pyramids? Where has sleekbooted Caesar gone? Who afterward will recall the cathedrals of the Rhine? History . . . is the Paradise of the lost. When we remember the martyrs we bring on the Messiah. (236)

In the final analysis, the Messiah brought by history, in Enoch's vision, is a Jewish one. Enoch may rebel against the Jewish God but he does not disengage himself from Jewish history. On the contrary, the more he distances himself from God the closer he binds himself to the Jewish tradition.

It is not only that he has a sentimental attachment to the languages of the Jews and is able to call both Tilbeck and McGovern not parasites but by the homely Yiddish designation for parasite, "*schnorrer.*" It is not even that the Yiddish words *schnorrer* (panhandler), *mamaloshen* (mother tongue, i.e., Yiddish), and *goldene medina* (the Golden Land, i.e., America) are a "sly gift" to the narrator from her stepfather. Rather, what is crucial here is that Enoch has succeeded in conveying his prophetic voice to his stepdaughter and has educated her in the ways of the Jewish value system. Under Enoch's influence, the narrator has begun her education:

I saw what he waited for, the extraordinary sign, the consecrated demonstration, which he did not dare to name Messiah. He was waiting for the deliverance of history. I saw him: he had been formed at Creation, he had been witness at Sinai, and he went on raptly waiting as those obsessed by timelessness always wait. He kept his bare secret vigil as devotedly as the high priest of the Temple in the moment of the utterance of the Name of Names within the Holy of Holies. He awaited justice for the wicked and mercy for the destroyed. He awaited the oblivion of devouring Europe. He awaited the just estimate of the yet-to-be-born. (236)

The narrator is the biological daughter of pagans and heathens. It turns out that she becomes the spiritual daughter of a Jew and is supremely aware of the differences. Should we have expected this virtual conversion to Judaism of the narrator? The possibility of such a turning is inscribed in the text, as indeed it is in all of Ozick's writings.

The Narrator

For Ozick, biology is not destiny. In *Trust,* environment plays a much more important role than does genetics. Stefanie is much more Allegra's daughter than the narrator because both Stefanie and Allegra attended Miss Jewett's and the narrator managed to avoid that environment. "When the creature enters the environment," the narrator says of Enoch, "the environment enters the creature" (524). In making this statement she might have been talking about her mother and Stefanie as well. She is surely talking of herself.

It will be remembered that the novel begins on the day the narrator is graduated from college. The moment described is not only a moment of transition. It also emphasizes that her experiences

are qualitatively different from her mother's. While Miss Jewett's
had fifty-four volleyballs in the gym closet, its library had seven
completely uncut—and therefore untouched—sets of Dickens. The
narrator on the other hand is what her mother calls abnormally
bookish; she reads much more than a graduate of Miss Jewett's,
even a novelist, would want to read. Her mother criticizes her
daughter for being too intelligent and for not having developed
physically, as though there were a causal relationship between the
two. "You have no bosom. . . . With you it's brain brain brain"
(456).

What is cause for criticism in her mother's eyes is viewed as the
height of desirability by the narrator herself, who repeatedly describes herself as the possessor of three traits and talents: conversation, bookishness, and character. She would think, for example,
that William's son would be attracted to a woman with those qualities. William's son, however, is governed by both biology and
environment. He chooses Stefanie, "the womanly child, the childlike
woman—in short, exactly what his father had married in my mother"
(259).

The vast majority of the intelligent, intellectual, and serious
conversation in this novel takes place between the narrator and her
stepfather. He will teach her about the role of history in human
affairs. She will approach the master as a seeker after knowledge.
But the narrator is not necessarily a disciple, and Enoch is not
necessarily a hero. One of his lessons is that one must not seek a
master, but, like a Parsifal in search of the Holy Grail, one must
seek to become a master oneself.

When the narrator confronts William, she does so with the need
to understand, with a desire to know. She is, using religious vocabulary, "a suppliant after truth" (313). She has never been looking
merely for an answer, however. She has more importantly been
looking for a way to go about seeking answers. "I went out," she
says, "like an explorer—not to find a destination but a route" (244).
In Europe, as a ten-year-old, the narrator's attention has been turned
by a letter her mother and Enoch had received from Nick. Although
she had had no idea of its contents, nor of the situation to which
it alluded, she was morbidly curious about the letter. She sees a
name in the letter—"Nick"—and tries to decipher and to decode
what she is certain is the letter's key word. Is it "confer" or "career,"
"cross" or "church," "curse" or "child?" One thing is obvious: this

word contains the key to her identity. And when her mother crumples the letter and puts it out of sight, the narrator describes her mother's gesture with a telling biblical allusion. She stuffed the ball of paper into her pocket "as though it were an invidious apple from the Tree of Knowledge" (134).

The search for knowledge is not a matter of desire but a matter of morality. The narrator explains that human history began when *homo faber*, "manufacturing man," became homo sapiens, "moral man," when he learned that being killed and killing others were the same act. Knowledge for the narrator is therefore an act, an event. "Knowledge is the only real event in the world" (586), she says. When she witnesses a kissing scene between William's son and Stefanie, she knows that something has happened, not in them, but in herself. She has gained knowledge, a moral act, the knowledge of good and evil.

When the narrator witnesses the scene of Tilbeck's copulation with Stefanie, she says, "I felt I had witnessed the very style of my own creation." Style and creation are also literary terms. There is a moment in the novel when the narrator feels that she may be like a bad chapter in a book, the infamous erotic chapter 12 in *Marianna Harlow*. In *Trust,* the narrator is a ripe candidate for a further error, this time, however, not an error of taste but of morals.

Tilbeck, the pagan, is completely free. He recognizes no limits to his activity and takes pleasure in treading on society's taboos. He will even venture to initiate an incestuous act with his own daughter, using the pretext of a scratch on her arm to make an approach. While he does succeed in kissing his daughter on the lips and in inserting his wine-perfumed tongue in her mouth, the sex act is not consummated. The daughter, aware of the irreversibility of the sex act, runs from the minotaur who is her father. Nick's penetration had been enough to teach the narrator about the seductiveness of passion. Her witnessing of the sex act with Stefanie suffices to teach her that what Nick has to give is not love but unadulterated sensuality. In the end, it is not sensuality that remains but only the idea of sensuality. Far stronger, and far more reaching, is the moral lesson that the narrator derives from her observation.

The narrator is several times described in the novel as straining to make sense of sounds she perceives only dimly in the distance. The words of the novel *Trust,* some of which may appear a bit muffled here, will become clearer as one approaches the stories that follow it.

The ending of the narrator's story is highly ambiguous. She reveals that Enoch has returned to his people's textual sources. What happens to her at the end? "Where I was and what I did during that period I will not tell; I went to weddings" (639). Her reticence to tell about herself is suggestive. Like Ruth Puttermesser of later stories, she does not marry. Nor does she "normalize" herself. We may conjecture that where she went was to a place similar to Enoch's. Both the narrator and the novelist, we will learn, have proceeded to undergo the education of a master.

In her interview with Bill Moyers, Ozick comments on Enoch Vand: "Though I never say so explicitly, I'm sure that this is one of the reasons that he returns to study texts, because he wants to understand and decode the world. . . . I do think the word 'decode' is very important, because the world is very cryptic to us. And I think Enoch Vand in that book, having been deep in great worldliness, was looking to break the code."[11] Cynthia Ozick, in virtually all of her subsequent writings, even when she will have been acknowledged a master, does nothing else than demonstrate to her readers the process of her continuing education, her attempts at decoding the world.

Chapter Four

Teaching and Preaching: "An Education" and "Bloodshed"

There is a didactic tone in much of Cynthia Ozick's writing. This strain is evident not only in *Trust,* in which the education of the main protagonist is the central theme, but also in later works such as *The Cannibal Galaxy,* which is set on the campus of a Jewish day school. This later novel contains, in addition, an analysis of the sources of the school's "Dual Curriculum"—an attempt at a synthesis of Jewish and Western cultural traditions. *The Cannibal Galaxy* also presents a central character, Hester Lilt, a philosopher of pedagogy and a teacher of severe lessons, who is described by her unwilling pupil, the day school's principal, as a whole school all by herself.

Nowhere is the didactic element more overtly central, however, than in the stories "An Education" and "Bloodshed." In these two stories a fine line is drawn between teaching and preaching. Perhaps their main lesson is, however, that all real learning is self-learning, that didactic writing, when practiced by an artist, gives way necessarily to autodidactic reading.

"An Education"

" 'An Education,' " Ozick informs us, "is the first story I ever wrote."[1] First published in 1972, it was actually written in 1964, on the heels of Ozick's completion of her massive novel *Trust.* It would not be surprising to find, therefore, on first looking into "An Education," that it deals with themes and contains patterns similar to those found in *Trust.* Such is indeed the case. Both narratives can be said to be about an academically successful young woman in search of a mentor from whom to learn a way of life. Both stories trace her intellectual itinerary until she reaches independence and maturity. Both tales illustrate a way of measuring oneself against one's proposed mentor and, finding him wanting, of coming to terms, out of personal strength, with the lost illusions of youth.

"An Education," an organic whole, shedding its own light, is divided into nine chapters. Each chapter depicts a scene in the education of the story's central figure, Una Meyer. The artistic burden of the piece—that "An Education" is a twice-told story and must be reread in order properly to be understood—is borne, modestly, by the centrally located fifth chapter and, more emphatically, by the story's ending.

There is another equally important division of the story, however, a ternary division that is discussed in chapter 5. "An Education" is a triptych, a portrait in three panels. The first panel depicts Una Meyer at the age of eighteen, an eager student of Latin who bursts with pride at her educational achievements in college. This portion of the story contains a measure of pure didacticism—some might say pedantry—as it leads its reader into the world of rhetoric and Latin love lyrics.[2] This panel depicts Una Meyer as exclusively devoted to matters of the mind and imagination. It also introduces two other characters called, ironically, Mr. Collie, a Latin teacher and pedant of the first water, and Mr. Organski, a doltish student of Latin in comparison to whom Una may indeed count herself among the intellectual elite. The names of these characters are obviously allegorical. Una—"one"—is both an everywoman and an individual. Mr. Collie is a dogmatic dog, and will disappear brusquely from the text. Mr. Organski, who will return to play a substantive role, is both the organ who introduces Una to sexuality and "organic" to Una Meyer's subsequent intellectual development. In truth, however, these names are mere decorations, nothing more than emblems, not yet symbols, and therefore their importance is limited and not overly to be stressed.

The second panel begins six years later. Una Meyer is now a twenty-four-year-old graduate student of the classics, a candidate for a Fulbright fellowship to Turkey to do research for a Ph.D. dissertation on left-handed Etruscan goddesses. As can be imagined, Una is vaguely dissatisfied with her life. On the one hand, she is no longer enthusiastic about her chosen field; on the other hand, although she does not actively wish to get married, she is unaccountably jealous of her engagement-ring-flashing cohorts in the university cafeteria.

She is in search of the feeling of exquisite happiness she had attained during her college years when she realized she was a member of an exclusive society. Since, in fiction, one who seeks always finds, Una comes upon a young woman named Rosalie, *sans* engagement ring, who is immersed in a book of cultural anthropology. Una engages Rosalie in an educational discussion, a discussion about the "perfectibility" of man. Rosalie offers to introduce Una to a "perfect" couple, Clement and Mary Chimes. Mary, a lawyer, is to begin a doctorate at Yale Law School as soon as she delivers herself of the baby she is carrying. Clement, who once studied with Margaret Mead, has changed fields and is now studying theology at the Union Theological Seminary in New York. The name "Chimes," Rosalie explains, is an Americanization of the Jewish name "Chaims." Mary and Clement, are, in addition to everything else, a perfect example of successfully assimilated Jews.[3]

The Chimeses are "perfect" in other ways as well. They are Renaissance figures possessed of the widest possible intellectual tastes, in art, philosophy, music, and language. Una is enraptured by the Chimeses and wishes she might enter into their society. Fortunately, the Chimeses, though without financial resources of their own, are generous with their selves. Previously they had graciously accepted Rosalie's invitation to move into her apartment. Now, they invite Una to share their New Haven living quarters. They accept Una's offer to contribute generously toward her room and board and are understanding when Una offers to rise early every morning to prepare their breakfast and to take care of the newborn Christina. Is Una being used? It depends on one's perspective. For Una, no sacrifice is too great because she does not feel that she is sacrificing anything. She has won her Fulbright and gleefully turned it down. She would rather bask in the glow of the perfect Chimes family than study ancient pagan religions. The story suggests that she has really exchanged one paganism for another.

Winter arrives. Despite the cold, Una feels an obligation to get the baby out from under foot and takes her for a stroll around the campus. Whom should she run into but Boris Organski, now a medical student at Yale? Boris alternates between teasing Una about her strange living arrangements and taking very seriously the infant's physical condition. The child is ill.

Boris begins to "court" Una after his own fashion. He picks undernourished Una up every evening after work—Una has meanwhile taken upon herself Clement's job—and takes her out for a

high-calorie meal. While she eats, he studies. He jokingly asserts
that he is fattening her up so that she will one day be fit to become
his mistress. Although the story does not say how much weight
Una gains on this regime, she does eventually wind up in Organski's
bed.

At the Chimeses, things grow progressively worse. Christina is
hospitalized. The couple fight, blaming each other and Una. On
the death of the baby, the Chimeses sell their books and move away,
never to be heard from again. The central panel ends with a fresh
revelation about Una's character: she refuses Organski's offer of
marriage.

As the third panel begins, Una is thirty-two years old. She has
finished her Ph.D., on a more benign subject than Etruscan goddesses, and has gone to teach at a small college in upstate New
York. There she runs into, of all people, Rosalie, recently widowed.
The two old acquaintances exchange rumors about the whereabouts
of the charming Chimeses. Having all these years refused Organski's
persistent offers of marriage, Una becomes a matchmaker and ar-
ranges for Rosalie to meet and marry Dr. Boris Organski. This
panel, as well as the story, closes ten years later as Una makes her
ultimate visit to the Organski family. The Chimeses have receded
even further into the background: there are not even rumors to
report. Everything in the Organski family is in order. Everything
is ordinary. Una decides that she will never come back.

The story is plain enough. Una now has a mind of her own. She
has had her education.

The story "An Education," as recapitulated above, is told from
the point of view of a caustic narrator. From this perspective, the
Chimeses are egocentric users of other people, Organski is a wise-
cracking but sensitive soul, and Una is a naive nincompoop in need
of an education about life. The end of the story brings with it a
revelation that forces us to reread the tale in another light, however.

The central chapter, chapter 5, hints at the story's basis in irony
and draws the reader's attention to the inevitability of multiple
readings. In this chapter the Chimeses have been trying to discourage
Una from taking up with Organski. They report to her that he is
jealous of their close relationship and has tried to set them against
her. It is obvious to the reader that the Chimeses are trying to
protect their claim on Una's loyalty. But what is going on in Una's
mind at the time? One would think that she would be swayed by

her mentor's arguments. She certainly voices no objections in Organski's defense. At the end of the chapter it is revealed that Una
is carrying in her pocket a supply of vitamins that Boris went out
of his way to procure free of charge for the Chimeses' ill child. The
bottle of vitamins stands in contradiction to the Chimeses' story.
It is, in a sense, a commentary on the story and forces Una to reread
it. Obviously, Boris is not the ogre the Chimeses say he is. (We
will see later than Boris is not the hero of the piece by any means,
but that revelation will be an indication of the story's complexity.)

The end of the story provides a similar disclosure that will force
us, the readers, to reread the whole story. As Rosalie and Una, at
the end, discuss their common experiences with the Chimeses, Una
reveals that just prior to meeting Boris she had begun to hate the
Chimeses. She was aware that they were hypocrites, schemers, plot-
ters, users, parasites. The story had given no indication of Una's
lucidity. There is a further surprise. She reveals that the death of
the baby had changed her attitude from hatred to pity. She had
gone from a position of inferiority to one of superiority. Without
our knowing it, the disciple had become a master. During the course
of the story Una had learned from Boris that the Chimeses were
"selfish," "shallow," and "not awfully bright after all."[4] But she
explains to Rosalie that this realization did not diminish her ad-
miration for them. The Chimeses had what Una sees as a certain
intactness. "You could see through them," she agrees with Rosalie.
"They were wonderful all the same, just *because* you could see through
them. They were like a bubble that never broke, you could look
right through and they kept on shining no matter what. They're
the only persons I've ever known who stayed the same from start
to finish" (126).

The major difference between the Chimeses and Una is that Una
does *not* remain intact from start to finish. She undergoes an educational process. Ironically it is the Chimeses who present themselves
as her mentors. Indeed, they are presented as educators above all.
For instance, the book Rosalie is reading when she first meets Una
is a book she has borrowed from the Chimes library. This is a library
with a difference, however, for, as Rosalie explains, "when you
return a book they ask you *questions* about it" (79–80). They are
not only teachers; they are also preachers. They do not refrain, for
example, from exhorting Una to abandon her Fulbright, and they
do so by using a vocabulary that has religious overtones. To accept

the Fulbright would be to go against her nature, says Mary, and, says Clement, going against your nature is "the same as going against God" (86). The Chimeses represent a religion where intactness, or perfection, is a given, and not something to be strived for. Una, it will be remembered, believes in the perfectibility of man, not necessarily in his perfection.

The Chimeses are presented to Una not as perfectible but as perfection itself. "They were perfect. Everything about them was perfect" (82). Their apartment is "exactly right, just what you would expect of a pair of intellectual lovers" (83). The baby the Chimeses give birth to is also perfect. Una "looked at her as on some sacred object which she was not allowed to touch too often" (92). "Whenever she lifted Christina, she felt she was holding treasure" (93–94). The Chimeses, who preach to Una a way of life, are transformed by Una into pagan idols. The story becomes "An Education" for Una when she realizes that her "teachers" are not objects for worship but rather subjects to be studied.

To understand the Chimeses one must realize that they live in a realm apart from reality, not in the supernatural, but in the domain of the extraordinary. They have the aura of a work of art, or of a stage play. They are theatrical not because they enact *King Lear* on the beach but because they put on a play in which they themselves are scripted. They are given to outrageous gestures—like cutting holes in doors to make room for stereo speakers—and they stage melodramatic scenes. "When all the lights were off and everyone was still, Clement and Mary came softly out of their bedroom in their pajamas, and, one by one, they kissed Una and Rosalie as though they had been their own dear children" (90). At the hospital, when other people would be overcome with grief, the Chimeses are on display. They play the role of concerned parents, are noticed by the hospital staff, and their performance exhilarates them. Even the death of their baby does nothing to diminish their brilliance. On the contrary, "they were glad to be interrupted. Fate had marred their perfect dedication and they did not despair. A brilliance stirred them. They were ready for something new" (122). We will learn later that there is something wrong with someone who does not despair, whose hope does not derive from despair. There is something wrong with the eternal optimist. It is this optimism, nevertheless, that draws Una to the Chimeses.

Una is not similarly attracted to Boris Organski. Rather, she is submissive to him. Una does not disagree with Boris when he informs her that "your friends are dangerous madmen" (103). He has analyzed them clinically and keenly. He himself is the subject of an analysis by the Chimeses. They notice right away that he has grave faults. "Medical types tend to think they're little gods," they say with some degree of accuracy. "He's pretty self-important, that guy. He's just looking to assert so-called authority" (108). Boris is clinical not only in his diagnosis of Christina's illness and the Chimeses' character. He is also clinical in his assessment of Una. He has analyzed Una's unwillingness to get married. "She was suffering from an ineradicable marriage-trauma. She had already been married vicariously; she had *lived* the Chimeses' marriage, she continued to believe in its perfection, and she was afraid she would fail to duplicate it" (125). Boris's analysis is likely to be correct, but at the same time it is a misreading of Una's text.

One of the reasons that Una does not wish to marry Boris is, as we have seen, that he presents himself, no less than the Chimeses, as a little godlet. Una refuses to become an idol worshiper once more, especially since Boris does not have the aura that the Chimeses possess. Of course, as a teacher, or perhaps as a preacher, Boris does have something to teach Una. He not only initiates her into the world of love, he also admonishes her to "abandon fantasy." "If you expose your liaison, you see, it will perhaps hint to them that you have an adumbration of a chimera of a life of your own" (113).

But Una Meyer is eager to live in a world of fantasy. At the moment her adventure begins she has already realized that left-handed Etruscan goddesses are not enough to fill the void she is feeling. She is world-weary, having decided that "there were no new revelations to be had in the tired old world" (80). Like Bleilip in "Bloodshed," she is in despair, and she sees immediately that the Chimeses are capable of realizing her most romantic desires. But Una is not merely a romantic. She is also an intellectual, a scholar. She is therefore ripe for an educational experience.

Over and over, it is emphasized to Una that she needs educating. The Chimeses, Rosalie, Organski all propose to be her teachers. Una does not reject their offers, but neither does she accept them. She is content to observe and to teach herself. The Chimeses, Rosalie, and Organski are not teachers but subject matter. Slowly, by accumulation, she comes to see that Clement is a faker, Rosalie is ordinary, and Boris is a bully. Clement, she sees, for example, cannot get beyond the grand gesture. Is he writing a long satirical poem, *Social Cancer*, or is he just proclaiming it written? "She hardly dared to articulate it, even to herself, but she secretly wondered whether Clement hadn't just gone back to sleep after breakfast" (100). Little does Clement know how right he is when he one day announces to Una: "You're on the brink of maturity, you could find yourself, your true métier, any day now" (109). But she does not give up her fantasy life so easily.

Una finds it easier to abandon Boris than to forsake the Chimeses. After their departure, Una persists in reading them into stories she sees in newspapers. She re-creates not only the texts she reads but also the Chimeses themselves. A firm believer in the redemptive powers of education, she is positive that they can be "repaired and reconverted by fresh educations" (123). Curiously, she has no interest in making her Chimeses into Jews once again. She is content that Clement become a Buddhist monk, so long as he gets a "fresh education."

The Ozick heroine, from Allegra's daughter, to Una Meyer, to the early Ruth Puttermesser, does not get married. For Una, who realizes that education is an eternal process, marriage—and by extension real life—must be continuously postponed. Una refuses Boris's offer of marriage because, as she says, "there's no education in it" (124). And yet Una, who has finally learned to live with imperfection, cannot endure that "her education should go on and on and on" (127). At the end, Una is confronted with an existential dilemma that causes her to despair. It is a despair that Una, thanks to her education, has earned.

"Bloodshed"

"Despair must be earned," cries the rebbe of "Bloodshed," another of Ozick's didactic and hortatory stories. "Bloodshed" is also about despair, what Cynthia Ozick will later call "existential dread." Despite the fact that the setting of the story is quintessentially Jewish—a Hasidic town—and that the protagonist is an assimilated Jew, the story is only superficially about "a confrontation between a secularized American Jew and an old-country believer," as Ruth Wisse asserts.[5] The only confrontations in the story take place *within* the characters themselves.

One must not be taken in by the uncanny resemblance between

Ozick's story and Philip Roth's "Eli, the Fanatic." As Wisse notes, in both stories the moral scales are tipped in favor of the old-world believer "not merely for his wry intelligence and personal courage, but also for having survived the Holocaust. In both works the protagonist capitulates to this superior moral force, admits the relative hollowness of his own comfortable existence, and recognizes, even if he cannot accept, the elevated spiritual situation of the other." Wisse's parallel is neat but not accurate. "Bloodshed," a highly original work, cryptic and symbolic, must be read as a function of its own encoding system.

"Bloodshed" is about one afternoon in the life of Jules Bleilip, a forty-two-year-old lawyer-turned-fund-raiser.[6] Like most of Ozick's main characters, Bleilip has a Jewish background, a background that is for the most part kept hidden from the reader. All we learn about him is that he remembers some Yiddish and Hebrew and is able to recall some Jewish ritual practices. We also know that, prior to his trip to the town of the Hasidim, he had read accounts of Hasidic lore. "Of their popular romantic literature he knew the usual bits and pieces, legends, occult passions, quirks, histories . . . pretty stories in the telling, even more touching in the reading—poetry."[7]

The poetry of "Bloodshed" is divided into two halves. In the first half it is recounted that Jules Bleilip, for no apparent reason other than curiosity, has come to the town of the Hasidim to visit his cousin Toby and her husband, Yussel. Toby has adopted the Hasidic way of life only since college; previously she too had been assimilated into the majority culture. It is not strictly accurate to say that this is a family visit. The family relationship is distant, tenuous, probably only a pretext Bleilip uses to gain access to the town itself. It certainly does not appear that Toby and Yussel have gone out of their way to invite Bleilip to their home. No festive meal is served. Precious little time is spent in their residence. In fact, Bleilip stays with his "cousins" only long enough to take Toby to task for having abandoned her youthful ambitions in favor of a society that restricts woman's role to that of homemaker. Toby argues that she has chosen this way of life, freely, because it affords her the opportunity to study Torah—the Jewish textual tradition—in her own way. Bleilip is also given a tour by Yussel of their house's electrical appliances, proudly displaying acceptance of the blessings of modernity. While these superficial conversations are going on, another current is flow-ing beneath the surface. Not so obviously, Bleilip has come in search of something beyond a debate with his relatives about tradition versus modernity.

Yussel understands this intuitively and uses the approach of the hour of the afternoon prayer as a pretext to invite Bleilip for an "audience" with the community's spiritual leader, the rebbe. The service is divided into three parts—this time not by Ozick but by Jewish tradition—beginning with *mincha* (the afternoon prayer service), followed by a study session, and concluding with *ma'ariv* (the evening prayer). This evening there will also be an epilogue, provided by Cynthia Ozick. The study session, in a story that focuses on teaching and preaching, will receive the most light and deserves the most attention.

After the very brief afternoon prayer, the men of the *minyan* (the prayer group), including Bleilip, sit themselves around a table for the exposition of the Law. This afternoon the men are continuing a discussion of the Mishnaic commentary on the laws of the Day of Atonement as it was celebrated during the time of the Holy Temple. Of course Bleilip does not understand the Hebrew, the Aramaic, or the Yiddish out of which this exposition is being woven. Somehow, however, by dint of concentration and memory, he understands that what is being described is a highly complex ceremony performed by the High Priest, involving changes of vestments, ritual immersions, and the sacrifice of animals, all in the name of atonement. Bleilip finds all these rites primitive and repugnant, a confirmation of his modernistic opposition to religion in general.

Examining the faces of the Hasidim sitting around the table, including the study leader, he tries to discern which one among them may be the rebbe. The rebbe is not the expositor of the text, but rather an ordinary-looking fellow who interrupts the expositor to teach the lessons of the law. The rebbe seems to eschew ritual as much as Bleilip does. His interpretation of the laws of the scapegoat of Yom Kippur (day of atonement), seems to coincide with Bleilip's. He teaches that, according to Jewish law, the scapegoat does not atone for men's sins; only man himself can atone for his sins. The high priest does not cleanse man of his sins. Only God can cleanse. The rebbe seems to be saying that not only are the laws being studied obsolete, but that they had no function in the time of the temple either.

The rebbe notes, however, that sacrifice is not out of date; it is practiced all the time. A survivor of the Holocaust like most of his adherents, he is only too aware of the modern propensity to shed blood. "For animals we in our day substitute men." It is important to notice that the rebbe sees *himself* as a part of the society that sheds blood, although it is clear that he has been only a victim, never an oppressor. The rebbe avers that there is a lesson to be derived from the juxtaposition of the temple ritual and Jewish history, and that is despair. But does the rebbe teach despair? No, he only mirrors it.

He turns abruptly to Bleilip and forces him to admit that the despair deduced by the rebbe from his texts—both commentary and history—resonated in his own soul. Bleilip denies that he is in despair. "I don't have a mistaken life," he cries. Whereupon the rebbe orders Bleilip to empty his pockets. A schoolchild confronted by a stern master, Bleilip pulls out from one of his pockets a toy gun. Is Bleilip contemplating suicide, trying to get used to the idea of suicide by fondling a toy gun in his pocket? Bleilip's intentions are never made clear in the story and the reader is invited to muse on this scene-stopping event as the congregation passes on to the evening service, and to subsequent dispersal to their homes.

At the conclusion of the service, only Bleilip and Yussel remain in the presence of the rebbe. The latter mysteriously orders Bleilip to empty his second pocket. This time a real pistol, loaded, is produced. Over his protests, Yussel is now dismissed: the rebbe understands that it is not he who requires protection. Bleilip will have his private audience with the rebbe, a thing he devoutly desires. During their tête-à-tête, the rebbe obtains from Bleilip the confession that he once killed a pigeon with his pistol. Bleilip has blood on his hands no less than the High Priest. But that is not the rebbe's lesson. The rebbe, a confessing confessor, admits that he himself sometimes does not believe. He explains that it is within the parameters of human behavior to have doubts. He also obtains from Bleilip the admission that he too sometimes believes. This is also the human condition. Besides, it is implied, if he did not sometimes believe, he would not have sought out the rebbe. Does the rebbe find Bleilip's belief a consolation? Engimatically, the rebbe deduces from Bleilip's belief—and not from his murder of the pigeon—the conclusion that "You are as bloody as anyone." The rebbe's conclusion requires interpretation.

In her homily on "The Riddle of the Ordinary," Ozick posits a fundamental dualism:

We all divide the world into the Ordinary and the Extraordinary. This is undoubtedly the most natural division the mind is subject to—plain and fancy, simple and recondite, commonplace and awesome, usual and un- usual, credible and incredible, quotidian and intrusive, natural and un- natural, regular and irregular, boring and rhapsodic, secular and sacred, profane and holy: however the distinction is characterized, there is no human being who does not, in his own everydayness, feel the difference between the Ordinary and the Extraordinary.[8]

The story "Bloodshed" is in a way an illustration of Ozick's thesis that the world is governed by an elemental polarity. That is why, perhaps, two teachers are needed: one to teach the law, the other to teach the lessons of the law. In this story there are, in addition, two guns; a real one and a fake one, an ordinary one and an ex- traordinary one. The extraordinary one is the one that comes instead of reality. The toy gun is like an idol and is therefore more to be feared than the real one it comes to replace. Ozick herself elaborates on the dangers of the "Instead Of" and exhorts her readers to understand the nature of the danger:

There is always the easy, the sweet, the beckoning, the lenient, the *in- teresting* lure of the *Instead Of*: the wood of the tree instead of God, the rapture-bringing horizon instead of God, the work of art instead of God, the passion for history instead of God, philosophy and history of philosophy instead of God, the State instead of God, the shrine instead of God, the sage instead of God, the order of the universe instead of God, the prophet instead of God. There is no Instead Of. There is only the Creator. God is alone. . . . God is One.[9]

"Bloodshed is also about the "Instead Of." It is certainly no coin- cidence that "Bloodshed" should contain an interpretation of a prac- tice in Jewish Temple law dealing with two types of sacrificial goats. According to the biblical account in Leviticus 16, the high priest was to take two goats: one to be an ordinary sin offering to God in the temple; the other to be sent out into the wilderness, to a place the Hebrew calls Azazel, and dashed to death as an atonement. Nobody knows the meaning of Azazel. Ozick indulges, therefore, in her own brand of etymology.[10] "What the word Azazel means exactly is not known—we call it wilderness, some say it is hell itself. . . . But whatever we mean by 'wilderness,' whatever we mean by 'hell,' surely the plainest meaning is *instead of*. Wilderness instead of easeful places, hell and devils instead of plenitude, life, peace. Goat instead of man" ("Bloodshed," 66). What the rebbe comes to teach is that there need be no *instead of*, there need be no hell.

There is a duality in the world to be sure. There are self-evident differences, of course, but for the man of belief these differences must be lived simultaneously. The rebbe tells the story of another duality, of another rebbe who believed that all people should walk around, not with two pistols, but with two slips of paper in their pockets. On one slip should be written: "I am but dust and ashes." On the other slip would be inscribed: "For my sake was the world created." This is a duality worthy of man, he preaches. A man should live in both despair and hope, the hope that comes from belief.

It must be emphasized that the belief the rebbe preaches is not one in rituals and in miracles. "He can't fly" (58), Toby admonishes her cousin. And indeed, the rebbe is presented as the "ordinary article, no mystic, a bit bossy, pedagogue, noisy preacher" (69). A teacher and a preacher, the rebbe has a very simple lesson to teach. "I do not believe in magic," he asserts. "That there are influences I do believe. . . . Turnings. That a man can be turned from folly, error, wrong choices. From misery, evil, private rage. From a mistaken life" (69).

The rebbe's powers are this-worldly and extend only to an uncanny ability to read the "other's" text. He has seen through Bleilip, like an X-ray, and knows that Bleilip has not yet been pushed over the precipice of despair, to be dashed irretrievably against the rocks. He knows that Bleilip is educable and that he has come for an education. Logically, the last place Bleilip ought to have come to in his quest is to a Hasidic village. He is a rationalist, a *mitnagged* (an enemy of the Hasidim). From his reading he has learned that Hasidism, with its purported emphasis on the mediatory gifts of the rebbe, had become "christologized." Ironically, Bleilip, the assimilated Jew, is a defender of the Jewish faith in its purest form. So is this unconventional rebbe. The rebbe shocks Bleilip because he is not a mediator between man and God. He is a mediator between man and his self. The rebbe's function is to tell the truth (the *emes,* in the rebbe's Yiddishized Hebrew). Reading Bleilip's text, the rebbe underlines Bleilip's existential dread. "You believe the world is in vain, *emes?*" (67). He tells his disciples all about Bleilip; he has a lesson to teach them too. "Man he equates with the goats. The Temple, in memory and anticipation, he considers an abattoir. The world he regards as a graveyard" (68).

The rebbe is not only a truth-teller; he is also a gifted pedagogue who takes his pupils' needs into account. He tells Bleilip those truths about himself that he is capable of using. Bleilip has come to the Hasidic town for one purpose, ironically, for the same purpose that Toby has come: to learn. "He never supposed he would get to the rebbe himself—all his hope was only for a glimpse of the effect of the rebbe. Of influences" (72). From the rebbe Bleilip got exactly what he came for, and this does not include magic or miracles. It consists of the rebbe's ability to speak from Bleilip's own heart, in the matter of despair, and to try to influence Bleilip to turn from that despair.

The rebbe reminds Bleilip that Jews are not South Sea Islanders, to be studied anthropologically, but that Judaism is an antique tradition from which one is enjoined to learn a value system. Why is it important for Bleilip to know that anyone who believes in God already has blood on his hands? Is it to cause him despair? Is it meant as a consolation? Is it to teach Bleilip that bloodshed is part of the human condition? Is it perhaps to teach him to accept the shedding of his own blood, that man's lot is "to be cut down" (66), that "instead of choice we have the yoke" (66)? No, the rebbe's assertion comes to teach Bleilip that belief is a choice made in an enduring value system. "For us there is the Most High, joy, life. For us, trust!" (67). "Bloodshed" is therefore an attempt to educate Bleilip, to initiate him into a culture and society that values "trust."

At the end of the adventure, the rebbe returns to Bleilip a gun-laden handkerchief, "for whatever purpose he thought he needed it" (72). The rebbe knows that he has gone as far as he could with Bleilip. He has had his influence. Whether Bleilip will perform a "turning" (the Hebrew word is *tshuva,* and is used for "repentence") will be a choice freely made by Bleilip. As at the end of *Trust,* as at the end of "An Education," the reader is free to believe that, whether under the influence of the teacher or as the result of a process, the protagonist will choose to be his own master, and, therefore, to take control of his own destiny.

In *A Fable for Critics,* James Russell Lowell (1819–1891), American poet and publicist and first editor of *The Atlantic Monthly,* wrote the following verses about himself:

> There is Lowell who's striving Parnassus to climb
> With a whole bale of *isms* tied together with rhyme, . . .
> The top of the hill he will ne'er come nigh reaching
> Till he learns the distinction 'twixt singing and preaching.[11]

Despite her anguish about her own devotion to high art, Cynthia Ozick is indeed striving to climb the Parnassus of prose fiction. As much as Lowell she senses the distinction between singing and preaching, but she does not accept it. She cannot accept it. She states her credo in the preface to *Bloodshed and Three Novellas:* "I believe that stories ought to judge and interpret the world" (4). For her a work of art must not only be but mean. Cynthia Ozick has come to learn that in the Jewish textual tradition singing *is* preaching, and that the only way to reach "the top of the hill" is to remain faithful to the aesthetic of one's tradition. Posterity will judge to what extent Cynthia Ozick has made a contribution toward formulating a new version of a Jewish aesthetic that values, as much as singing, both teaching and preaching.

Chapter Five
A Jewish Fantastic: "The Pagan Rabbi" and "Levitation"

Among the many stories in the Ozick canon that have supernatural elements, several belong firmly in the fantastic genre and may be counted among its most masterful representations. This chapter examines two of Ozick's most powerful and at the same time most representative efforts, "The Pagan Rabbi" and "Levitation."

For many years, Ozick has been asking herself, and us, how it is possible to be both Jewish and a writer. For her, the term "Jewish writer" is an oxymoron—like "pagan rabbi"—in which each half of the phrase is antithetical to the other and cancels it out. If writing is pagan, how is the Jew to handle the overwhelming need to write? One answer is to stifle one's impulses. Many of Ozick's stories are, at least superficially, polemics against storywriting. Another response is to "compose midrashim," tales that fall within the Jewish textual tradition.

"The Pagan Rabbi" and "Levitation" are both difficult and interesting: difficult because they contain both polemics against writing and midrashim; interesting because they have a problematic mystical element that is also within the Jewish textual tradition. Ozick comments on the mystical tendency to be found in many of her stories. Her attitude to the "mystical enterprise" may be somewhat surprising: "I myself am hostile to the whole mystical enterprise. I'm a rationalist and I'm a skeptic. But there's something in me that is fascinated by this surrender to the mystical blur between the creator and the created. It's really a fictional theme for me. I reject it intellectually and emotionally. But it's where the stories come from."[1]

Is this statement a confession, or is it a literary *profession de foi?* Does it mean something when you make a literary theme out of an attitude you reject? Can a writer make a poetics out of contradiction?

What, exactly, is this "something" that Ozick finds in herself? Can we pinpoint its source? These are some of the questions that pose themselves to anyone attempting to relate the oeuvre of Cynthia Ozick to the genre of the fantastic.

The narrator of another of Ozick's fantastic stories, "Puttermesser and Xanthippe," commenting on the pervasiveness of golem-making in Jewish history, makes an observation similar to the one offered by Ozick concerning her own writing:

> Puttermesser was no mystic. . . . Her mind was clean; she was a rationalist. . . . What interested Puttermesser was something else: it was the plain fact that golem-makers were neither visionaries nor magicians nor sorcerers. They were neither fantasists nor fabulists nor poets. They were, by and large, scientific realists. . . . Even Rabbi Elijah, . . . the Vilna *Gaon,* once attempted . . . to make a golem! And the Vilna *Gaon* . . . was . . . the scourge of mystics. . . . If the Vilna *Gaon* could contemplate the making of a golem, . . . there was nothing irrational in it.[2]

Obviously there is "something" in the Vilna *Gaon,* in the most Jewish of Jewish writers (where the term is *not* an oxymoron), that is also "fascinated by the surrender to the mystical blur between the creator and the created."

The fantastic is an elusive genre, as Tzvetan Todorov has explained in his seminal work on the subject, because by its very nature it is fluid, dynamic, evanescent, characterized by change.[3] It does nothing more, Todorov writes, than occupy a duration. It is characterized by a blur, by the hesitation of the reader implicit in the text as to whether the incident he is reading about will resolve itself into one of two neighboring genres, what Todorov calls the uncanny (*l'étrange*) or the marvelous (*le merveilleux*). The uncanny (a term taken from Freud's 1919 essay[4]) describes a situation in which a supernatural event is explained rationally. The marvelous describes a situation in which the supernatural is simply accepted as such. "The fantastic is that hesitation experienced by a person who knows only the laws of nature, confronting an apparently supernatural event."[5] In his analysis of the *problems* posed by the fantastic, Todorov emphasizes that it is a literature "which postulates the existence of the real, the natural, the normal, in order to attack it subsequently."[6] The fantastic is governed by a poetics of contradiction.

For Ozick, who also attacks what she postulates, there is a nuance of "the real" that may be of consequence. Todorov implies that the fantastic text, an experience of the limits of the real, may be the quintessential artistic text. Ozick answers the question "What is Art?" with a liturgical, almost homiletical declaration: "It is first noticing, and then sanctifying, the Ordinary. It is making the Ordinary into the Extraordinary. It is the impairment of the distinction between the Ordinary and the Extraordinary." She goes on to say in the same essay that the Jew has a very important trait in common with the artist: "Nothing that passes before him is taken for granted, everything is exalted."[7]

"The Pagan Rabbi"

Take, for a first example, the plot of "The Pagan Rabbi." Two young men, sons of prominent rabbis, had been classmates together at a rabbinical seminary. One—the narrator—drops out of school and marries Jane, a gentile girl, an incident which causes his father to sit *shiva* (a seven-day mourning period) on his account. He subsequently goes into his uncle's fur business in upstate New York, is miserable in his marriage because his wife is frigid (he calls her a puritan), gets divorced, moves back to New York City, and, deciding to deal in writers and writing, opens a bookstore. The other—Isaac Kornfeld—continues his rabbinical studies, becomes a professor of "mishnaic history" (whatever that is), publishes brilliant monographs on Jewish subjects, and causes his father to beam broadly with pride. He subsequently marries Sheindel, a *sheitel*-wearing Jewish woman, and together they have seven daughters. Kornfeld winds up committing suicide by hanging himself from a tree with his tallith.

Almost everything about these two parallel lives is ordinary, recognizable, sociologically accurate, and, until the strange, brutal fact and manner of the suicide, utterly realistic. The key, the most important fact in the narrative, is not, however, the tallith. The element that moves the tale from the realistic to the fantastic is the tree from which Isaac Kornfeld hangs himself. He may have been a rabbi, but, as the narrator learns when he goes to pay a condolence call on the widow, he has become a "pagan rabbi," a teller of seemingly supernatural stories and a person who has himself lived inside these stories. Sheindel describes a series of her husband's literary inventions:

These were the bedtime stories Isaac told Naomi and Esther: about mice
that danced and children who laughed. When Miriam came he invented
a speaking cloud. With Ophra it was a turtle that married a blade of
withered grass. By Leah's time the stones had tears for their leglessness.
Rebecca cried because of a tree that turned into a girl and could never
grow colors again in autumn. Shiphra, the littlest, believes that a pig has
a soul.[8]

A difference between Ozick's fiction and classical nineteenth-
century fantastic literature is apparent. Reality is not only social
order. It is also natural order, cosmic. The fantastic in Ozick's tale
resolves itself into something more than the marvelous, and, despite
appearances, into something more than a mere fairy tale. What
Ozick is describing in her story about Isaac's stories is the development of the narrative of the family life of Rabbi Isaac and Sheindel
Kornfeld into a story belonging to the Jewish fantastic, with its
judgment of the world.

Isaac Kornfeld, a Jew, would frequently go out into the field to
daydream. This action bursts with significance, places the tale firmly
within a certain Jewish textual tradition.[9] The epigraph to Ozick's
story, taken from *Mishna Avot,* performs the first step of this function: "He who is walking along and studying but then breaks off
to remark, 'How lovely is that tree!' or 'How beautiful is that fallow
field!'—Scripture regards such a one has having hurt his own being"
(3). The connection is clear: there is a danger to one's very Jewishness
inherent in an aesthetic appreciation of nature. Ozick has made
much of the fundamental opposition between paganism and the
Jewish idea.

In this story, the very choice of the name "Isaac Kornfeld" places
Ozick in the Jewish textual tradition, in the company of no less a
Jewish writer than Rashi, the Jewish commentator par excellence.
"Isaac Kornfeld" clearly alludes to the Scriptural tale of another
Isaac, a young Yitzhak, son of Abraham, who, awaiting the arrival
of his bride, goes out into the field to daydream. There is, first,
the linguistic connection between "Isaac Kornfeld" and *Vayetzeh
Yitzhak lasu'ah basadeh"* (Gen. 24: 63). And there is a connection
between Rashi and Ozick. Rashi recalls a midrash on what Isaac
was "doing" in the field. Rather than have him daydream on the
erotic consequences of a marriage, Rashi reins in the dreamer and
has him praying instead (*"lasuah: leshon tefila"*). Ozick's midrash

tells of what happens when one goes out into nature for nonliturgical purposes.

Isaac Kornfeld, it must be emphasized, was also a writer and not only of scholarly monographs. The story contains, *mise en abyme*, [10] Isaac's text. This text may be interpreted, variously, as the suicide note of a madman (and thus the fantastic story resolves itself into the uncanny), as the description of a supernatural occurrence (in which the story would resolve itself into the marvelous), or as an allegory or parable. Isaac's verbatim text has three "readers." Sheindel, who knows the text by heart, reads the first half to the narrator; the narrator reads the other half out loud. The reader implicit in the text, the reader who knows that he is in the genre of the fantastic, wavers between Sheindel's marvelous reading and the narrator's uncanny one. The "letter" is addressed to someone called "creature," and "loveliness." It is a Jewish text and like many Jewish texts, it begins inside the story of the Exodus. It contains a brilliant midrash against diaspora living (based on a highly intuitive, almost pantheistic mysticism). The two philosophical points of Isaac's midrash are that idolatry does not exist—because death does not exist—and that, in the plant world, in the world of trees, in the world of nature, the soul is able to be free.

The next stage in Isaac's *itinerarium mentis* (and in the reader's road to the fantastic) is his "discovery" (on the outside as it were, in the field) of wood nymphs: He has seen a nymph save the life of one of his daughters drowning in a stream. He comes to the conclusion that there are only two ways to communicate and commune with these free-floating souls. To experience ecstasy (to stand outside of himself), he must either die or copulate with nature.

He tries the latter first. In what Ozick could only have meant to be the description of an abomination, Isaac Kornfeld fornicates with an oak tree and succeeds in achieving some sort of ecstasy this way. He even conjures up the presence of a nice pagan girl, Iripomoňoéià (the "apple of his eye"), who informs him that his soul has stepped out of his body and is now visible. Isaac looks at his soul and is mortified by what he sees. Isaac Kornfeld's soul, walking in the field, studying Talmud, is Jewish! The soul does not even notice Iripomoňoéià, denies her, "passes indifferent through the beauty of the field" (35) and is faithful to the rabbinic dictum that Ozick had quoted for us in the epigraph of her story. When Isaac Kornfeld confronts his Jewish soul, he learns that to have a Jewish soul is not to be free in nature but to be bound to law. According to Kornfeld's soul, the page of Talmud is a garden, the letters on the page are birds, and the columns of commentary on the page are trees. When Isaac Kornfeld learns that he cannot be a Jew and a writer and teller of stories at the same time, and, moreover, when he learns that he cannot live inside his stories, he decides to die.

If the story ended here, the fantastic would have dissolved into nothing more than allegory, with a clear message: If you want to be a Jew, give up writing and all that enterprise entails. But it does not end here. It ends with the reactions of the narrator and Sheindel to Isaac's tale.

Todorov, for whom the end of a work of art is art itself, and for whom the subject of writing is writing itself, warns against the use of the fantastic genre for allegorical purposes. He sees only two possible resolutions for the fantastic:

At the story's end the reader makes a decision even if the character does not; he opts for one solution or the other, and thereby emerges from the fantastic. If he decides that the laws of reality remain intact and permit an explanation of the phenomena described, we say that the work belongs to another genre: the uncanny. If, on the contrary, he decides that new laws of nature must be entertained to account for the phenomena, we enter the genre of the marvelous. [11]

He does recognize, however, that, using a strict definition of allegory, where the double meaning of words is indicated in an *explicit* fashion and does not proceed from the reader's interpretation, whether arbitrary or not, the fantastic lends itself to an allegorical resolution.

Cynthia Ozick, who has called for a liturgical component in Jewish literature, balks, however, at the use of the term *allegory* for her own works:

Two stories—"The Pagan Rabbi" and "Usurpation"—intend to be representative of certain ideas; but I think of them rather as parables than allegories. In an allegory, the story *stands for* an idea, and the idea can be stated entirely apart from the story, in a parable, story and idea are so inextricably fused that they cannot be torn free of each other. In this sense, I hope I've written an occasional parable. But I would never seek out allegory, which strikes me as a low form. [12]

Whether we use the term *allegory* or *parable,* or indeed neither of these, we can agree with the comment of Ruth R. Wisse about the ending of an Ozick story: "Her reader is expected at the conclusion of her stories to have an insight, to understand the point of events."[13] Ozick's warning against allegory should be heeded in considering the end of this supernatural tale.

Sheindel, it is clear, is on the side of Rashi. There is only one thing a Jew ought to do in a field, and that is to pray. It would be even better to make a fence about the law and not go out into the field at all. The fantastic, she seems to be saying, is not a place for Jewish rabbis. For the narrator, and even more for the reader implicit in the text, the ending is more problematic. The narrator is a product of the Enlightenment and has even failed as a product of the Enlightenment. And yet, when he goes home, the narrator flushes all his house plants down the toilet. He apparently agrees with Sheindel's judgment of the world. Does he thereby also accept Sheindel's reading of the story? Not entirely. When he met Sheindel, in her grief, he was attracted to her. He fell in love with her and even contemplated marrying her and normalizing his life in Judaism. In the end, however, the narrator rejects Sheindel because he cannot accept her severity. He is aware of the dangers of the Enlightenment. But he would rather be normal. The act of consigning the house plants to New York's sewers is a mere gesture, however significant. The narrator will, we are certain, continue to live in the world. And after "The Pagan Rabbi," Cynthia Ozick will continue to write fantastic short stories in which she investigates further the liturgical possibilities of the Jewish fantastic.

"Levitation"

The title of "Levitation" places that tale in the "key"[14] of the supernatural, creates at the threshold of the story the atmosphere of the uncanny in which the reader expects to find himself immersed. Once inside, however, the reader finds depictions of human beings and descriptions of events and surroundings so everyday that the expectations created by the title are contradicted. Are we in the *heimlich* or the *unheimlich?*[15] The reader's hesitation at this point creates the "moment"—amounting to the duration of the reading of the literary text—that Todorov says characterizes the fantastic.

The critic Joseph Epstein has asked whether "The Pagan Rabbi" and especially "Levitation" are examples of the new "liturgical" fiction, the new "literature attentive to the implications of Covenant and Commandment" that Cynthia Ozick has set herself to write. Epstein finds these stories "willed and schematic" "even where I cannot precisely figure out the scheme."[16] Epstein had thought at first that the difficulty lay in what he perceived as Ozick's inability to end a story successfully. (The ending of "Levitation" is given by Epstein as the most blatant example of the defect, but the charge has been made against many of Ozick's short stories, including "The Pagan Rabbi.") He later came to the conclusion, he tells us, that what he found objectionable in Ozick's writings had to do precisely with the subject that interests us here: Ozick's "fantastical" fiction. "I like Miss Ozick's work least," he writes, "when she is readiest to let her imagination rip; I like it best when she brings her Jews down to earth."[17]

Epstein's concerns—with endings, with the fantastic, and with earthiness—are related. They are concerns of both Ozick and literary theoreticians.

In a response to a question about her attitude toward the beginnings and endings of her stories, Ozick declared: "I am never attentive to the end, at least not until I get there, because I trust the end to be implicit in the beginning."[18] Jurij Lotman, who has made a systematic study of the structure of the artistic text, notes, "The act of making, of creating, is an act of beginning. . . . The fundamental question is not how it ended but where it originated."[19] As we have seen in both Todorov's theory and Ozick's practice, the fantastic short story is anchored in reality, derives from reality, and has its origins in reality.

"Levitation" is more evidently about writers and their writing than is "The Pagan Rabbi." It is "about" two writers, second-rate novelists, whose subjects are Jewishness and ordinariness. It is also about contradictions, including the contradiction between Jewishness and ordinariness. The one taboo of Lucy and Jimmy Feingold is that they may not write about writers. To write about writers who do not write about writers—as Ozick does here—is to create a contradiction. It is also to create an uncanny effect of mirroring, where the mirrors do not so much reflect reality but refract it, causing a feeling of reverberation, of shimmering. In addition, Ozick does not hesitate to include other texts in her text, the verbatim quotation of several lines from the writings of her characters and an almost verbatim regurgitation of Jimmy's readings in Jewish history.

The setting for the "levitation" of the title, its shell, its outer frame, is made up of the concrete details of the real life of two writers living in New York City. Feingold makes his living, in real life, as a powerless editor at a publishing house—nervous about his editorial decisions, rejecting manuscripts for ignominious reasons. Although a writer, he is ordinary. He has a "nice plain pale face, likeable."[20] He is recognizable. Every New Yorker will also recognize Ozick's portrayal of the vicissitudes of New York existence as true to life:

New York: They risked their necks if they ventured out to Broadway for a loaf of bread after dark; muggers hid behind the seesaws in the playgrounds, junkies with knives hung upside down in the jungle gym. Every apartment a lit fortress; you admired the lamps and the locks . . . and the police rods on the doors, the lamps with timers set to make burglars think you were always home. Footsteps in the corridor, the elevator's midnight grind; caution's muffled gasps. (8)

In the intensity of this realism, there is a hint of the transformation—if not yet the sanctification—of the ordinary into the extraordinary. As she had done with Isaac Kornfeld, Ozick incorporates the writing of her characters into her own. Lucy, in her novel, turns Ozick's realistic description of New York into a hauntingly Kafkaesque one. Upper West Side apartments, Lucy writes, "have mysterious layouts. Rooms with doors that go nowhere—turn the knob, open: a wall" (6). Short stories, by writers of fantastic fiction, have similar layouts.

Novelists, it appears, have a power they do not demonstrate in their daily lives. (The word power appears in Hebrew, *oz,*—half of Ozick—in the epigraph of *Levitation.*) Feingold and Lucy do not know how to harness that power, and so they decide to give a party and invite all the powerful people in the world of literature. That none of the powerful come is an indication that we are to look for meaning not in the plotting of the protagonists but rather in the plotting of the author.

Something happened in the three rooms of that West Side apartment. And while that something was happening something else was going on in the triptych formed by the three rooms. What happened was that a story of the ordinary—a party of mediocre people—almost imperceptibly turns into a story of the extraordinary—the levitation of a roomful of Jews.

Ozick delights in portraying the realization of this *tour d'adresse*. The party itself is like a work of fiction in which the characters are seen to come to life. Ozick indicates the point at which this transformation begins to take place by noticing "something in formation." This is precisely like the fantastic moment of a story: "It seemed about to become a regular visit, with points of view, opinions; a discussion. The voices began to stumble; Feingold liked that, it was nearly human" (10). Then Lucy notices the distinctions between the rooms of the party. The central panel of the triptych—the center hall—is empty, waiting to be filled. In the dining room are the non-Jews (and a sprinking of Jews), talking about theater and film, "junk," according to Feingold. That frame of the triptych contains a portrait of sterile realistic art.

Lucy, the daughter of a minister who read psalms from the pulpit and unwittingly caused his daughter to convert to the Judaism of the Ancient Hebrews and to marry "out of her tradition," observes the scene of the third wing of the triptych from its threshold, on the outside, in the frame. It is through her eyes, the eyes of a novelist (but not of the author of the story) that the reader sees the levitation of the title, and much, much more. It is through her eyes that we see what happened and also what was going on.

Feingold himself is holding forth in the living room (peopled exclusively with Jews) about "God," which in his case means Jewish suffering at the hands of the Christians. He quotes chapter and verse about the blood libels of the Middle Ages. There is a "pagan rabbi" at the party as well, the one who had administered Lucy's conversion. He eats kosher cake brought from home in a plastic bag and at the same time entertains some very serious doubts about the existence of God. This friend from the seminary has also brought a friend, a refugee, an Elie Wiesel-like survivor of the Holocaust and witness to it. It is he who urges Feingold in his narration to "come to modern times." For Lucy, this witness is exactly the ingredient needed to give a voice to Feingold's text. It is this refugee's Jesus-like face of suffering and his haunting voice that cause the first stage of Lucy's hallucination and bring the story to its most intensely fantastic moment. The refugee's voice has the power the Feingolds were looking for in giving the party in the first place. His very whisper can carve statues in which every Jew, for Lucy, is a Jew on the cross. After the Crucifixion, in this triptych, the Ascension. And so, Lucy sees all the Jews levitating on the voice of the refugee.

The story is not yet over, however, and we are going to be asked to look further than the hesitation inherent in the fantastic. There is still a panel, the central panel, to be filled. Lucy fills it by entering, with her mind's eye, into the shadow of another tale. She tergiversates, turning her back on the first conclusion. She sees herself in a little city park on a Sunday afternoon in early May, with her two little boys, to whom she had furtively been telling stories of little Jesus. They are there for an anthropological demonstration of musicians and dancers from Sicily, not "artists" but real peasants who will sing and dance to a song that celebrates the Madonna of Love. The primitive folk music of this ancient people is intensely erotic, sending the dancers into a trance, causing in them an ecstasy similar to the one experienced by Kornfeld. Lucy has an illumination: "Lucy is glorified. She is exalted. She comprehends . . . before the Madonna there was Venus. . . . The gods are God. . . . Everything is miracle! Lucy sees how she has abandoned nature, how she has lost true religion on account of the God of the Jews" (18).[21] Ozick is not merely indicating the essential contradiction between Judaism and Christianity, nor is she indicting Christianity for its pagan roots. She is positing a fundamental difference between Western and Jewish storytelling. Lucy comes back from her illumination to reality, to the reality of a departing female guest—from the dining room, of course, where they are discussing "the impact of romantic individualism"—who is afraid of being ambushed in the laundry room of her New York apartment house. In the living room, however, all the Jews are still in the air. And that's the way the story, finally, ends.

We are no longer sure through whose eyes we see these continually levitating Jews, through Lucy's or through Ozick's. The story ends without ending, leaving the reader in doubt, and the Jews in a fantastic tale that refuses to resolve itself into either the uncanny or the marvelous.

This is the conclusion that vexes Joseph Epstein. But he is looking merely for its allegorical meaning. He writes: "I recognize that Miss Ozick is reaching for something deep and special here. Can she be referring, metaphorically, to the inherent *luft*iness of the Jews, to the spirituality that can set them apart, especially when they speak of themselves among themselves? No doubt she is, and she is no doubt referring to more as well."[22]

In his commentary on the tale, Epstein also writes one of the story's possible conclusions, usurps Ozick's story to compose a midrash on it that urges the Jews to come back down to earth. "I may sound more like a landlord than a critic here, but I react to the story by asking, 'Madam, what is that living room doing on the ceiling? Madam, I implore you, get those Jews down, please!' "[23] Epstein's landlord enters into the logic of the text, takes the fantastic seriously, like Sheindel. But Epstein's landlord misses the point. The "point" that Ruth Wisse enjoins us to look for at the end of an Ozick story is not in the supplying of its ending. The point of "Levitation"—and of "The Pagan Rabbi," "Usurpation," and "Puttermesser and Xanthippe," all tales embedded in the genre of the fantastic—is that there is, despite Ozick's extrafictional proclamations to the contrary, a Jewish way of writing fiction, a way that "rejects intellectually and emotionally the surrender to the mystical blur between the creator and the created" and is "at the same time fascinated" by it. The something in Ozick is not necessarily a pagan streak common to all writers of the Western tradition; it can also be the hesitation between two contradictory solutions to a literary dilemma, out of which the fantastic, including the Jewish fantastic, is made.

Chapter Six

A Jewish Realism: *The Cannibal Galaxy*

In a 1976 essay in *Commentary*, Ruth R. Wisse, describing what she perceived as a turning point in American Jewish writing, identified Cynthia Ozick as the leader of a movement of writers who were self-consciously defining themselves as Jews and who were attempting to express their artistic vision in Jewish terms.

While Wisse does not include Philip Roth in this movement, she does suggest that "it is Philip Roth, and not Cynthia Ozick . . . who can best afford to write about American Jewish reality." Roth's American suburb is more "real" than Ozick's European-style shtetl. For those, like Ozick, who wish "to weave new brilliant cloth from [the] ancient threads [of Judaism], the sociological reality of the present-day American Jewish community would seem to present an almost insurmountable obstacle."[1]

In her 1983 novel *The Cannibal Galaxy* and in the 1980 novella "The Laughter of Akiva," from which the novel derives, Ozick has succeeded in overcoming the "almost insurmountable obstacle." Taking Judaism seriously as a cultural alternative, Ozick has written not only what Wisse has called act 2 of the drama known as "American Jewish Fiction," but act 3 as well. Ozick has now taken on American Jewish reality. Her second revolution is made all the more dazzling by the fact that she has woven her tapestry using what some, at least, will recognize as traditionally Jewish narrative techniques.[2]

Narrative Techniques

The "some" will include those who accept Erich Auerbach's conclusions in chapter 1 of *Mimesis*, his seminal study on the representation of reality in Western literature. As Auerbach reminds his readers, it is Aristotle and Plato to whom we owe the Greek term *mimesis*, in the sense of artistic representation. He traces modern

realism to innovative nineteenth-century French novelists like Stendhal and Balzac, who "took random individuals from daily life . . .
and made them *the subject of serious, problematic, and even tragic representation*" (my italics).[3] It is to ancient Greek literature that Auerbach turns for the purpose of comparing and, more importantly,
contrasting the Western way of representing reality with the specifically Jewish way.

Homeric style, he argues, knows no background, "only a foreground, only a uniformly illuminated, uniformly objective present."[4] "Homeric heroes . . . wake every morning as if it were the
first day of their lives."[5] Homer's basic impulse is to represent
phenomena in a fully externalized form, visible and palpable. In
Jewish literature, as epitomized for Auerbach by the biblical narrative of the Binding of Isaac, the *Akedah*, "the decisive points of
the narrative alone are emphasized, what lies between is nonexistent;
time and place are undefined and call for *interpretation;* thoughts and
feelings remain unexpressed, are only suggested by the silence and
the fragmentary speeches, the whole, permeated with the most
unrelieved suspense and directed toward a single goal . . . remains
mysterious and *fraught with background*" (my italics).[6]

Abraham's actions are explained not only by his character but
also by his history. His faculties may be fully engaged in the event
at hand but he remains continually conscious of what has happened
to him earlier and elsewhere. His thought and feelings are entangled
in many layers. According to Auerbach, this specifically Jewish
representation of specifically Jewish reality has "doctrine and prom-
ise" incarnate in it and is therefore a teaching text. It contains a
secret second meaning that must be subtly investigated and
interpreted.

An investigation of *The Cannibal Galaxy* reveals that its characters—random or not so random individuals taken from daily Jewish
life—are also made the subjects of serious, problematic representation. Moreover, each of the main characters is profoundly "fraught
with background," a background that is at times mysterious and
often contains a secret second meaning, a background that calls for
and even demands interpretation.

Indeed, a leitmotiv of the novel is a phrase that seems to reappear
with urgent frequency. It is a description of the world—not, as the
psalmist has it, as "a vale of tears"—but as a "vale of interpretation."
As early as 1970, in her essay "America: Toward Yavneh," where

she called for the adoption of American English as the new Jewish language, Ozick made the following prediction concerning the direction the "New Yiddish" literature would take: "The liturgical literature produced by New Yiddish may include a religious consciousness, but it will not generally be religious in any explicit sense: it will without question 'passionately wallow in the human reality;' it will be touched by the covenant. *The human reality will ring through its novels and poems, though for a long time it will not be ripe enough for poetry; its first achievements will be mainly novels*" (my italics).[7]

Ruth Wisse was not the only one to remark that fantasy, the depiction of *another* world, was central to Ozick's early literary inspiration. Harold Fisch, "introducing" Ozick in a 1974 article, makes a similar point. "Cynthia Ozick's fiction is marked by a fertile strain of fantasy which gives her a radical freedom in dealing with contemporary problems. She also maintains a firm grasp of ideas even while exuberantly exercising her gift of fantasy."[8] He, too, notes, by the way, that her work represents a new phase in American Jewish writing.

In an interview with Eve Ottenberg published in the *New York Times Magazine,* Ozick maintains that she is "hostile to the whole mystical enterprise. I'm a rationalist and I'm a skeptic." She does concede, however, that "there's something in me that is fascinated by this surrender to the mystical blur between the creator and the created." Ozick's conclusion on this matter is illuminating for most of her fiction. "It's really a fictional theme for me," she says. "I reject it intellectually and emotionally. But it's where the stories come from."[9]

The mystical enterprise is where the stories come from, to be sure. But that is not the only place they come from. Sometimes, as in "The Laughter of Akiva," they originate in the reality of the American Jewish community, in a community that is living its life as Jews, as Jews immersed in American culture. In both "The Laughter of Akiva" and *The Cannibal Galaxy,* from the very story told, from the plot itself, it is clear that Ozick has turned to literal representation and imitation of American Jewish reality.

The Story and Its Source

The story "comes from" a particularly American institution in Jewish life, the day school. The day school is the most up-to-date avatar of Jewish education in America. First was the heder, then the "afternoon Hebrew school" and the "Sunday school." Now there is the day school, which combines a secular curriculum with a Jewish one, in one prolonged day under one roof and central administration.

Ozick, in both the novella and the novel, inserts her rationalist, skepticist scalpel into the flesh of one of these schools—on the shores of Long Island Sound in a suburb of New York, or on the shores of some great lake in American's heartland—and, after making a perfect incision, she probes around from the inside like a surgeon. The result is an anatomy lesson about an important "community" in American Jewish life. Readers will recognize the day school principal, the children, the teachers, the parents, and the elaborate graduation ceremonies. One thing is certain, Ozick does not give a romanticized picture of the workings of this complicated body. Her portrayal is candidly clinical—until, that is, the emotions of her characters intervene. It is then that we realize that, for Ozick, "accurate portrayal" of reality is not an end but a means. Ozick's mimesis is not Greek, or even in the tradition of the great nineteenth-century realists. Her mimesis, in Auerbach's terms, is Jewish; in the spirit of the biblical author, its goal is not mere representation, but interpretation. For the sake of clarity, this analysis will focus on the novel rather than the novella. One of the points of both texts is Ozick's insistence that we judge from the later text, not the earlier.

Auerbach characterizes Jewish representation of reality as being "fraught with background." In significantly different ways, Ozick supplies similar European backgrounds to both of the main characters of this American novel. The biographies of both Joseph Brill, the day school principal, and Hester Lilt, the writer who enrolls her little daughter at the school for the regulation eight years of elementary education, are so heavily weighted with background that nearly all the "foreground events" that take place in the narrative must be interpreted in the shadowy light of what has taken place "elsewhere and earlier." While Joseph Brill's background is given, there is much in it that remains to be interpreted. It consists of a childhood spent in prewar Paris, in the teeming Jewish quarter known as the *Pletzl* (similar to London's East End and New York's Lower East Side); of an adolescence spent discovering the broader world of art and science; and of a young adulthood spent, during the Holocaust years, hiding in a convent cellar, while his parents, his teacher/rabbi, and several of his brothers and sisters are sent to the gas chambers. Most significantly, the whole novel—except perhaps for the ending—can be found in this expository section.

It is the details of his background that loom large in Joseph Brill's later life. Ozick provides one of the keys to the novel by introducing the following curious item concerning Joseph's childhood: that there were two ways to go from home to his father's fish store—the direct way, leading through the Jewish quarter, and the "roundabout way," leading past "the loveliest house in the world." The seemingly innocuous childhood fancy of taking oblique routes assumes tremendous importance when one realizes the extent of the literary allusion inherent in it. Did not the little Marcel of Proust's *Remembrance of Things Past* also have two ways, one leading past the house of Swann the Jew, the other past the chateau of the lovely Duchesse de Guermantes, a figure of intrigue? The intriguing character in little Joseph's case is another literary figure, the famous seventeenth-century *épistolière*, Madame de Sévigné, who is credited with having molded the literature of France. It is to her house (now become a museum) that Joseph is drawn in his "roundabout way." From the very beginning, Joseph is torn between two worlds, between two cultures: Jewish life, represented by his rabbi and family, and Western civilization, represented by Madame de Sévigné.

A great deal of foreshadowing takes place in the early pages of the novel. Not only is Madame de Sévigné a writer like Hester Lilt, but she is overwhelmed by an obsessive passion for her daughter, as Hester Lilt will prove to be. Just as "Madame de Sévigné's unreasonable passion for her undistinguished daughter had turned the mother's prose into high culture and historic treasure,"[10] so, too, Hester Lilt's brilliant prose will be interpreted by Brill as having at its base a similar passion for her own daughter.

In fact, the novel's emblem reveals itself to be Brill's obsessive efforts to decode both art and reality. Another foreshadowing event in the novel's exposition concerns a statue of Rachel that Brill finds in the museum of his roundabout way. Naively, he thinks it is a statue of Rachel the Jewish matriarch; in reality, he learns later in an illuminating discovery, it is of another Jewess, the nineteenth-century French tragedienne Rachel, who, in her interpretation of neoclassical French culture, brought it back to life for the French. Misinterpretation and "discovery" are the stuff of which Greek literature is made. Ozick engages Jewish themes with this device.

An even more significant foreshadowing occurs when Joseph encounters Claude, a quintessential French aesthete, the novel's most
pure representative of Greek culture, a Louvre incarnate. At one
point, Claude takes Joseph to hear an old writer read from a work
in progress. The portion recorded by Ozick turns out to be, in
miniature, a casting of Joseph's later life as school principal, in a
world where children are not seen as growing old. This "interior
reduplication" of the later plot is—it must be pointed out—a
gentile casting of Joseph's life. It leaves out the crucial Jewish side
and the even more crucial struggle and accommodation between the
two ways.

Struggle and accommodation are the twin forces of Joseph's Holocaust years. But it is not with horror and terror that he struggles;
it is with books. To his convent cellar he has taken with him one
of Rabbi Pult's books, a text of rabbinic law and lore. Once in the
convent cellar, he is provided with the library of a recently deceased,
very liberal, priest. Randomly riffling the pages of two of his books,
he has an illumination: the texts of the two cultures—Jewish and
Western—can be accommodated: "Rav and Proust . . . both measured the world, one by passion for the ideal, the other by passion
for the sardonic detail. How different they were! *And neither told a
lie.* This was a marvel, that two souls, two such separated tonalities,
so to speak, could between them describe the true map of life" (28).

On confronting these texts, Joseph Brill decides that he will
devote his life to a symbiosis of the two cultures. He will establish
a Jewish day school with a dual curriculum and will turn out Jewish
geniuses. (This obsession with genius is only latent in his background, a general given of French culture.) The only trouble is, he
learns when he has established himself in a middle-class Jewish
community in America, geniuses do not reveal themselves as such
in an elementary school setting. Furthermore, America is not Europe. Both Judaism and Europe are "in history," but America is
not. Jews in America have abandoned the very memory of their own
past. After thirty years of uninteresting foreground (which Ozick
does not bother with), Joseph Brill settles into a comfortable mediocrity. Until, that is, Hester Lilt comes to register her child.

Here, at last, is the genius Joseph Brill has been looking for.
Alas for him, as brilliant as the mother is, the child, during eight
years of schooling, reveals herself to be despairingly dull. Curiously,
the despair is all Joseph Brill's, not the mother's. She seems confident

that her daughter will turn out to be a duplicate of herself, a genius of originality.

Ozick's representation of Hester Lilt's background is at opposite poles with that of Joseph Brill. While his background requires interpretation, it is nevertheless given. Hester Lilt's background (like, later, her daughter's) remains completely hidden. It is no accident that the writer's name is Hester: the Hebrew expression describing the hiding of the face of God is *hester panim*. Twice during the novel Joseph Brill tries to get Hester Lilt to reveal her background: "She gave him little: she had left the middle of Europe long ago, decades back, on one of those Children's Transports, but he could not discover from what beginning she had been rescued. In nationality she seemed to be a bit of everything; it was the brush of his native consonants he thought he had momentarily heard. He listened in vain for her earliest place" (50).

Hester Lilt's Story

Hester Lilt's life is indeed "fraught with background." She does not care to reveal it because more important then the Jewish reality she represents is the mystery to be interpreted. This is the other side of Auerbach's coin. That interpretation is more important than background for Ozick is made abundantly clear in a later passage in the novel when Hester Lilt does finally reveal her background to Joseph Brill. Unfortunately, he cannot make head or tail of her story; he does not understand it. More significantly, the reader who is witness to the scene is not supplied with the text of Hester Lilt's background, only with the author's reporting of it. Hester Lilt gives Brill a convoluted European story, facts he cannot fathom. Ozick gives the reader none of the facts: "The more she delivered, the more she withheld. She meant him to seize everything and nothing. She knew herself to be a flake of history, someone destroyed, finished; old, the way the world after its destruction is old; whatever had once mattered did not matter now. *She was all future; she cut the thread of genesis*" (92; my italics).

What counts for Hester Lilt, as for Madame de Sévigné, is latency, the background that leads to the possible. In fact, this is Brill's own definition of reality: "*What we deem to be Reality is only Partial Possibility, coarsely ground into mere dumb matter*" (5). At the end of the novel, Beulah Lilt, the dullard pupil, turns out to be an original artist whose work, obviously like her childhood, is endowed with latency.

Hester Lilt is indifferent not to background but to event. Her obsession is with the Jewish quality of interpretation. This is evident both in the titles of her works and in the parables for which she has a particular predilection. Hester Lilt is an "imagistic linguistic logician." She uses language—and silence—to show *things* clearly, and to leave *meaning* hidden. A listing of some of her titles demonstrates her didactic duality: *Metaphor as Exegesis; Divining Meaning; Interpretation as an End in Itself;* and *An Interpretation of Pedagogy.* These titles and these images lend themselves to and indeed call for interpretation.

Joseph Brill devotes himself to interpreting Hester Lilt, and after a series of near-comic pratfalls, succeeds in decoding her metaphors, theories and images. He learns that nothing she has said is without significance, even her silence, even her babble. Hester Lilt has taught Joseph that there is no language without effect, that, in the vale of interpretation, the "purity" of babble is inconceivable. If there is no language without consequence, how much more consequential are an author's formal writings. The question remains: Is Hester Lilt's writing Jewish? Since she does not engage in mimesis, it is not easy to tell. For Joseph Brill, the literary analyst, "It was difficult to say whether it had 'religious overtones'; sometimes it seemed to; sometimes not. . . . It came to him, turning and turning those rare pages, that she might have been a poet; but she had relinquished everything lyrical, everything 'expressive'. . . . She dealt in scrutiny and commentary" (54). The reason for Joseph Brill's confusion, therefore, is that Hester Lilt is not a writer of fiction; background is extraneous to her. She does, however, comment on fiction. She interprets Jewish fiction—midrash—and in doing so rewrites it.

To understand how Jewish Hester Lilt is (in Auerbach's terms), one need only compare her with one of the other female characters of the novel, Iris, the young woman whom Brill, in his determination finally to be normal, marries in his old age. It is neither insignificant nor coincidental that—in the vale of interpretation where the purity of babble is inconceivable—Iris is a Greek name, the name of a Greek goddess. It is also not without interest that Iripomoňoéià is the name of the dryad who entices the pagan rabbi of Ozick's most famous short story. This fact freights the present text with a new sort of background. Before Iris moves in with her new husband, on the grounds of the Jewish day school, she has been living with a family of Greeks. She herself is a pure Greek vessel. Neither background nor history interests her ("I'm not in history!" she asserts [116]). Iris is not interested in her husband's background either and cannot even begin to guess that the meaning of Joseph's life derives from the fact that he is "fraught with background."

The allusion above to Ozick's earlier chef d'oeuvre is not an offhand remark. All literary works may be said to be fraught with a background of their own. Sometimes a writer rewrites events; sometimes, other people's texts. In the case of a writer such as Ozick, with an oeuvre of her own to mine, it is not strange to find her rewriting herself. In fact, Joseph Brill's accommodation of the two cultures is but one resolution of the dilemma of Isaac Kornfeld, the pagan rabbi (discussed in chapter 5). "He [Joseph Brill] longed for a noble scholarship—the pleasure-pain of poetry, and the comely orderliness of numbers and the logical passion of Gemara, all laced together in an illustrious tapestry" (75). That there is a poetry side to Brill is evident in his reaction to the yearly commencement exercises. Concerning commencement, when the hymn *Eliyahu Ha-Navi* is chanted alongside the robust singing of *Chevaliers de la Table Ronde,* Ozick comments, using the indirect free style of quotation: "Ah, how he fell with these into the poetry side of life" (118). Brill even goes out of his way to hire as a teacher—against his better judgment—a version of the pagan rabbi, a Rabbi Sheskin who turns Scripture into story, who encourages dreaming and drawing in class, and who admonishes Naphtali, the child of Brill's old age who specializes in making exhaustive and exhausting lists, to ponder the fourteen lines of a sonnet, the brevity of a phrase in Talmud, the smaller melodies of Mozart, and, most significantly for a rabbi, the veins in a leaf.

The World of Joseph Brill

Rabbi Sheskin represents, therefore, the poetry side of Joseph Brill's life. Brill's son, Naphtali, represents the culmination of Ozick's representation of the serious and problematic side of his life. Brill had become convinced throughout his long tenure as a principal that the children contained the mothers. His initial fear of fathering a child, reflecting perhaps a fear that the child will contain that part of himself he sees as a failure, is surpassed by his desire to see his own latent visionary genius replicated. In truth, Naphtali does contain Joseph Brill, the part that loves categories, divisions, classifications, types, and orderliness, the part that has grandiose visions. Mutatis mutandis, Naphtali has the same dreams that Joseph had had in his convent cellar:

Naphtali had changed his mind about becoming a teacher: he thought of empires. He thought he would found companies, induce them to accrete, and then forcibly amalgamate them: he would work day and night, grow very rich, and be tapped by the President for, say, Secretary of Transportation. He would resuscitate cross-country land mobility, commanding untried alliances among buses and trains; he would air out the crackling grease of the bus-stop cafeterias that lay across the breast of the nation; he would wash the windows of the dozing trains; in the cities he would plant twin silver tracks in black urban asphalt, and bring streetcars to life again. How pleased the President would be! (159)

For Ozick, Naphtali's visions do not constitute a vindication of Joseph Brill's life the way Beulah Lilt's visions seem to do for Hester Lilt's. The reason is clear. In this work, the only real achievement is in the realm of art, where a new language can be created and where true originality is possible. This is of course the meaning of the scene in which Brill takes his son Naphtali to New York to view an exhibit of Beulah Lilt's paintings. The revelation Brill has of true genius is akin to a "discovery scene" in Greek literature (cf. the discovery of Odysseus). Like Eurycleia, he finally understands: "He understood she was acclaimed. He understood more: the forms, the colors, the glow, the defined darkness, above all the form of things—all these were thought to be a kind of language. She spoke. The world took her for an astonishment. She was the daughter of her mother" (156).

If *The Cannibal Galaxy* were a Greek text, the revelation of Beulah Lilt's genius might be considered a tragic denouement for Joseph Brill: his whole life might have been for naught. But *The Cannibal Galaxy* is a Jewish text, a Jewish representation of reality. In tragedy, one has the feeling that time is running out and there is no place to go. In the Jewish value system, there is always the possibility of *t'shuva,* repentance. The recognition that one has erred can be followed by a correction, by *t'shuva*.[11] At the end of the novel, in what is not to be construed as an ironic twist of fate but as a deliberate act of "penitence," we learn that Joseph Brill—living in retirement in Florida—has himself chosen the category for an award to be given at his beloved commencement exercises. The Joseph Brill Ad Astra Award is to be given "to the eighth grader with the most creative potential regardless of class standing" (161). In a school where the only criterion for success had been good grades, the award itself signifies not only that Joseph Brill has accomplished *t'shuva,* it recognizes that children can do so as well, and "turn out" better than their grades would project.

In her *Commentary* essay, Ruth Wisse personifies American Jewish literature by describing its "career." She makes clear that "marginality" and "victimization," the themes most closely associated with the Jew of the early period of this literature (in the works of Saul Bellow, Bernard Malamud, and Philip Roth), are not *necessary* to a Jewish literature. The interpretation proposed here of Cynthia Ozick's realism demonstrates that American Jewish writing is also capable of a human—and profoundly Jewish—act of *t'shuva,* of returning not only to the Jewish heritage but to the Jewish heritage's style of writing. It is now also clear that it is no longer necessary to write mystically of shtetls, golems, and miracle makers to create an authentically Jewish atmosphere. By using the tools of traditional Jewish writing—freighting her characters with meaningful background, calling for interpretation and commentary, treating her subjects problematically—Cynthia Ozick has shown, in *The Cannibal Galaxy,* that it is possible for Jewish writing—at the same time—to be "touched by the covenant" and "passionately to wallow in the human reality."

Chapter Seven

Rewriting Others: "Usurpation (Other People's Stories)"

"The Pagan Rabbi" (1966) and "Levitation" (1979) are not the only stories in the Ozick canon that have supernatural elements. "Usurpation (Other People's Stories)," first published in 1974, may also be counted among the most masterful representations of the fantastic story. It is linked to "The Pagan Rabbi" (and by extension to the later "Levitation") in other significant ways as well. Like "The Pagan Rabbi," "Usurpation" was awarded the O. Henry Prize for best short story of 1974. In addition, Ozick binds "The Pagan Rabbi" and "Usurpation" into the same bundle, calling them both parables, in which "story and idea are so inextricably fused that they cannot be torn free of each other."[1]

In the preface to *Bloodshed and Three Novellas*, the volume in which "Usurpation" has found its permanent home, Ozick, responding to an unfavorable review, enunciates her literary credo. For her, "a story must not merely *be* but mean. . . . I believe that stories ought to judge and interpret the world."[2]

An Outline

"Usurpation" begins as though it were a commentary, an essay about writing, a piece of literary criticism. It even sounds more like reportage than story. Like her other fantastic short stories, it begins in the "real."

The narrator, herself a published but obscure writer, has gone to the "Y" (obviously New York City's famous 92nd Street Y) to hear a famous writer read his latest, as yet unpublished story, "The Magic Crown."[3] Recognizing as she hears it that the story contains elements that are grist for her own literary mill, the narrator, in the manner of writers before her, like Boccaccio, Shakespeare, and Dostoyevski,

90

wishes to appropriate the story for herself, to "usurp" it, to "rewrite" it in her own style.

Strangely enough, at the conclusion of the public reading, the narrator is approached—accosted might be the way the narrator would put it—by a young man, also a writer. Claiming that he is a relative of the characters in the story whose public reading has just been completed, the young man thrusts a manuscript into her hands, imperiously demanding that she convey it to the "famous writer." Instead, the narrator "rewrites" this story, too.[4] That this story concerns another writer, the Hebrew novelist and Nobel Prize winner S. Y. Agnon, should not surprise us. "Usurpation" is, after all, about "other people's stories." Coincidentally, the rewritten story about Agnon—but not the "real" one—contains a silver crown.

There is a difference, however. Malamud's crown was a piece of chicanery, represented by a charlatan wonder-working "rabbi" as a magical device for healing the sick. In Ozick's—or, rather, we should insist, the narrator's—plot summary of the Malamud tale, it is not actually given to the protagonist to see a magic crown. Rather, it is explained, he was merely momentarily mesmerized. Finally, the crown performs no magic. The ailing person for whom the curing crown was sought dies.

In the story about Agnon, as retold by Ozick, the crown becomes a metaphor for Jewish literary fame and talent.[5] This crown had been worn by the ancient Hebrew prophet Isaiah, by the medieval Hebrew poet Solomon Ibn Gabirol, and by the modern Hebrew poet Saul Tchernikhovsky. Agnon acquired the crown by gaining renown.

But the story wishes to take the metaphor of the crown literally. It also wishes to move thereby into the realm of the fantastic. "Tchernikhovsky was already dead when he brought me this" (143), says "Agnon" to the student-writer as he presents him a box containing the physical crown. In addition to the ghost of Tchernikhovsky, the story contains another supernatural element. The crown is not only a metaphor for poetic-literary eminence. It has magical powers beyond the curative. Anyone who wears it, whether he or she deserves it or not, immediately gains the eminence of the previous wearers and, magically, becomes a cornucopia of stories. "What a load he carries, what inventions, what a teeming and a boiling, stories, stories, stories! His own; yet not his own" (149). The rest of the retold "Agnon" story concerns the struggle of the ghost of

Tchernikhovsky to recover the crown from its undeserving possessor (the student-writer) and to restore it to its metaphorical use. Fortunately for Tchernikhovsky, the defender of the poetic faith, the crown not only provides a ready-made bibliography for its wearer; logical in the extreme, the crown also accelerates its possessor's aging processes. One must after all account rationally for such a vast bibliography, however mystically acquired. The young student-writer looks into a window and beholds an uncanny, terrifying reflection: an old man. He has aged rapidly; within a brief time he will suffer a heart attack and, like the father for whom Malamud's protagonist had sought the curative crown, he too will die.

If Ozick's story ended at this point, we might have here a neat fantastic short story, resolved in the supernatural, in which Ozick shows how by rewriting "other people's stories," one can enter into the realm of Jewish midrash, where—as Warren Harvey demonstrates—a story about a metaphor taken literally becomes a commentary on that metaphor and an eternally organic component of it. But an Ozick story rarely stops after its first ending.

In a 1982 essay, Ozick insists that "what literature means is meaning." In "the literature of midrash, or parable," she explains, "there is no visible principle or moral imperative" that can be seen apart from the story. "The principle does not enter into or appear in the tale; it *is* the tale; it realizes the tale. To put it another way: the tale is its own interpretation. It is a world that decodes itself."[6]

"Usurpation" may also be read as a story that is its own interpretation. While not a midrash in the manner of "The Pagan Rabbi," it is nevertheless written in the midrashic mode.

The Midrashic Mode

Midrash is a term that describes the rabbinical method of adding an interpretative texture to a narrative text. It is a type of biblical interpretation in which the rabbis of the talmudic era commented on biblical narrative by rewriting it. The rabbinical story, however, never violated the "intactness" of the biblical story. The rabbinic method recognizes, however, that once a biblical story is seen to have other stories latent within it, the original can no longer be divorced from the new story. The new story is henceforth one of its implied interpretations.

James Kugel, a Judaic scholar who has written extensively on modes of biblical interpretation, suggests that "midrash's precise focus is often what one might call surface irregularities in the text; a good deal of the time it's concerned with (in the broadest sense) *problems.*" To elucidate his notion, Kugel uses the metaphor of the oyster. "The text's irregularity is the grain of sand that so irritates the midrashic oyster that [the midrashist] constructs a pearl around it."[7]

An analogy to sculpture may provide further clarification of the midrashic enterprise. It is obvious that a sculptor may not fashion his statue ex nihilo. Rather, he may be said to find in a piece of marble that statue whose form is inherent in the raw block. All the sculptor need do is remove all the extraneous pieces of marble and produce a work of art. A midrashic sculptor would begin his work at this point. Seeing perhaps a surface irregularity, or noting a difficulty with the sculptor's execution, the midrashist would enter into the statue through the noted irregularity (the "problem") and extract a completely new statue from the one at hand, all the while leaving the original intact.

The new statue would be seen as an interpretation of the old one, a commentary on it. Of course, once this original statue has been "worked on" in this manner, it can never again—by those who are familiar with the "interpretation"—be taken simply for what it was. Not only that, but henceforth it must be dealt with as a function of *all* the latent situations that have been made patent. That is the midrashic mode.

The implications of this mode for the reading of texts are far-reaching. One need only note that once a "midrash" has been written on a text, the text can no longer be read chronologically. One has to find a way to refer to its midrash as well. Also, midrash is not merely a method of *reading* a biblical text. What is fascinating about the method is that to talk about one's reading of a text is to rewrite it. The rewritten text is not merely an interpretation of the original text, however. In the hands of a supreme artist, like Ozick, for example, it becomes a work of art in its own right.

This is what happens in "Usurpation." The stories of Malamud and Stern remain intact. The rewritten stories and the frame story of the rewriter are inextricably fused into a new story at the point where the "writer" of the Agnon story brings his visitor, the re-writer, to the home of the crown-making "rabbi" of the Malamud tale. It is revealed that this "rabbi" is not a rabbi at all, nor does he claim to be one. The newspapers, reporting on his trial and incarceration for fraud, those same newspapers where Malamud found his story and rewrote it himself, have called him "rabbi," and, as his wife acknowledges, he has seen no reason to issue a demurral.

If not a rabbi, what is he then? Like the narrator, like the student, like Malamud, like all the wearers of the crown, Isaiah, Ibn Gabirol, Agnon, and Tchernikhovsky—especially Tchernikhovsky—he is a writer.[8] Although we have seen that he has created real-life fictions (the crown that "heals"), the "rabbi's" texts, boxes and boxes of texts, include both commentaries—biblical commentaries—and stories—Holocaust stories—that judge both God's work and His world.

It is not insignificant that the "rabbi's" first name, in Ozick's recension of his story, is Saul, like Tchernikhovsky's. A photograph in a frame even reveals that he physically resembles Tchernikhovsky. (That is to say, he resembles the narrator's image of Tchernikhovsky in the retold Agnon tale.) But there is also a difference. Unlike the pagan Tchernikhovsky—whose poem "Before the Statue of Apollo" the narrator professes to admire—this Saul speaks out against the magical components that make paganism out of religion.

The Tchernikhovsky Problem

Saul Tchernikhovsky clearly presents a problem in this text. He is a writer of the pagan idea and "clearly chooses the company of Canaanite idols" (11) in preference to the company of Jewish poets. The idols, however, "predictably anti-Semitic," react to Tchernikhovsky as a Jew; the last word of the story is their venomous castigation of their colleague: "kike."

The tension Ozick portrays between the pagan and Jewish worlds is reflected in the poem by Tchernikhovsky to which Ozick's story alludes. The poet Tchernikhovsky claims in no uncertain terms:

> I am the Jew; your adversary of old! . . .
> The waters of every ocean on earth
> With all their multitudinous uproar
> Could not completely fill the gulf that yawns between us.
> Heaven itself and the ample plains could not,
> Stretching, annihilate the abyss dividing
> The Torah from your adorers' cult.[9]

And yet, despite the seemingly unbridgeable chasm, Tchernikhovsky does bow down before the statue of Apollo, the "symbol of light

in life, the symbol of life itself, and of courage and of beauty."
How is one to explain this contradiction?

Eisig Silberschlag writes that in this poem Tchernikhovsky "endeavored to find a link between the Jewish God of the desert and the Greek god of light." He claims that the "poet felt that the Jews were sufficiently removed from the Pagan world to borrow safely some of its saner qualities."[10] Ozick feels no such thing. She does not try to bridge a gap that is ultimately unbridgable. Nor does she try to harmonize views that are at best contrapuntal. To put it another way, she will live with Tchernikhovsky's contradictions, the way midrash does. She will not harmonize Tchernikhovsky with Isaiah, Ibn Gabirol, and Agnon, but will use their insurmountable differences for a Jewishly meaningful purpose. This she does with the creation of her own Tchernikhovsky, the "rabbi" Saul. And it is from this Saul-not-Tchernikhovsky that the reader is to extract meaning from her tale.

Like others of Ozick's fantastic short stories, "Usurpation" ends both enigmatically and ambiguously, without resolving all the disharmonies. As the story draws to a close, it is revealed that everyone in the final scene—the student-writer, Saul's wife, the picture of Saul himself within the frame—is wearing a little silver crown. Breaking out of the frame, the figure in the picture of Saul-not-Tchernikhovsky levitates to the ceiling, "as if gassed," adds Ozick.[11] Once again we are placed in the realm of the supernatural. The writer who has ascended has it in his power to offer the narrator a choice—God or Apollo, law or levity. She chooses Apollo, and is rewarded with a cornucopia of stories. But she herself realizes that her pagan fertility is illusory. In the pantheon of the poets where both Agnon and Tchernikhovsky live on, Agnon receives both worldly and other-worldly rewards. Tchernikhovsky tries to abandon his tradition and his tradition's strictures for the freedoms of paganism. The Canaanite idols at whose altar he would worship, however, hurl anti-Semitic epithets at him and remind us in strong terms of his marginality and foreignness.

Analysis

How are we to deal with "Usurpation"? The story's very architecture, highly complicated, as this attempt at plot summary has demonstrated, lends itself to analysis.

"Usurpation" is much more than a fantastic short story. It is a complex frame story, in which meaning is conveyed both in the flesh and in the skeleton of the work. There are, indeed, several types of framing devices in "Usurpation."

A pair of parentheses can sometimes act as lines of demarcation, setting the remarks contained within the parentheses off from the main body of the text, highlighting them, and giving them a meaning different from the meaning conveyed in the main body of the text. There are several parenthetical structures in "Usurpation," each one playing that function. The first of these is the story's subtitle, "(Other People's Stories)." Perhaps "Usurpation," set off from its subtitle, is *not* "(Other People's Stories)," but entirely Ozick's own. Is that the hint of the initial frame through which one enters into the world of fiction? Two parenthetical remarks made in the body of the story serve to remind the reader that, while Ozick is working with other people's stories and is bound by the givens of her sources, these represent no more of a constraint for the real artist than the fourteen lines of a sonnet. The following is one example of Ozick's use of the parenthetical remark, demonstrating that she is indeed rewriting her own version of other people's stories: "(Quite so. A muddle in the plot. That was the goat's story, and it had no silver crown in it. I am still stuck with these leftovers that cause seams and cracks in my own version. *I will have to mend all this somehow. Be patient. I will manage it.* Pray that I don't bungle it.)" (147; my italics).

The frame underlines the contrapuntal disharmonious nature of this work of art. The last sentence of the parenthetical remark, an interpellation of the reader, asking him or her to intervene in the fiction, may be seen as an effort to rupture the frame so that real life and the life of fiction may mingle freely. This notion will be analyzed subsequently.

First there is the matter of the preface to *Bloodshed and Three Novellas*. A preface seems like an unseemly piece of writing, especially from a writer like Ozick. Ruth Wisse is especially harsh in this matter:

Like a prizefighter who cannot stop punching at the signal of the bell, Miss Ozick adds a preface to her four novellas to push her meaning home. It is she herself who "explains" her final story ["Usurpation"], reducing it like a tendentious reviewer to a moral function. . . . The preface tells us when the stories were written, why they have been included here, what they are about. This is not footnoting, like Eliot's notes to "The Waste Land" to which the author ingenuously compares it, but self-justification and special pleading. [12]

Ozick agrees with Wisse, to some extent, if not about her own prefaces, then about prefaces in general. "In general," she writes in the preface, "a piece of imaginative writing that cannot make its principles plain without a set of notes is justifiably regarded as a failure. Stories cannot carry suitcases stuffed with elucidations" (9). Stories must speak for themselves unless they are made out of frames, and especially may they have these casings when they are written in the midrashic mode, where the commentary—as in a preface— is more important fictionally than the story itself. Ozick may have sensed this midrashic component of the frame when, in an interview, she asserted that "The Preface to *Bloodshed* is a piece of fiction like any other. 'Preface' is the title of the fiction". [13] It is in her equation of commentary and fiction that Ozick reveals that, for her, meaning—usually found in the commentary—is what must be sought in the fiction.

Perhaps, then, the meaning of "Usurpation" ought to be pursued in other fictional frames of "Usurpation" as well, and not merely in the preface. Photographs play an important thematic role in Ozick's fiction. In "Usurpation" it is the picture *frame* that counts. The picture of the "Saul" who looks like Tchernikhovsky breaks the boundaries of the frame and in a preternatural moment ascends.

"Usurpation," to a great extent, is about the rupture of the artistic frame and the violation of the artistic space. Boris Uspensky, a theoretician of fictional frames, has explained, "Efforts to violate the borders of the artistic space, generally speaking, seem to be motivated by the understandable desire to bring together, as closely as possible, the represented world and the real world, in order to achieve the greatest degree of verisimilitude—of realism—in the representation." [14]

The narrator of "Usurpation" does much more than achieve a greater degree of verisimilitude when she violates the space of the Malamud story. Her version of it does in truth *begin* in reality; it does indeed read like an essay in which the reporter invites his reader into the real world of public readings of stories by famous writers. Of course, a story about stories is suspicious enough. But we are led off the track when we learn that the story being read by "Ma-

lamud" is itself not invented. "The famous writer . . . took it from
an account in the newspaper" (133). The story has not yet been
transformed into a "story," a framed work of art. Not only is it
being read aloud, it has not yet been published in a book. It is in
the realm of story *telling,* not story *writing.* It hesitates between the
real world of public readings and the artistic world of fiction. The
narrator believes that she may yet "act upon" a story that she recognizes as worthy of herself and that still has no palpable existence.
She expresses the burning desire "to leap upon the stage with a
living match and burn the manuscript on the spot, freeing the crown
out of the finished tale, restoring it once more to a public account
in the press" (135). So strong is her desire to violate the artistic
boundary that she is even moved to utter a pagan prayer to the
magic crown: "Almighty small Crown, annihilate that story; return,
return the stuff of it to me" (135). It is not the pagan prayer that
is here crucial. It is the assertion that "Malamud's" story was the
narrator's to begin with, that, in fact, it is "Malamud" who is the
usurper. "Usurpation" is, as we have conjectured, not about "other
people's stories," but about Ozick's own. Decidedly, it is about her
own.

I must emphasize here that the story of a public reading of a
story on a stage contains another cadre—the theatrical frame. A
reading is a performance after all. The narrator ruptures that frame
by presenting herself not merely as a spectator, who has paid for
her ticket and naively becomes absorbed by the action on the stage.
She is also a participant in the action, changing not only the course
of the dramatic action but also its focus. While a public reading is
"really" happening onstage, something else, something more dramatic perhaps, is going on in the audience. A totally new drama,
the one between the student-writer and the narrator, is being created.

It is not insignificant that the narrator characterizes the student-
writer as a "goat." David Stern's story is about the passion of a new
Jewish religious theater, and he even places it within the context
of Greek tragedy, which is an outgrowth of the dance of the goat-
mask, the *tragos,* of certain Greek pagan rituals. The part of Stern's
story that relates his creation of a Jewish religious theater is contained
in, and very artfully framed by, the epithet "goat."

After the narrator has finished retelling the story told by "Stern,"
she adds a postscript that returns us to the realm of reality. This
postscript—a commentary—is a borderline of another sort. "Well,

that should be enough," she writes. "No use making up any more of it. It is not my story. It is not the goat's story. It is no one's story. It is a story nobody wrote, nobody wants, it has no existence" (157). How can the narrator affirm that the story has no existence? Palpably, it does. Perhaps the story is not important. The commentary—that is, the rewriting of it—is. The "goat" will be permitted to get his revenge during a moment of manifest fictional absurdity. The goat will become an impossible reader performing an impossible act. "I looked up one of your stories," he tells the narrator. "It stank, lady. The one called 'Usurpation.' Half of it's swiped, you ought to get sued. You don't know when to stop. You swipe other people's stories and you go on and on, on and on. I fell asleep over it. Boring! Long-winded" (175).

Now, how did the character in the story get out of the story and obtain a copy of it to read? He did so by breaking the artistic frame. And how did he get back into it in order to inform the narrator of his judgment? This is accomplished by a process—let us call it "infolding"—thanks to which several frames, without explaining away their divergence, can be made to mesh and overlap, like intertwining spirals. The point is that, impossible or not, the story— Ozick calls it elsewhere "the story that never was" (159)—is not important. It is the frame that matters. Or more properly, since the structure must not only "be" but "mean," it is the meaning found in the frame that should concern us here. It is the commentary.

The Meaning of the Commentary Frame

Commentary is a basic activity of "Usurpation," central to its action. We have already seen examples of the commenting mode. But there is much more, an overwhelming quantity of commentary. "Agnon" does not shy away from giving a laudatory literary opinion of predecessor Ibn Gabirol. He also has some negative things to say about Tchernikhovsky's poetic pantheism. "Tchernikhovsky" comments on an Agnon story, "Messiah," about why the Jewish redeemer one day refused to appear on earth. [15] "Tchernikhovsky" creatively misreads Agnon's story and thereby makes it suit his own anti-Agnonian purpose. Ozick, of course, will not be satisfied merely to misread, no matter how creatively. The midrashic mode is not only an approach to reading. It is also a way of rewriting. Ozick rewrites the story, and Agnon's "Messiah" becomes yet another of the usurped stories of "Usurpation."

The most "usurped" of these stories is of course David Stern's. Stern's story is not only about Agnon, the religious writer; it also contains a theory of a Jewish religious theater. This idea is maltreated by Ozick in a manner that we shall soon see. Stern's story is also a commentary on a commentary, a commentary on the talmudic statement that affirms that "any man in whom there can be found haughtiness [*ba'al ga'avah* is the Hebrew term Ozick uses to describe that man], is to be considered an idol worshipper".[16] "Ozick" in her commentary on "Stern's" story, says that "the only good part in the whole thing was explaining about the *ba'al ga'avah*" (163). She latches on to this notion of the arrogant man as idolator and explains that one of the reasons she has, as a writer rewriting his story, chosen to kill off the student-writer is to punish *him* for his literary arrogance. She punishes him not for wanting to supplant Agnon by attaining his magic crown, but for wanting to supplant God by creating a "religious" literature. "It is an excellent thing to punish him. Did he not make his hero a student at the yeshiva, did he not make him call himself 'religious'?" (157–58).

Ozick's quarrel with religion needs to be clarified here. For indeed, as is hinted at in "Levitation," she does have a quarrel with that term. Her position is elucidated in the language of the least eminent of the writers she "usurps" in "Usurpation," the "pagan rabbi" Saul, him of the magic crowns. It is not at all surprising that her position in so critical a matter be elucidated in her commentaries on the works of a character she has herself created. Given all the other acts of infolding we have already witnessed and analyzed, it seems logical that Ozick should act as her own critic and rewriter.

Saul in "Usurpation" is himself both a commentator and a story writer. One text found in Saul's archive—a box under a bed—contains a commentary on the scene in Exodus 33 in which God refuses to reveal to Moses His "way" of doing things:

A Jew don't go asking Ha-shem[17] for inside information, for what reason He did this, what ideas He got on that, how come He let happen such-and-such a pogrom, why a good person loved by one and all dies with cancer, and a lousy bastard, he's rotten to his partner and cheats and plays the numbers, this fellow lives to 120. With questions like this don't expect no replies. . . . Ha-shem says, My secrets are My secrets, I command you what you got to do, the rest you leave to Me. This is no news that he don't reveal His deepest business. From that territory you get what you deserve, silence. (167)

Curiously, Cynthia Ozick expresses views similar to Saul's. Her commentary is also on a biblical text:

The King James Bible says, "I am that I am." But the Hebrew says: being is being or essence will be essence. The Hebrew does acrobatics with the root of "to be," and it's a non-answer. The only answer is to ask the question; the answer is that God is ontology. God has no Jewish definition; God is *the* question about the universe. Deuteronomy says your job as a human being is simply to discharge your obligations to your fellow human beings—i.e., to keep the Commandments—and you mustn't think about the nature of the Creator. And that's what Deuteronomy 29:28 says: "the secret things" aren't our human concern, we can't make a portrait of the Unknowable. This is the direction of a great, mammoth, volcanic high imagining which in a fundamental sense really does set Judaism apart from all other concepts.[18]

This consonance between the ideas expressed by "Saul" and those offered by Ozick is striking. Could it be that, in "Usurpation," Saul, and not the narrator, is Ozick's *porte-parole*? There is ample evidence for such speculation.

Frame-ups

"Usurpation" may be characterized not only by its frames but also by its frame-ups. The narrator is presented as one who lusts after stories, as a reader of stories who is able "to finger out the magic parts." More than once the narrator will assert an attitude that she consequently contradicts by her practice. "I'm not interested in ideas," she says. "I hate ideas. I only care about stories" (176). Of course, if there is anything clear about the narrator it is that she is a personification of the idea.

Contradictions are wallowed in. The narrator will aver that she detests plot summaries, for example, even as she is giving one. True, it is not exactly a summary of the plot that is presented but rather the Ozickian version, a personal rewriting of a previous text. The narrator will display erudition about the Maimonidean concept of the Messiah, for example, and then apply that concept to Zionist thinker Theodor Herzl. At the same time she will protest: "How

I despise writers who will stop a story dead for the sake of showing off!" (158). Her assertion that "practical action is my whole concern, and I have nothing but contempt for significant allusions, nuances, buried effects" (159) is not merely an inconsistency. It is such a blatant disharmony as to constitute a significant allusion itself.

These frame-ups come from the world of literary commentary. They are internal to the story. What are we to make of that outer frame found in the preface? How do Ozick's remarks there fit in with the attitudes expressed by the narrator within the story? "Usurpation," she says, "was in my view the opposite of mystery; it expressed not possibility but resolution. It was the incarnation of an *idea;* it had a purpose; it led to a point" (8). "Usurpation" is also a diatribe against storytelling in general:

Usurpation is a story written against story-writing; against the Muse-goddesses; against Apollo. It is against magic and mystification, against sham and "miracle," and, going deeper into the dark, against idolatry. It is an invention directed against inventing—the point being that the story-making faculty itself can be a corridor to the corruptions and abominations of idol-worship, of the adoration of the magical event. (11)

Fiction in the mind of Ozick is commentary. She makes the point in a piece of commentary, the preface, which in an interview she has called "fiction." Ozick has succeeded in blurring the distinction—in her mind and in her work—between fiction and commentary. That much is evident from her handling of a story written by Saul the biblical exegete. It is a Holocaust story that Ozick reproduces within her own story. Significantly, this is not a rewriting of Saul but his own writing. Of course, it will turn out to be Saul's rewriting of Ozick. The smaller text will prove to be an interior duplication in miniature of the text in which it is set. It is important to recount a full measure of Saul's story here.

Saul's Story

A man's son is scheduled by his Nazi captors for death in the concentration camp. The father, frantic, tries to find someone to bribe, someone who will see to it that another boy is taken in his son's place. As he meditates his plan, his conscience is bothered and he seeks out a rabbi for advice. May he save his son's life at another's expense? The Rabbi answers: "The law is, Don't kill." The father obeys the law, with tragic consequences. Saul intervenes in his own story to comment: "Ha-shem looks at what's happening, here is a man what didn't save his own boy so he wouldn't be responsible with killing someone else. I blew in man so much power of my commandments that his own flesh and blood he lets go to Moloch, so long he shouldn't kill. That I created even one such person like this is a very great miracle, and I didn't even notice I was doing it. So now positively no more" (170).

Unfortunately, Saul's deduction of what goes on in God's mind is only wishful thinking. There is, tragically, more. Everybody in this story will go up in smoke, not only the father and the son, but also the boy whom the father spared by not carrying out his plan to use him as a replacement. Saul laments that if there is a miracle, it should not be that there is one pious commandment-keeper in the world, one who would not kill another to save his own son. It should be to stop the murderers altogether. "The father," Saul comments further, "on account of one kid eats up the one miracle that's lying around loose. For the sake of one life the whole world is lost" (170). But, Saul remarks, that is not Judaism: "The sages say different: If you save one life only it's like the whole world is saved. So which is true? Naturally, whatever's written is what's true. What does this prove? It proves that if you talk miracle, that's when everything becomes false. Men and Women! Remember! No stories from miracles! No stories and no belief! (170–71). The story is not only a parable. It is also a diatribe, like the larger story in which it is encased, against certain conventional views of religion in which miracle plays a central role. The narrator's response to Saul's speculation is, "I can't digest any of this" (171). Of course she cannot digest any of this because her outlook has been digested by Saul. It also means that to digest would be to explain away differences. If what is written—in all its inconsistency—is true and at the same time indigestible then we are left with a cosmic literary bellyache.

The "Magic" of Jewish Storytelling

Earlier in the story, the narrator had admitted that she was drawn to the magic aspect of "Malamud's" story. "Magic," she admits, "is what I lust after. And not ordinary magic, which is what one expects of pagan peoples; their religions declare it. . . . As for me,

. . . I am drawn to what is forbidden" (134). She realizes of course that the Jewish idea is exactly the opposite of magic. Nevertheless, a tangle of contradictions, she reveals an inner aspiration: "Some day I will take courage and throw over being a Jew, and then I will make a little god, a silver godlet, in the shape of a crown, which will stop death, resurrect fathers and uncles; out of its royal points gardens will burst" (135). Her problem is that the Jews have no magic.

One lesson that one may learn from Saul's commentary on his own story is that the Jews, like the narrator, have a history of temptation. "The Jews have no magic," the narrator admits. "And yet with what prowess we have crept down the centuries after amulets, and hidden countings of letters, and the silver crown that heals: so it is after all nothing to marvel at that my own, my beloved subject should be the preternatural—everything anti-Moses, all things blazing with their own wonder" (134–35). The narrator equates the Jewish dynamic, which is a tension between theological theory and daily practice, with her own.

As she has admitted many times before, Ozick in her preface declares, "storytelling, as every writer knows, is a kind of magic act" (10–11). In the preface she reveals another curious coincidence of her own tension with that of previous Jewish writers who have worn the crown of literary glory. What she did not realize when writing "Usurpation" was that "Ibn Gabirol had worried over the theme that obsesses my tale." The worry is whether Jews ought to be storytellers altogether. "Ibn Gabirol wondered whether the imagination itself—afflatus, trance, image—might offend the Second Commandment" (10). Ozick is comforted by the fact that Ibn Gabirol felt as she does about storytelling and yet he wrote poems. The commentary in the preface reveals that Ozick is constantly rethinking her attitude toward the tension between the second commandment and the story-writing instinct and that rethinking is in essence rewriting.

Ozick reveals that she has made great strides in her thinking since the writing and rewriting of "Usurpation." She says, "I used to see the imagination in very rigid terms as the enemy of the moral life and of moral seriousness. I now see something else, that you cannot be a monotheist without a very developed imagination, because you have to imagine, you have to envision and imagine that which there is no evidence for whatever".[19] Ozick continues by making the distinction between two kinds of imagination. "The mammalian imagination results in idol-making. The higher imagination, the imagination that can imagine the unimaginable, the imagination that invented monotheism—this posits God."[20]

We see here that by a process of constant rethinking of her philosophical outlooks Ozick is able to progress from the notion of magic to a highly developed sense of the prophetic. She does this by framing out her stories in the midrashic mode. In particular, as we have seen from "Usurpation," stories can as a matter of aesthetic principle carry within them their own organic interpretation. That is because stories that interpret themselves also interpret the world. Jewish stories do carry a baggage of elucidations. Rewriting others is not what "Usurpation" is about. It is about rewriting oneself, continually and continuously mulling over the metaphysical problem of writing as a proper Jewish activity.

Chapter Eight
Rewriting Herself:
"The Shawl" and "Rosa"

Many are the writers—both novelists and critics—who have come to the conclusion that writing is an activity based not only in reality but also on previous writing. In Bernard Malamud's novel *God's Grace,* a modern rewriting of the Flood Story of Genesis, the hero, when asked where stories come from, informs his companion that stories come "from other stories."[1] In *The Anxiety of Influence,* Harold Bloom asserts that "one cannot write a novel without remembering another novel."[2]

In "Usurpation (Other People's Stories)" (1974), Cynthia Ozick demonstrated that she had no anxieties whatever about being influenced by previous writers. To the contrary, she publicly arrogated to herself the right to rewrite other texts, basing herself on a long literary tradition that goes back at least as far as Boccaccio and Shakespeare in the Western world, and to the domain of rabbinic literature in the Jewish tradition.

"Usurpation" provides hints of a second phase to the rewriting phenomenon. In Ozick's case, rewriting does not limit itself to other people's stories but extends to her own work as well. The short story "Puttermesser and Xanthippe" is in many ways a sequel to the earlier "Puttermesser: Her Work History, Her Ancestry, Her Afterlife." Ozick's novel *The Cannibal Galaxy* is a rewriting of her earlier short story "The Laughter of Akiva," placing greater emphasis on the background of her main protagonists, emphasizing the dual role—of culture and of cruelty—that Europe has played for her Jewish heroes.

Perhaps the summit of Ozick's art as rewriter—that is to say, as a writer—is attained in a pair of short stories published in the *New Yorker* in 1980 and 1983, respectively: "The Shawl" and "Rosa."

"The Shawl"

"The Shawl" tells the story of a woman and two girls caught up in that "place without pity" known as the Holocaust. Rosa, a mother governed by strong maternal instincts, will try to overcome a Nazi policy that dictates that infants are not to be spared. Rosa's teenage niece Stella has no motherly instincts. She will be governed exclusively by the instinct of self-preservation.

The story has two loci: the road on which the Jews are forced to march to their final destination, and the concentration camp itself, presented in miniature as a barracks and a yard surrounded by an electrified barbed-wire fence.

The story revolves about the shawl of the title, seen by Rosa as her daughter Magda's only defense against the Nazis. It is used as both a wrapping in which to hide the child—a container—and as a security blanket with which to pacify her so that she will not cry out from hunger and thereby betray her existence to the oppressors. The story has one incident. One morning on the *Appleplatz* Rosa hears the cry "Maaa . . . aaa!" and notices her daughter, shawlless, crawling on the ground. Rosa is faced with a tragic dilemma. If she tries to run and snatch up the baby, the baby will not stop crying and the Germans will discover both "criminals." If she runs back to the barracks to find the comforting shawl, perhaps the baby will be discovered, during the brief moment of delay, by a German soldier. Rosa opts for the shawl and hurries back into the barracks. Stella, obviously in an effort to keep from freezing, instinctively trying to cling to her own life, has taken Magda's shawl and covered herself with it. Rosa grabs the shawl and runs back out into the arena. But it is too late. A German officer has picked the child up and is heading toward the electrified fence. The maternal instinct and the instinct for self-preservation wage a silent battle within Rosa as, helpless, she observes the Nazi electrocute her daughter by hurling her against the fence.

In two thousand finely wrought words, that is the story of "The Shawl." It is obvious, however, that the power of the story derives not merely from the plot, as starkly riveting as it may be, but from the concentrated style of the author.

Ozick, like a French symbolist poet of the nineteenth century, paints not "the thing itself" but the *effect* produced by the "thing." The effect of a concentration camp is achieved here by both indirection and concentration. How do we know that we are in a place that harbors crematoria? Ozick writes only of an "ash-stippled wind." How do we know that Magda is the fruit of an illicit liaison with a non-Jewish, "Aryan" man? Not by her blue eyes, nor by the color of her hair, which resembles the color of Rosa's star, but by the word *their* set off by italics: "You could think she was one of *their* babies."

The concentrated world of "The Shawl" extends beyond its fictional borders into other worlds. Ozick's use of metaphor here is crucial. Rosa, marching on the road with the baby in her arms, is a "walking cradle." Stella's weakened knees are "tumors on sticks," her elbows "chicken bones." Magda in the shawl is "a squirrel in a nest." The shawl's windings form "a little house." Magda's round face is "a pocket mirror" in which her ascendancy can be seen. More ominously, Magda's tooth, jutting up in her mouth, is "an elfin tombstone of white marble." Providing a moment of sad comic relief, the shawl itself, blown in the wind, is a "clown." At the end, the scream Rosa represses is "a long viscous rope of clamor." Rosa's skeleton is not merely a frame on which her flesh is draped but "a ladder up which a scream might climb."

These images are intended to produce, by indirection, the effect of physical and mental torture. No scream is ever produced on Rosa's viscous rope, no scream climbs up her ladder. In this story there is—strictly speaking—not one word of dialogue among the protagonists. The only sound that passes anyone's lips is Magda's semibestial infant cry, "Maaaa . . . aaa!". Aside from that one cry, even Magda is characterized by silence. "Ever since the drying up of Rosa's nipples, ever since Magda's last scream on the road, Magda had been devoid of any syllable; Magda was mute."[3]

Of conversation between Rosa and Stella there is no indication. Stella's "I was cold" comes "afterward." In place of dialogue Ozick puts the double voice of nature and technology. Just as the language of metaphor succeeds in dilating the scenic space and in creating a world wider than the space occupied by the text, so too the language spoken by nature succeeds in enlarging the confining space of the barracks, indicating both other places and other times.

Ozick's nature speaks in murmurs. "The sunheat [in the arena] murmured of another life, of butterflies in summer. . . . On the other side of the steel fence, far away, there were green meadows speckled with dandelions and deep-colored violets; beyond them, even farther, innocent tiger lilies, tall, lifting their orange bonnets." This moment of lyricism provides relief in the tension-filled drama; it constitutes a delaying tactic at the precise moment of the greatest horror.

The language of technology performs a different function. The fence surrounding the barracks is electrified. In the deathly silence characteristic of "The Shawl" Rosa can discern its pathetic hum. "Sometimes the electricity inside the fence would seem to hum. . . . Rosa heard real sounds in the wire: grainy sad voices."

The voices within the wire are quite possibly the voices of Jewish history, the voices of those who have already gone up in fire. These are not voices of warning; they are voices of lamentation, of poetry. They constitute a striving to turn lament into a liturgical voice of triumph. They have come to urge Rosa to act courageously. When Rosa appears on the margins of the arena, shawl in hand, she sees her child being carried aloft by a helmeted soldier. "The voices told her to hold up the shawl, high; the voices told her to shake it, to whip with it, to unfurl it like a flag." The voices vainly urge Rosa to become a hero.

At another moment the electric voices of the fence take on the identity of the voice of the child Magda; soon those two voices will indeed be one and the same. "The electric voice began to chatter wildly. 'Maamaa, maaamaaa,' they all hummed together." The moment that Magda "splashed against the fence, the steel voices went mad in their growling, urging Rosa to run and run to the spot where Magda had fallen."

Rosa's instinct for self-preservation overcomes both her maternal instincts and any heroic urges she may have had. Rosa does not obey the voice of the electric wires because she knows that "if she let the wolf's screech ascending now through the ladder of her skeleton break out, they would shoot." Rosa's story in "The Shawl" ends with her making the same use of the shawl that Stella had done, and, incidentally, as Magda had done, as a life preserver. Rosa takes the shawl and stuffs her mouth with it. Stifling speech, she preserves life.

Because Rosa has denied the tragic, heroic moment, she has left Cynthia Ozick with a problem. Surely there is more to this woman Rosa than her actions under superhuman stress. It is on the pretext of this problem that Ozick will enter into "The Shawl" and pull out a midrash on it, the prize-winning story "Rosa," a rewriting of "The Shawl."

"Rosa"

"Rosa" takes place approximately 35 years after the events described in "The Shawl." Both Rosa and Stella have survived the ordeal. After the war, Zionist rescue organizations had made an effort to induce teenager Stella to be rehabilitated in a Youth Aliyah setting in Palestine. Rosa, who had herself been brought up in an assimilated non-Zionist family, blocks these efforts and whisks Stella away with her to America. There, aunt and niece live what it is probably no exaggeration to call an eccentric existence. Rosa is still resentful of Stella's role in Magda's death; Stella is unable to "normalize" her existence in marriage and family. This double spinsterhood is remarkable for the way Rosa Lublin chooses to earn a living: she opens an antiques shop.

The shop specializes in both real and metaphorical mirrors. Every customer who enters the shop is offered not only things "used, old, lacy with other people's history"[4] but also a story of Jewish suffering at the hands of the Nazis. In particular, Rosa offers to her "clientele" not the story of "The Shawl"—of that there is no direct mention— but a story of the tramcar that used to pass through the center of the Warsaw Ghetto.

Obviously frustrated by her customers' total indifference to the story she has to tell, and unable and unwilling to adapt to life after her traumatic experience, Rosa goes mad and, one day, smashes up her store. In order to save her aged aunt from prosecution and a possible sentence, Stella works out a deal with the authorities whereby Rosa will leave New York and retire to Miami Beach.

Such is the background against which Cynthia Ozick's story is set. The word "background" is used here because only at this point does "Rosa" the short story begin, in a rundown retirement hotel in Miami Beach. To the casual and disinterested observer, Rosa looks like a "madwoman and a scavenger" (1), indifferent to life. She rarely ventures out into the hot Florida sun, taking her meals— a cracker spread with Welch's grape jelly or a single sardine from a tin can—standing up in her kitchen. Her shabby dress would lead one to believe that she is negligent of her person.

On the day the story begins, Rosa makes what appears to be a superhuman effort to do a wash at the local laundromat. There she meets Simon Persky, a relative of Israeli politician Shimon Peres and a near-widower whose wife had been institutionalized for mental illness. It appears that Persky, who otherwise fancies himself something of a ladies' man, has been sent by fate to rehabilitate Rosa. Although unaware of the extraordinary past life that Rosa has led and equally unconscious of the extraordinary inner life that Rosa has been leading, Persky does not treat Rosa as "the ordinary article," but rather as an individual of intrinsic worth. After her encounter with Persky, Rosa returns alone to her hotel room with her laundry—curiously, minus a pair of underpants. The missing pair of pants will become an obsession with Rosa throughout the course of the story; her suspicions will be directed at her new acquaintance.

She has another obsession, not evident to the casual observer, and that is to write letters in Polish to her dead daughter Magda. In these letters Rosa displays a cultured background, a literary style, and a vivid imagination. She conjures up Magda either as an adult woman, a professor at Columbia University, or as a sixteen-year-old girl dressed in frilly clothes. Rosa's letters have two main themes: complaints about Stella's stubborn resistance to Magda's continued existence, and reminiscences of Rosa's beautiful home life in prewar Warsaw.

Rosa also writes to Stella, to whom she must, for appearances' sake, feign that Magda is indeed dead. In her last letter she has asked Stella to send her a package: a box containing Magda's shawl, religiously preserved all these years. Despite Stella's misgivings that her aunt is engaged in some mad form of idolatry, she informs Rosa that the shawl is on its way.

Rosa receives other mail as well. This includes a series of letters and a box containing a scholarly manuscript from Dr. James W. Tree—the name is suggestive, especially in a work by the author of "The Pagan Rabbi," in which the main protagonist hangs himself from a tree—a professor in the "Department of Clinical Social Pathology" at the "University of Kansas-Iowa." Dr. Tree is doing research on a theory of "Repressed Animation"—souls in hiding?—and would welcome the opportunity to make a case study of Rosa's reaction to her "stress resulting from incarceration, exposure, and malnutrition." Rosa does not respond to this cold, clinical intrusion into "other people's suffering" except to burn Tree's insistent letters.

Does Rosa resist *all* intrusions? Eventually, she will not resist Persky's warm, humane, personal, value-laden intervention in her life. At the end of the story she will have the telephone in her room reconnected, symbolically renewing contact with the outside world. More importantly, she will begin to make room in her inner life for Persky's continuing presence.

The Relationship of the Stories

While "Rosa" is many ways a continuation of "The Shawl," it is not strictly speaking a sequel to its predecessor. Both stories are independent works of art and neither "needs" the other to be considered complete. One might say, however, that once the reader has knowledge of both stories, neither story can be approached without reference to the other. Once again Cynthia Ozick has entered, and drawn the reader into, the midrashic mode.

The similarity of "Rosa" to Ozick's earlier midrashic writing is striking. Like Isaac Kornfeld, the main character of "The Pagan Rabbi," like Jimmy and Lucy Feingold, the authorial couple of "Levitation," like Hester Lilt, the "imagistic linguistic logician" of The Cannibal Galaxy, and like almost all of the personages depicted in "Usurpation," from the narrator, to the "goat," to "Saul-not-Tchernikhowsky," Rosa is a writer. Taken by itself, it is perhaps not significant that Rosa spends much of her life in Florida cooped up in her room with a writing board on her knees composing letters. What is significant is that these letters written to her dead daughter Magda are works of fiction. What is even more compelling is that "to her daughter Magda she wrote in the most excellent literary Polish" (1). Rosa's parents, no less than Rosa's literary predecessors in Ozick's oeuvre, are thinkers and writers. Her father she describes as a philosopher; her mother, she reveals, published poetry. Stella, as if in criticism, calls her aunt a "parable-maker" (17), but the reader attuned to nuances in Ozick will realize that that title is a badge of honor.

When Rosa was a high school student in prewar Warsaw, she had been praised by one of her teachers for her "literary style." Ozick intervenes in the story (using a free indirect style of quotation) to comment on the linguistic power accorded to the writer. "What a curiosity it was to hold a pen—nothing but a small pointed stick, after all, oozing its hieroglyphic puddles: a pen that speaks, miraculously, Polish" (19). Of course Ozick is commenting not only on Rosa's power but on her own ability as a novelist to create a fiction in which she can write in English and force her reader into accepting that what he is reading is indeed "literary Polish." After all, says Ozick, what is writing but an "immersion into the living language: all at once this cleanliness, this power to make history, to tell, to explain. To retrieve, to reprieve!" And that is not all.

Writing, she concludes, is something more: the making of fictions. In her own words, writing is: "To lie" (19–20). Rosa, for her part, explains her own fiction-making capacity to her daughter in her own way: "to those who don't deserve the truth, don't give it" (19). The fictions that Rosa creates are based in fact, located in history. Their goal is to make the past meaningful. Simon Persky, obviously in an effort at bonding, claims that his past is identical with Rosa's. After all, like her, he was born in Warsaw. More than once Rosa will protest to him vehemently: "My Warsaw isn't your Warsaw." First of all, since Persky left Europe in 1920 for America, he did not experience the degradations of the Warsaw Ghetto. In addition, Persky, insulated in Polish Jewishness, had had nothing at all to do with Polish culture. Rosa's Poland is unfathomably different:

In school she had read Tuwim[5], such delicacy, such loftiness, such *Polishness*. The Warsaw of her girlhood: a great light: she switched it on, she wanted to live inside her eyes. The curve of the legs of her mother's bureau. The strict leather smell of her father's desk. The white tile tract of the kitchen floor, the big pots breathing, a narrow tower stair next to the attic . . . the house of her girlhood laden with a thousand books. Polish, German, French; her father's Latin books; the shelf of shy literary periodicals her mother's poetry now and then wandered through, in short lines like heated telegrams. Cultivation, old civilization, beauty, history! Surprising turnings of streets, shapes of venerable cottages, lovely aged eaves, unexpected and gossamer turrets, steeples, the gloss, the antiquity! Gardens. Whoever speaks of Paris has never seen Warsaw. (5–6)

There are, then, two types of Warsaw, Rosa's and Persky's, and the lives lived in these two cities are not comparable. Life itself, for Rosa, can be further divided, as she puts it, into three phases: "the life before, the life during, the life after. . . . The life after is now. The life before is our *real* life, at home, where we was born" (28). (From the word "was" we know that Rosa is not speaking "literary Polish" but immigrant English, and she is speaking it to Persky.) Persky wants to know what the "life during" was. "This was Hitler," Rosa answers. This is the life of which Persky has no inkling. This is the life about which the people coming into her store were indifferent. Rosa admits that "before is a dream" and can therefore be preserved only in the fantasy world of fiction. Furthermore, when one looks at the superficiality of modern life, and here Rosa means modern *American* life, one concludes that "after is a joke." What Rosa wants to force her interlocutor to understand is that "only during stays. And to call it life is a lie" (28).

How is one to render an account of the "during" that "stays"? "The Shawl" is one of the stories of the enduring "during," presented as a brutal, simple truth. Rosa has another story to tell about the "during," about the time contained between the lovely "before" and the superficial "after." It concerns the tramcar that went through the heart of the Warsaw Ghetto. What was extraordinary about that tramcar was its very ordinariness: "The most astounding thing was that the most ordinary streetcar, bumping along on the most ordinary trolley tracks, and carrying the most ordinary citizens going from one section of Warsaw to another, ran straight into the place of our misery" (34). Amazingly, the ordinary streetcar passengers did not even see the extraordinary setting in which they were riding. They could not imagine, much less notice, an "other" for whom an ordinary head of lettuce might take on pastoral dimensions, representing all of nature. "Every day they saw us—women with shopping sacks. . . . Green lettuce! I thought my salivary glands would split with aching for that leafy greenness" (34).

"Rosa" is a story in the Jewish mode to the extent that it demonstrates to the reader the extraordinariness that lies hidden in Rosa's very ordinariness. In one of her letters to her daughter Magda, Rosa protests that Stella's accusation that Magda's father is a non-Jew, a German, and possibly a Nazi, is a slander. She does admit that after Magda's death she had been "forced" more than once by Nazi soldiers. She insists however that her relationship with Magda's father, her admittedly gentile father, was most ordinary: "Take my word for it, Magda, your father and I had the most ordinary lives—by 'ordinary' I mean respectable, gentle, cultivated. Reliable people of refined reputation" (19). The ordinariness of which Rosa speaks is extraordinary on several counts. Hers was not the life that most Polish Jews in America speak of. Persky did not know of such thorough acculturation. In addition, compared with the uncultivated "joke" that life has become in the "after" of America, the ordinary life of prewar Europe is in itself extraordinary.

Extraordinariness may indeed be the key to "Rosa." Behind the "madwoman and the scavenger" that we see, there is a rich extraordinary background, a background that includes more than an affair with a gentile and an illegitimate child. It is a background that includes even more than the reading of an exquisite Jewish-Polish poet, Julian Tuwim. The Lublins had fine art at home, including an authentic Greek vase, no less suggestive of eternity than Keats's Grecian urn. In addition, "we had wonderful ink drawings, the black so black and miraculous, how it measured out a hand and then the shadow of the hand" (35).

It is in Rosa's developing relationship with Persky that "Rosa" gives further meaning to what Ozick has called "the riddle of the ordinary."[6] Before his retirement, Simon Persky had been a button manufacturer. That button is magnified by Rosa into a major metaphor for ordinariness. She compares Persky's background to her own in its terms: "She considered Persky's life: how trivial it must always have been: buttons, himself no more significant than a button. It was plain he took her to be another button like himself, battered now and out of fashion" (26). Time and again Rosa returns to this image, apparently seeming mad to one who has not yet fathomed the poetry of her language. "I'm not your button, Persky! I'm nobody's button!" (30).

Rosa is unfair to Persky. He is not trivial. He, too, is not a button. Not only that, but he means to deal with Rosa as a person of intrinsic worth. He recognizes that there is something of the extraordinary in her. (He would probably believe that of everybody, like Ozick.) At one point in the story the conversation between Persky and Rosa turns to books. Persky is impressed to learn that Rosa reads only in Polish and, moreover, that she does not read mere "books" but is interested only in real "literature." Noticing that Rosa has no books in her home, Persky humanely offers to drive Rosa to the library. This gesture of warm humanity is taken as such by Rosa: "A thread of gratitude pulled in her throat. He almost understood what she was: no ordinary button" (28).

If Rosa is to be admired for her extraordinariness, Persky himself is to be given consideration for the fact that his very ordinariness contains a grain of Jewish heroism. Persky's outlook on life—one is tempted to call it a philosophy—is based on his simple humanism. Persky counsels Rosa that in life what is needed is perspective, what is required is moderation. To Rosa's assessment, for example that her quarters are "cramped," Persky answers: "I work from a different theory. For everything there's a bad way of describing, also a good way. You pick the good way, you get along better" (27). When Rosa complains to Persky that Stella is trying to wipe out the memory of all that Rosa cherishes, Persky advises her to be moderate,

even in her effort to do such a noble thing as to commemorate the
past. "Sometimes a little forgetting is necessary . . . if you want
to get something out of life" (28).

It is clear that, before the encounter with Persky, Rosa has wanted
little if anything from life. After all, the "life after" is a joke. Rosa
does not want to be normal, like Persky. She prefers a life that is
lived on an entirely different plane, a plane that involves art, creativity, the imagination, a plane that with some justification might
plausibly be called pagan.

In reminiscing about her parents' home in prewar Warsaw, Rosa
recalls that her mother was attracted to the object of her maid's
religious adorations: a statue. In Ozick's writings, this type of attraction always verges on the idolatrous. Magda's shawl becomes
Rosa's substitute for her mother's statue of the Virgin and Child.
The shawl is a religious icon that Rosa feels the urge to kiss. In a
letter informing her aunt that the requested shawl is in the mail,
Stella takes the opportunity to preach to Rosa: "Your idol is on its
way. . . . Go on your knees to it if you want. . . . You'll open
the box and take it out and cry, you'll kiss it like a crazy person.
Making holes in it with kisses. You're like those people in the
Middle Ages who worshipped a piece of the True Cross, a splinter
from some old outhouse as far as anybody knew" (12). Stella's
assessment of Rosa's behavior in the presence of the shawl, as brutal
as it may appear in its rationality, is on the mark. Indeed, Rosa is
very close to being an idol worshiper. Even Rosa's letter-writing
activity is ambiguous. On the one hand, it is an aesthetic outlet
for a deep emotional strain, on the other, it is the expression of a
pagan mentality.

When Rosa prepares to write her highly creative letters to Magda,
she first meticulously sets the scene. Is she preparing a canvas for
painting or an altar for devotion? Even the act of preparing the
paper with which to write Magda is an ambiguous one. The act of
receiving Magda's shawl, however, is clearly idolatrous.

Rosa has received in the mail a package that she is certain contains
her beloved shawl. Rather than rip it open victoriously, she delays
opening the box as much as possible. In so doing, she makes herself
into a statue:

She put on her good shoes, a nice dress; . . . she arranged her hair,
brushed her teeth, poured mouthwash on the brush, sucked it up through

the nylon bristles, gargled rapidly. As an afterthought she changed her bra and slip; it meant getting out of her dress and into it again. Her mouth she reddened very slightly—a smudge of lipstick rubbed on with a finger. *Perfect, she mounted the bed on her knees and fell into folds.* A puppet, dreaming. Darkened cities, tombstones, colorless garlands, a black fire in a gray field, brutes forcing the innocent, women with their mouths stretched and their arms wild, her mother's voice calling. After hours of these pitiless tableaux, it was late afternoon. (20; my italics)

The perfection achieved by Rosa in this tableau is that of a work of art creating other works of art. Rosa has succeeded in making herself into a *tableau vivant*, perfect, ready to investigate the contents of her treasure chest. Instead of opening the box, however, she dreams of her brutal past, a dead civilization, painting, in her mind's eye, *tableaux morts*. The connection between these *tableaux morts* and the *tableau vivant* that Rosa has transformed herself into is striking. One contains the other. And, although hours pass at this activity, both are frozen in time. The dreaming activity is not merely a hiatus between the desire to open the package and its opening. The dreaming activity—the artistic activity—itself becomes central, and leads to further artistic activity. Reintegrating reality after her dream, Rosa does not return her attention to the box with the shawl in it. Instead, she returns to the underpants that were mysteriously missing from her laundry.

How are underpants different from a shawl? The latter represents the life of the imagination. It represents the dangers of the life of the imagination, to be sure, but it also represents the attempt to give meaning to history. The underpants represent present reality in all its commonness, in all its ordinariness. They represent the need to regain meaning in life.

Rosa will now go out into the Miami evening in search of her underpants. She will go out, therefore, "to retrieve, to reprieve." On the sands of Miami Beach she will find decadent reality in the form of homosexual lovers. She will also find a way of framing her life.

The "Container" and the "Contained"

One of the most vivid techniques adopted by Ozick in "Rosa" is the striking opposition between images of the "container" and the "contained." The word "container" is found only once in the entire story, applied metaphorically to Stella, but it appears to have been enough to set the image humming. Stella looks innocent on the outside; she has "the face of a little bride." Rosa, nevertheless, harbors a great deal of resentment of Stella, for a complex set of reasons, including blame for Magda's death. To Magda, Rosa writes of Stella: "You could not believe in what harmless *containers* the bloodsucker comes" (2; my italics). The very sentence implies a distinction between the container and the contained. Miami Beach, with what Rosa calls its trivial residents, is another type of container, "a box for useless buttons" (26). The button metaphor is here contained within the container metaphor. Her own place of residence, a container within a container, a single-room apartment in a Miami Beach retirement hotel, is described as "a dark hole" (1). And yet, when Rosa is able to conjure up Magda's presence, the room is magically transformed into a magnificent surreal palace, in which the buttons on Magda's dress are the stars of some extraordinary heaven:

The whole room was full of Magda: she was like a butterfly in this corner and in that corner, all at once. Rosa waited to see what age Magda was going to be: how nice, a girl of sixteen, girls in their bloom move so swiftly that their blouses and skirts balloon, they are always butterflies at sixteen. There was Magda, all in flower. She was wearing one of Rosa's dresses from high school. Rosa was glad: it was the sky-colored dress, a middling blue with black buttons seemingly made of round chips of coal, like the unlit shards of stars. (32)

When Rosa ventures out into the Sodom and Gomorrah of Miami's beachfront, the sand in which the lovers lie enveloped is compared to the volcanic ash of Pompeii. "The sand was littered with bodies. Photograph of Pompeii: prone in the volcanic ash. Her pants were under the sand; or else packed with sand, like a piece of torso, a broken statue; the human groin detached, the whole soul gone, only the loins left for kicking by strangers" (22). Time is here doubly frozen, once by lava and once by the art of photography; both of these contain time. The underpants themselves are at one and the same time the thing contained (in a photograph) and the container for a work of art (the statue of a torso). Rosa is compelled to look for her pants in the sands of Miami Beach perhaps because she feels a need to convert them into that work of statuary.

Her suspicions lie elsewhere. She believes that Persky, in a fit of perversion, has stolen her pants. Only a sense of decorum and respect for Persky's humanity prevent her from confronting him with her suspicions. Nevertheless, her imagination will still think in terms of intertwining containers: "She wanted to tell him he was under suspicion; he owed her a look in his jacket-pocket. . . . If not his jacket, his pants. But it wasn't possible to say a thing like this. Her pants in his pants" (25).

The most striking use of the image of the container and the contained can be found in Ozick's use of the metaphor of electricity. It is on this point that the continuity of "Rosa" with "The Shawl" is most apparent. In "The Shawl" Rosa is frozen by the hum of electricity; the electrified fence of the concentration camp is the container for voices that cry out to Rosa. In "Rosa" the metaphor of electricity is extended to encompass two other types of expressiveness. When Rosa writes letters to Magda, she writes "inside a blazing flying current" (35). Rosa's writing is contained and expressed by an electric hum. The second type of electric current has to do with the fact of Magda's blond hair and with the fact that Magda is the product of Jewish and Aryan strains: "She was always a little suspicious of Magda, because of the other strain, whatever it was, that ran in her. . . . The other strain was ghostly, even dangerous. *It was as if the peril hummed out from the filaments of Magda's hair, those narrow bright wires*" (33; my italics).

As with Stella, so with Magda: what is inside the container is dangerous. Rosa herself is tempted to exteriorize her feelings; it is quite likely that she fears that, doing so, she will empty herself of all content.

There are two other containers in "Rosa," the package from Stella containing Magda's shawl, and a package from Dr. Tree, containing a scholarly study of another type of "containering," called by Ozick "repressed animation." Dr. Tree's package comes first. Rosa mistakes its contents for those of the other package. She treats it as though it did indeed contain the object of her idolatrous worship. In order to maximize the feelings of her inner life, she delays opening the package and exteriorizing her dreams. "She tidied all around. Everything had to be nice when the box was opened" (13). This retarding tactic is expanded into the episode of her foray into Miami Beach underlife.

On Rosa's return to her hotel she is greeted by the faithful Persky. In what she thinks is an act of religious self-sacrifice, she offers to

Persky the honor of opening the package. "What her own hands longed to do she was yielding to a stranger, a man with pockets; she knew why. To prove herself pure: a Madonna" (29). What Persky, the man with pockets, is a container for remains to be seen. Rosa wishes to display herself for the world to see; she wants to remain the statue she had created previously. The box contains not Magda's shawl but Dr. Tree's treatise.

Just as Rosa had destroyed her store—the store that contained stories—Rosa will destroy the treatise, sending the Tree up in flames. Subsequently, the "real" package from Stella arrives. Neither the container nor its contents will any longer hold interest for Rosa. It is her own contents that interest Rosa now, and she feels she is losing hold of them. "It was not possible to be hoodwinked again, but Rosa was shocked, *depleted,* almost as if yesterday's conflagration hadn't been Tree but really the box with Magda's shawl" (30–31; my italics). Rosa feels empty of content. The former owner of a store that specialized in mirrors sees in Simon Persky a possible mirror for her own humanity.

Rosa's room had been tidied up, prepared for a pagan ritual, the worship of the dead. It turns out by some "miracle" to have been prepared instead for life. Persky arrives. "Her room was miraculously ready: tidy, clarified. . . . Destiny had clarified her room just in time for a visitor" (27). In this encounter with the "visitor" Rosa gets a further inkling that she is quite willing to be brought back to life. One of the signs of her newly expressed "animation" is her decision to have her telephone reconnected. At first, when she hears the telephone ring (the sound coming by the way from wires, contained in them), she thinks of the telephone as a dead idol that can magically be brought to life. In a pagan gesture, she will even take the telephone and wrap it in the shawl, making the shawl a container for repressed animation.

When Persky, a gentleman come to call on a lady, has his presence announced via the telephone, the shawled telephone will be described as "silent god, so long comatose." Like Magda, the telephone can be "animated at will" (35). Unlike Magda, however, the telephone announces not a dead past but a future that contains Persky's version of life. In the closing scene of the story Rosa takes the shawl off the telephone, thus divorcing it from Magda. The shawl that contained Magda and at the same time repressed Rosa's animation will now repress Magda. "Magda was not there. Shy, she ran from Persky. Magda was away" (36).

Given Cynthia Ozick's attitude toward background and history, one may be confident that Magda will not be "away" for good. Rather, having written "Rosa" as a midrash on "The Shawl," Ozick means for the two stories to stand not in a diachronous relationship one to the other, a relationship in which one story would follow the other chronologically. Rather, Ozick means for the two stories to stand next to each other in a synchronous relationship, in which one story "always" contains the other and comments on it. Just as the mirrors in Rosa's store are meant both to freeze time and to record its passing, so too these two stories, "Rosa" and "The Shawl," are mirrors of themselves and mean to give meaning to both history and life.

Chapter Nine

Repairing the World, Repairing the Text: The Puttermesser Stories

Cynthia Ozick is not a "woman writer." Tinged with overtones of anger, Ozick's voice rises to indignation at the mere suggestion that she might fall into that category. In interviews and in both her analytical and polemical essays, Ozick rejects the term outright. She reveals that her rejection stems directly from and is completely consonant with her conception of the world as a place in need of repair, as a place to which it is desirable to try to bring the messianic idea of redemption.

In the television interview with Bill Moyers, Ozick asserts that for her the term "woman writer" is antifeminist. It is antifeminist, she suggests, because it tends to segregate women, and may tend to "lead to a situation where we're going to have writers and then we're going to have women writers, instead of everybody being subsumed under the glorious rubric of writers."[1]

Ozick's most elaborate analysis of the term "woman writer" can be found in her 1977 essay "Dissent," a classic example of cogent argumentation. In this essay, Ozick argues that the term "woman writer" is a political term. She insists further that "the language of politics is not a writer's language. Outside its political uses, 'woman writer' has no meaning—not intellectually, not morally, not historically."[2] The logical conclusion to such an assertion is that because, as she puts it, "a writer is a writer," he or she is free of all contingencies, including biological ones. Not only does the writer have freedom. The writer has creative power. The writer can create a multiplicity of identities. "When I write, I am free. I am, as a writer, whatever I wish to become. I can think myself into a male or female, or a stone, or a raindrop, or a block of wood, or a Tibetan, or the spine of a cactus."[3] Literature, Ozick reminds us, is not life. "In life, I am not free. In life, female or male, no one is free. In life, female or male, I have tasks; I have obligations and responsibilities."[4]

Lest one get the idea that the tasks and responsibilities of which Ozick speaks arise from biological premises, Ozick sets out, in subsequent essays, to combat not only Freud's assertion that "anatomy is destiny," but also what she sees as a neo-feminist capitulation to the restrictions of biology and anatomy. She does this, first, by setting up a dialectic between the notions of "intrinsicness" and "instrumentality" and, then, by embedding the notion of "intrinsicness" firmly within the Jewish tradition. Although as late as 1985 Ozick in an interview revealed that her idea of instrumentality is still evolving,[5] it is clear from her statements in this interview, as well as in her 1984 piece, "Torah as Feminism, Feminism as Torah," that her notion of the centrality of the intrinsic value of every human being is derived from the Jewish textual tradition, especially the narrative of Hannah in the First Book of Samuel.

For Ozick, who has been called a "religious" writer, Judaism is nevertheless, first and foremost, a humanism. Ozick states her position in the negative, in answer to the question "What is antifeminism?": "It's using, it's seeing woman, not as intrinsically valuable, intrinsically human, but rather as an instrument toward another end, toward a societal end, toward a religious end. The world offers an infinite list. But it seems to me that the text of Torah itself is the source of feminism. Context and text and intrinsic support for anti-instrumentality. You mustn't *use* a human being. And this is what feminism is about. This is the heart of feminism."[6]

Obviously, Ozick is as aware as any reader of the paradox inherent in her words. A person who has intrinsic value also has no tasks. In the performance of tasks, a person may *choose* to be an instrument of a policy, an ideology, or an idea. Indeed, as Ozick's oeuvre illustrates, a person may choose to be an instrument for the repair of the world.

Ozick's feminism does not exclude the messianic idea of repair. Indeed, one might say that to a great extent her notion of feminism is itself a messianic idea, that without the full participation and integration of women in all the tasks of society—especially the Jewish tasks—the world is flawed. In the section of her essay "Notes toward Finding the Right Question" entitled "On Jewish Repair and Renewal," Ozick wonders why the most sincere scholars of the Torah do not rise as one to demand a repair of the flawed fabric of

the Jewish people.[7] At stake here is not the alleviation of the suffering of the female half of the Jewish people—that is to say, the
mere correction of an injustice—but, rather, it is the biblical commandment of "Justice, justice shalt thou *pursue*" (my italics) that is
being infringed. The lack of justice does not harm merely the oppressed. The abstention from pursuing justice actively destroys the
world.

It is therefore an understatement to say that Cynthia Ozick is not
a woman writer. That she is a feminist writer, according to her
definition of the term, is evident not only from her essays on the
subject but also from her fiction. The 1971 short story "Virility,"
the tale of a literary hoax perpetrated by an untalented "male writer"
who publishes his *Tante* (Yiddish for "aunt") Rifke's poetry as his
own, is the most polemical and the most interesting of Ozick's
purely feminist stories. In this story, *Tante* Rifke's verse, usurped
by her nephew, is received by critics and public alike as the con-
summate expression of one man's virility. He is consequently show-
ered with fame and riches. After a series of successes—*Virility I,
Virility II, Virility III*, etc.—the hoax is penetrated, and *Tante*
Rifke's last book of verse is published as her own. It is received
with disdain as a failure of flaccid woman's writing, soft and sentimental. The polemical conclusions to be drawn from this story
are obvious. Much more subtle, because in them Ozick blends
feminism with the idea of the repair of the world, are the Puttermesser stories.

The First Puttermesser Story

The title of the first of the two Ruth Puttermesser stories is
suggestively misleading. The title's length alone—"Puttermesser:
Her Work History, Her Ancestry, Her Afterlife"—promises a narrative brimming over with events. At the end of the story, however,
another title suggests itself as more appropriate, something on the
order of "Nothing Happened." On still closer examination, one
realizes that the title nevertheless contains the story's essence: the
story is a triptych, as the ternary rhythm of the title suggests, whose
three panels make up not the biography of Ruth Puttermesser, with
its sequence of events, but more precisely a portrait of her person-
ality, in which diachrony, the sequence of events, is subordinated
to a synchronic meaningfulness. The story focuses not on the events

themselves but on the role the events play in conveying the essence of a character.

The story may be divided into three parts *not* indicated by the subtitle. One may speak of Ruth Puttermesser's two jobs and of her Hebrew lessons as the three main narrative blocks of text.

There are important minor details as well. At the beginning of the story, Ruth Puttermesser is depicted as something of an eccentric. She is unconventional, not because at age thirty-four and Jewish she is unmarried, but because she prefers to live in her old childhood apartment on the Grand Concourse in the Bronx, a neighborhood gone to seed and abandoned by the upwardly mobile middle-class Jews who had built it into a postwar paradise.

Two other important characteristics that go undeveloped in the story are her activism on behalf of Soviet Jews and her feminism. The former betrays a concern that is a veritable leitmotiv in Ozick's work, concern for the oppressed of the world as expressed in recent Jewish history. This is evident in works as varied as *Trust,* Ozick's lengthy first novel, where Enoch Vand goes in search of victims of Nazism after the war, then in both of Ozick's more recent novels, *The Cannibal Galaxy* and *The Messiah of Stockholm,* where the Holocaust is the backdrop against which her characters' dramas are played out, and in several short stories that feature Holocaust survivors.

Ozick's feminism is also touched on only lightly here. Puttermesser is presented immediately as "something of a feminist," but "not crazy." While she resents having "Miss" put in front of her name, she does not attribute whatever injury she is made to suffer at the hands of those who wield power over her to her gender.

The first job that Ozick describes is a case in point. Having served, matter-of-factly, as editor of her law school's law review, the most prestigious and most promising position a graduating law student may have, Puttermesser goes to work for a "blueblood" law firm, Midland, Reid. Like everyone else fresh out of school, Puttermesser is put in the back office, doing the tedious research that the more senior associates require. Over the years, very few of her ilk are groomed for eventual partnerships, and those who are all seem to be cast in the racial mold of the senior partners.

In this general atmosphere, Puttermesser feels no personal discrimination. She tacitly recognizes that, from the perspective of the Jews, power in America is in the hands of a gentile elite. Nor does

she see this "fact" as a flaw. The partners of Midland, Reid are
well-born, well-bred, refined, and pleasant. Aristocrats, in short.
They themselves are confident that the power they hold is theirs by
right. They neither abuse nor misuse their power. They merely *use*
it. They are enlightened. As can be seen from the comically entertaining description of Puttermesser's farewell luncheon with the
partners—as she takes leave of the firm, like so many others before
her, of her own free will—the partners are only vaguely aware of
Puttermesser's cultural tradition. They assume she is leaving the
firm because there are few suitable (i.e., Jewish) marital prospects
for her at their firm. They misread the Jewish marital customs,
mistaking the marriage canopy for a canvas, and the breaking of
the glass for the shattering of a whole set of dishes. It is as though
they had read about these customs in *National Geographic*.

The Midlands and the Reids are enlightened power-holders who
rule by what seems to be divine right. There is not much one can
do to repair a world ruled thus except to carry on revolutionary
activities. This is not an option for Ozick. So Puttermesser leaves.

From Midland, Reid, Puttermesser moves on to a civil service
job in the New York City bureaucracy. There, as Assistant Cor-
poration Counsel in the Department of Receipts of Disbursements,
Puttermesser encounters another type of power, not the power of
birth and privilege, but the power of democratic politics. It is as
if the Revolution has taken place. This bureaucracy has another type
of power, the bureaucrats' power to stop things from happening.
In this sort of corporate body, in fact, nothing *can* happen; the
organism merely breathes. True, there are spurts of innovation immediately after every election, but these soon subside, giving in
quickly to the laws of nature, which resist change.

In this section of the story, Ozick provides the portrait of Ruth
Puttermesser by reflection only. She is seen as an image of the city
commissioner for whom she works. The portrait of this commissioner, a blue-eyed German Jew named Guggenheim who had do-
nated money to the incumbent mayor's campaign, is masterful,
worthy of La Bruyère, the great seventeenth-century French verbal
portrait painter. In concise, taut sentences, taking up a page at
most, Ozick gives us the very essence of a modern aedile, moderately
rich, superficially polished, and royally ignorant of everything, including especially the workings of his own department.

Is this the man whom Ruth Puttermesser is destined to marry?

Is this a story in which something as "active" as a marriage is destined to take place? Decidedly not. At this crucial point in the narrative—crucial because it presents itself as a turning point— Ozick intervenes in her own narrative to impede its progress, unwittingly imitating one of the many city bureaucrats her story implies:

> Now if this were an optimistic portrait, exactly here is where Puttermesser's emotional life would begin to grind itself into evidence. Her biography would proceed romantically, the rich young Commissioner of the Department of Receipts and Disbursements would fall in love with her. She would convert him to intelligence and to the cause of Soviet Jewry. He would abandon boating and the pursuit of bluebloods. Puttermesser would end her work history abruptly and move on to a bower in a fine suburb.[8]

But instead of grinding itself into evidence, Puttermesser's emotional life is ground to a halt. She will not marry. Rather, she will sublimate any private emotional stirrings into a dream of a better world. And here we move on to the third panel of Puttermesser's portrait, a panel painted under the sign of the dream.

This dream relates to the deep strivings of Ruth Puttermesser and to the profound and rich cultural tradition of which she needs to feel herself a part. Earlier in the story we had learned that Ruth Puttermesser studies Hebrew in bed. Now we learn further that Puttermesser is taking Hebrew lessons, not at the local University or at an Israeli-style *Ulpan,* but from her Great-Uncle Zindel, who, while teaching her the language, also passes on to her some grains of her tradition. She has learned from him the Jewish notion of *gan eydn,* a combination of the Garden of Eden, with which it is eponymous, and a messianic postlife, a "World to Come."

Puttermesser's own dream of *gan eydn* represents an advanced case of childishness. In the world to come, Puttermesser will sit under a green tree, with a box of little fudge figures on one side of her and pile of library books on the other. There she will eat without tooth decay—a seemingly indifferent detail whose importance will become evident only at the end of this chapter—and read to her heart's content. The utopia described by Puttermesser's biographer is not so much a *locus amoenus,* a pleasant geographical location, as it is unrestricted time. It is also time recaptured, the time of her childhood, when the Crotona Park branch of the New York Public Library existed for her. Paradise, therefore, because it once existed, is something accessible. It is not in the heavens. It is not even in a magical realm. Only in hindsight does paradise seem magical, and then only in the telling of it.

Paradise is centered on texts. In this paradise Puttermesser will read from three categories of books. For the purposes of the present analysis, the division of Puttermesser's ideal library into fiction, nonfiction, and biography is suggestive. After all, the Puttermesser story is presented as a biography, neither fiction nor nonfiction. What does it mean to write in a genre that is somewhere in between fiction and nonfiction? Like the fantastic, biography for Ozick seems to be not a fixed genre, but a moment, a moment that hesitates before resolving itself into either fiction or nonfiction.

The example of Great-Uncle Zindel is more than merely instructive. Like his great-niece, like the Rosa of a later story, Zindel is an eccentric, an old Jew who lives alone among Spanish-speaking blacks. Zindel teaches his niece not only Hebrew grammar but also, himself an initiate into Jewish mysticism, the power of the combinations of the letters of the Hebrew alphabet. The Zindel episode hints therefore at a third source of power in the story: the Jewish textual tradition. The mystical quality of this power is carefully hidden behind Zindel's zaniness. It is also masked by Zindel's teaching of other lessons, not anthropological but moral, that one may derive from a sort of popular comparative philology. Zindel's teaching is moral in another way as well. In marrying certain pregnant-looking Hebrew letters, Zindel implies Ruth Puttermesser ought to get married and give birth.

At the text's suggestion that Puttermesser might marry City Commissioner Guggenheim and settle with him into a life of comfortable normalcy, the author intervened to put a stop to such a development. Here as well, at Zindel's veiled and not-so-veiled suggestion that Ruth marry and bear children, there is another authorial intervention. In a stroke of narrative genius, Ozick does not now assign to the *narrator* the task of speaking in her own voice. Rather, it is a second narrator who irrupts into the text and addresses herself to the first narrator. This second narrator tells the "truth" about Zindel. "Stop. Stop, stop!" the second narrator cries out. "Puttermesser's biographer, stop! Disengage please." The speaker has ruptured the artistic frame and will now proceed to destroy the fantastic text. "Though it is true that biographies are invented, not recorded, here you invent too much. A symbol is allowed, but not a whole scene: do not accommodate too obsequiously to Puttermesser's romance. Having not much imagination, she is literal with what she has. Uncle Zindel lies under the earth of Staten Island. Puttermesser has never had a conversation with him; he died four years before her birth" (35–36).

The rupture of the artistic frame informs us that while Puttermesser's dream of *gan eydn* may have been *based* in reality, her story about the progenitor of the dream, its source, is a fantasy. Ruth Puttermesser never met the man who gave her Hebrew lessons. The Hebrew lessons, moreover, never took place. And neither did the teaching of Jewish mysticism. As at Midland, Reid, as in the City Bureaucracy, "Nothing Happened."

It is curious that although "the scene with Zindel did not occur," the narrator finds it important to aver that her character, Ruth Puttermesser "loved the voice of Zindel in the scene that did not occur" (37). The Zindel scene apparently has a reality that transcends reality. It exists precisely to balance the scenes at Midland, Reid and the New York City bureaucracy. Both the law partners and Commissioner Guggenheim have a background, whether real or not, on which they can call. The fiction that Puttermesser creates, it is revealed, derives from her need for a link with history. "Surely a Jew must own a past," (36) says the narrator.

It turns out that Puttermesser's parents, in their strivings toward Americanization, had broken all ties with their past. So successful was their generation at making that rupture that it is no surprise that the Midlands and the Reids are innocent of finding value in Jewish tradition. Conjuring up this history herself, Puttermesser sees, behind and beyond her blandly Bronxian parents, the teeming of the shtetls of Poland, where Jews had built a thousand-year Jewish culture. But because Ruth Puttermesser is disengaged from this culture by her upbringing, she sees it only dimly, if at all.

The second narrator interrupts Puttermesser's Zindel fantasy because Ruth Puttermesser must learn where she came from before she may know where she is going. Her work history is not sufficient. Her desire to see in the New York City bureaucracy the poetry that Hart Crane saw in New York City is inadequately encompassing. The second narrator asks the first: "Hey! Puttermesser's biographer! What will you do with her now?" (35). The reader attuned to Ozick's writings knows what she will do: she will put her heroine in a library for ten years so that she might catch up on her Jewish heritage.

But the reader in harmony with Cynthia Ozick also knows that the seeds for Puttermesser's subsequent development have already been planted. "Puttermesser is not to be examined as an artifact but as an essence" (38), Ozick insists. The essential qualities of Ruth Puttermesser have already been given in this 1977 story. And since Puttermesser is nevertheless to be examined, an analysis of several of the themes prevalent in this first story will prove fruitful for an analysis of the larger issues broached subsequently by Ozick in "Puttermesser and Xanthippe."

First of all there is the positive role that Ozick attributes to the notion of *les mots de la tribu*. The partners at Midland, Reid guess that behind and beyond the Jewish law review editors they hire there is a whole array of tribal customs. For them the customs may be quaint and colorful, they betray nevertheless a certain primitiveness. They guess that Ruth Puttermesser is leaving the firm so that she may be faithful to her tribe's marriage customs. And they are witness to the atavistic behavior of the young athletic Jews in the firm whose disgruntlement betrays their origins as members of a tribe of yeshiva students.

Cultural anthropology reveals quaint behavior, it is true. It can also reveal a rich cultural tradition. Hebrew is not merely the age-old language of the Jews. For Puttermesser's biographer it is perhaps a code for the world's design. Here we get beyond narrative to meaning:

In bed she studied Hebrew grammar. The permutations of the triple-lettered root elated her: how was it possible that a whole language, hence a whole literature, a civilization even, should rest on the pure presence of three letters of the alphabet? The Hebrew verb, a stunning mechanism: three letters, whichever fated three, could command all possibility simply by a change in their pronunciation, or the addition of a wing-letter fore and aft. Every conceivable utterance blossomed from this trinity. It seemed to her not so much a language for expression as a code for the world's design, indissoluble, pre-determined, translucent. The idea of the grammar of Hebrew turned Puttermesser's brain into a palace, a sort of Vatican; inside its corridors she walked from one resplendent triptych to another. (23–24)

It is crucial here that the Hebrew language with all its meaning-fulness is presented here not only as a code but as a religious re-pository for Jewish art. There is not only a *Génie du Christianisme;* there is a *Génie du Judaïsme* as well. Just as the Vatican houses great works of religious art so too does the Hebrew language shelter and display its own works of art, triptychs of another sort, formed by the three letters of the Hebrew root.

Not only Hebrew but also Yiddish provides an insight into the inner workings of Jewish culture. Great-Uncle Zindel, in the scene that did not occur, comments on Ruth's name, Puttermesser, which means, literally, "butterknife" in Yiddish. His comment is not merely philological; it also reveals the workings of a value system. Here is what Zindel has to say about "knifes":

> "My father, what was your great-great-grandfather, didn't allow a knife to the table Friday night. When it came to *kiddush*—knifes off! All knifes! On Sabbath an instrument, a blade? On Sabbath a weapon? A point? An edge? What makes bleeding among mankind? What makes war? Knifes! No knifes! Off! A clean table! And something else you'll notice. By us we got only *messer,* you follow? By them they got sword, they got lance, they got halberd. Go to the dictionary, I went once. So help me, what don't one of them knights carry? Look up in the book, you'll see halberd, you'll see cutlass, pike, rapier, foil, ten dozen more. By us a pike is a fish. . . . A *messer!* Puttermesser, you slice off a piece butter, you cut to live, not to kill." (34–35)

The word *messer* is a *mot de la tribu* because of its ability to evoke a civilization behind its common meaning. Puttermesser is attracted to the legend of Great-Uncle Zindel because she feels a need to see behind the America of her parents, who delude themselves, perhaps, that their history is the same as that of the Midlands and the Reids. Puttermesser, who has no tangible link with the history of the Jews, has to go out of her way to find one. She must claim an ancestor even if she has to invent him out of the grain of his truth. So Puttermesser the lawyer becomes a writer of fiction. Zindel is merely the beginning. Of the rest she can have merely an inkling.

Of course there is a way to gain knowledge of the past—and that is through books. Hence her utopia. Although Puttermesser's thirst for knowledge is universal (her reading list shows that she wants to know *everything*), the realization of her utopia will be a purely per-sonal one. Puttermesser's vision of utopia resembles nothing so much

as her lost childhood. In her childhood, Puttermesser had had paradise, in the form of the Crotona Park Branch of the New York
Public Library. Curiously, however, in her utopia, there are no
people; there are only sweets and books. Other people do not seem
necessary. Nor are there overriding social problems to be dealt with.

There is a tremendous variety of nonfiction subject matter on
Puttermesser's reading list, a list meant to encompass the universe.[9]
There is anthropology, zoology, physical chemistry, and philosophy.
The interest in books about the linkages of genes, quarks, primates;
theories about the origins of the races; religions of ancient civilizations; and the meaning of Stonehenge betray an interest in the
sources of modern civilization. Sources are important for Ozick.
Among the works of fiction are books by Balzac and Dickens,
Turgenev and Dostoyevski, Tolstoy and George Eliot, all nineteenth-century novelists who lie, perhaps, at the source of Ozick's
mode of narration.

If there are exterior influences on Ozick's writing, there is also a
more powerfully felt organic source. Ozick will conjure this source
up, first, by creating out of a grain of truth—the "fact" that the
Zindel she describes did in reality exist—a Jewish past. She will
give herself a Jewish history. In the subsequent Puttermesser story,
"Puttermesser and Xanthippe," Ozick creates that Jewish history
not out of a grain of truth but out of a grain of sand.

The Second Puttermesser Story

Puttermesser's story does not pick up exactly where it left off.
Puttermesser is twelve years older now (forty-six) and has finally
moved from her childhood apartment on the Grand Concourse in
the Bronx—forced out by urban decay—to a more adult mode of
life on Manhattan's fashionable East Side. In the interim she has
picked up a lover, a married man, fifty-two-year-old Morris Rappoport, to whom has been transferred Puttermesser's concern for
Soviet Jews.

It is the Sunday morning after Morris Rappoport has left his
mistress, in a huff at having his amorous advances rebuffed in favor
of a text. Puttermesser, who used to study Hebrew in bed, ostensibly
giving equal time to Hellenism, is now reading Plato. Obviously,
in the intervening twelve years, Puttermesser, the diligent autodidact, has been studying Gershom Scholem as well. Scholem (1897–

1982) was the author of a monumental body of scholarship on Jewish mysticism. [10] Puttermesser has been initiating herself into this aspect of the Jewish tradition, providing herself with the intellectual past whose lack she earlier felt and whose void she tried to fill with the creation of Zindel.

Now, a biological urge intervening, it is not an uncle she will create, but a daughter. Apparently, during the Saturday night of her rupture with Morris, she had created out of the soil of her apartment's potted plants the form of a teenage girl. Inadvertently, she breathed life into this creature. Without realizing that she was carrying out rituals described in Scholem's essays—including the combinations of the Hebrew letters—she created in her own image a traditional Jewish golem.

It turns out that the golem could not have come at a better time, both from Puttermesser's viewpoint and from that of the decaying city of New York. Puttermesser will soon be fired from her job in the Department of Receipts and Disbursements, displaced by a political appointee, and is in need of a new mission in life. New York City, on the other hand, decaying rapidly both physically and morally, is in dire need of repair.

It will be repaired thanks to the miraculous appearance of the golem, a bundle of unbridled energy, who comes up with the idea of making Ruth Puttermesser mayor of the city of New York. The golem also comes up with a plan to resuscitate, reform, reinvigorate, and, most importantly, redeem the city of New York. Thanks to the golem's energy and to Puttermesser's moral stance, derived from the verse in Deuteronomy, "Justice, justice shalt thou pursue," both the idea and the plan are realized. Puttermesser becomes mayor and New York City is redeemed, transformed into a bright, shining Garden of Eden of civic uprightness.

It is in the nature of utopias that they do not last. Scholem teaches that it is an "attribute" of the golem that it will eventually destroy what it has created, including its creator. Puttermesser's desire for daughters is translated into the creation of a female golem, a doppelgänger. The golem created by Puttermesser, her literary double, also has desires—how can she not?—and these are expressed by a voracious appetite not only for food (remember the fudge of the earlier *gan eydn*) but also for sex.

The golem wishes to express more than her creator. No longer willing to be merely an instrument, she has acquired an individuality of her own and wishes to express her own intrinsicness. She does this by copulating with every man of power she can find. But when Eros enters Gracie Mansion, orderliness flies out. The city, an organism obeying its own biological laws, reverts to its former state. Mayor Puttermesser has been destroyed; the Garden of Eden has been destroyed. In order to save New York City from further destruction, the golem will have to be returned to her former state of earth.

As in the earlier Puttermesser story, it is as if "Nothing Happened." Nevertheless, while it may be true that, from the point of view of the plot, nothing goes forward, from the perspective of art, in the realm of idea and meaning, in the domain of the creative imagination, a great deal is going on.

The desire for daughters is a case in point. Ruth Puttermesser at age forty-six is the same feminist she was at age thirty-four. That is to say, she is not at all interested in feminist polemics, or in a politics whose goal might tend to segregate women. True, when Morris Rappoport, her former lover, returns to attempt a reconciliation, he concedes that this might be unseemly since, as mayor, Puttermesser has to be above suspicion, like Caesar's wife. The mayor interrupts to respond that she has "to be Caesar." Although she recognizes the uses of power, aggressiveness is not in her value system. "Though she deemed herself a feminist, no ideology could succeed for her in aggrandizing force. Puttermesser was not aggressive. She disdained assertiveness."[11] She takes it for granted that woman's place is at the center, making no distinction between man's and woman's place. Thus, for example, in her utopia, "due process is honored by intelligent lawyers, both women and men" (134). She is also careful not to say "poetess," insisting that gender is irrelevant to the role that poets are called upon to play. "A little-known poet who specializes in terza rima is put in charge of Potter's Field. For each sad burial there, she composes a laudatory ode" (134). It is significant that Ozick, who makes her leading character into a powerful mayor, also arrogates to a woman the right to be "little known," and to perform a humble task, without diminishing her intrinsic value.

Despite Ozick's crusade in her essays against the Freudian notion that "biology is destiny," Ozick adorns her literary creations, Xanthippe as well as Puttermesser, with the biological urge to procreate. Thus she writes that although Puttermesser "knew that she would never marry, . . . she was not at all reconciled to remaining child-less." "Sometimes," the narrator comments, "the thought that she would never give birth tore her heart" (91). It is by no means insignificant that, in an interview, Ozick avers that she may indeed return subsequently to Puttermesser as a character for her fiction. "I think I'd like to marry her off some day. I would like to have her married and normal."[12] Ozick is perhaps in this matter no different from Puttermesser's mother in Florida and the imagined Great-Uncle Zindel, both of whom want no less for their Ruthie.

The relationship of mothers to daughters is a recurring motif in Ozick's fiction. Hester Lilt's attitude to her daughter Beulah, in *The Cannibal Galaxy*, Rosa's adoration of her daughter Magda in "The Shawl" and "Rosa" are intense.[13] The desire to have a daughter depicted in "Puttermesser and Xanthippe" represents an increase in the intensity of the relationship, despite, or perhaps because of, the real absence of daughters.

The golem Puttermesser creates, Xanthippe, is a direct result of Puttermesser's desire to have a daughter named Leah. "Huge sly Xanthippe," Ozick writes, "gargantuan wily Xanthippe, grown up out of the little seed of a dream of Leah!" (156). At first, however, there is a denial of maternity. When Xanthippe insists on calling Ruth her mother, the creator protests, "I didn't give birth to you." Most tellingly, the narrator adds, immediately after Ruth's denial, the seemingly gratuitous statement: "She would never give birth" (97). Is the genetic relationship here the crucial one? Ozick explores that question in her later novel *The Messiah of Stockholm*. At one point, in the present story, not knowing how to explain away the presence of a teenager in her home, Ruth thinks of passing her off as an adopted daughter. Having a daughter is after all one way of being mature, responsible for life, like nurturing house plants.

Xanthippe, however, is simultaneously like and unlike Putter-messer's dream of daughters. The narrator insists that "the girl did not resemble Puttermesser at all; she was certainly not one of the imaginary daughters" (92). The reason for making this distinction becomes clear when one searches for the source of Puttermesser's desire for daughters, the desire for self-expression: "She imagined daughters. It was self-love: all these daughters were Puttermesser as a child. She imagined a daughter in fourth grade, then in seventh grade, then in second-year high school. . . . *O infelix Dido,* chanted the imaginary daughter, doing her Latin homework" (91). Ozick has insisted that Beulah Lilt was herself as a child. Rosa imagines her murdered daughter Magda at different ages, wearing the clothes the mother wore at that stage.

The world created by these mothers is a fictional world. The desire for procreation is transformed into the realization of a desire to create a text. The role of daughters is similar to that of literary creations. This does not of course mean to equate giving birth with literary creation. Xanthippe insists: "I am your offspring, you are my mother. I am the execution of the grandeur of your principles" (124).

This literary desire for daughters is a way of expressing the desire to recapture a lost childhood. Both the first and the second Puttermesser utopias are characterized by a return to childhood. They are also characterized by the power to fulfill desires, however childish. Ozick makes the connection between desires and powers herself. She notes that Puttermesser has "desires as strong and as strange as powers" (139). One of the conventions of the literature of the golem is that the golem has no sexual appetites, cannot procreate, and, in addition, is denied the power of speech. Ozick contravenes these conventions. Her golem not only eats voraciously and grows out of all human proportion but she is also, once initiated into sex by Rappoport, a devouring sexual mechanism. Additionally, Puttermesser, who recognizes Xanthippe is her doppelgänger, wants her golem to be able to procreate as well. "She was ready to disbelieve. A golem cannot procreate? Ah, but its blood is as hot as human blood. Hotter! A golem lusts tremendously, . . . yearns hugely after the generative, the fructuous. Earth is the germ of all fertility: how then would a golem not dream itself a double? . . . A golem cannot procreate! But it has the will to; the despairing will; the violent will. Offspring! Progeny! The rampaging energies of Xanthippe's eruptions, the furious bolts and convulsions of her visitations—Xanthippe, like Puttermesser herself, longs for daughters! Daughters that can never be!" (145). The creation of Xanthippe is therefore the realization of both psychological and biological desire. There is another sense in which genetics plays a role in this story and that is the sense in which the source of Ozick's creation of a golem is a literary one.

Peter Brooks, in his study of "design and intention in narrative," pursues the notion of desire as "that which is initiatory of narrative, motivates and energizes its reading, and animates the combinatory play of sense-making."[14] Brooks's feeling that the desire for meaning is the very motive for narrative proves very useful in this chapter's explanation of the meaning of Ozick's "Puttermesser and Xanthippe." The narrator of Ozick's tale expressly avers that Puttermesser's desire for a Leah—that is, for a natural daughter—is what leads the narrative to create Xanthippe, not merely a golem, but a fictive daughter in the full sense, one who is all story.

  The Sources of Xanthippe.   In this sense, the desire for Leah is one of the sources of "Puttermesser and Xanthippe." There are other sources as well. By creating a magical Xanthippe, Puttermesser, who has read them, immerses herself into these other sources.

  Reading oneself into other people's stories is a major theme in Ozick's work in general. It is so in this story in particular. The example of Leon Cracow is pertinent. Cracow is a functionary in the office where Puttermesser works. Because he sees himself maligned in a second-rate novel about one John McCracken Pyle ("That's practically Cracow," he says), a man who "goes to prostitutes," he is suing its author. Puttermesser, consulted by Cracow, urges him on. "She believed in the uses of fantasy. 'A person should see himself or herself everywhere,' she said. 'All things manifest us' " (91). This episode is more than merely a private joke, as one might have surmised. The reader has witnessed Xanthippe's claim that she is, as a creation of Puttermesser's mind, the latter's vehicle for self-expression. Just as importantly, Ozick finds it important to inform the reader that the phrase "all things manifest us" is not Puttermesser's creation, but a quotation engraved in stone on the façade of her Grand Concourse apartment building.

  Pithy Bronx inscriptions are not the total extent of the sources of "Puttermesser and Xanthippe." There is a way in which the whole story may be said to derive from the Sunday edition of the *New York Times* and from a verse in Goethe's *"Erlkönig."* On the Sunday morning on which the story begins Puttermesser notices that Rappoport has left his copy of the massive newspaper behind on the floor, unopened. She picks it up, dreamily thinking of daughters. The dead weight of the newspaper reminds her of Goethe's poem and she imagines a scene in which her imaginary daughter, now in high school, recites the line "In its father's arms the child was dead." This line is given as the genetic source for the heavy figure made of earth that Puttermesser finds on her bed: the golem. Later on in the story, expanding the metaphor of the *New York*

Times as a physical model for the golem, the narrator will remark that all the societal ills that the golem has come to remedy are to be found in the articles in Rappoport's *Times,* thus emphasizing the role of the "real" narratives in the newspaper as a source for the fictional narrative. It is most telling that at no point does Rappoport's paper ever get read. It is enough that the narrative be there— like a picture in its newspaper frame—for it to give birth to a further frame, that of the golem.

Of course, the main source for Ozick's fiction is Gershom Scholem's essay, "The Idea of the Golem,"[15] which Ozick cites as the machine that generated her narrative. She goes further; she extracts from Scholem's essay a brief history of golem-making. Her précis includes recipes for concocting a golem, the suggestion that golem-making might be akin to idolatry, and the hint that, while golem-making may lead to idol worship, it does stem from the maker's laudable desire to imitate the creator. True to Ozick's form, the narrator does not fail to note that Scholem makes a distinction between non-Jewish and Jewish golem-making, the former using as its ingredients blood, sperm, and urine, the latter only earth, water, and the divine afflatus. She cites the precedent of a female Jewish golem, disqualified by the rabbis because of the elements— wood and hinges—out of which it was constructed.

The true genetic source for the Puttermesser golem, however, is the story narrated by Scholem of Great Rabbi Judah Loew of Prague (1520–1609), the "Maharal," a quasi-mayor of the city who created a golem to save his community's Jews from anti-Semitism. Puttermesser, a creature of modernity, creates the golem not to save the Jews but to save the city itself. One might also say that while the Maharal's golem was "classical," Puttermesser's was influenced by the romantic tradition. And, if Loew's golem-making method is "ordinary," Puttermesser will go out of her way to make her method extraordinary.

It will be noted also that Ozick insists that her model is not at all a mystic but a practical man. This is an aspect that interests Ozick's character most of all. The narrator also adduces from Scholem the example of Rabbi Elijah, the Gaon of Vilna, a paragon of Jewish rationalist thought, who once thought of creating a golem. The precedent of the Vilna Gaon is brought in order to justify the narrator to herself and to reassure her readers that the seeming Jewish impropriety of any magical act does not obtain here. Ozick rehearses the long tradition of golem-making in Jewish mythology in order to illustrate a tension in Jewish life that she finds useful. On the one hand the Jews create golems; on the other hand the golem itself encourages its own destruction.

This tendency to self-immolation of the created object may be analogous to Cynthia Ozick's career-long preoccupation with the dangers of idolatry inherent in fiction-making. This is as much as to imply that the golem-making of "Puttermesser and Xanthippe" may be a parable for the fiction-making of Cynthia Ozick.

What is important at this point, therefore, is the use Ozick makes of her "classical" source. One of the traditional roles of the golem, for example, is to serve as water-carrier for its master. Puttermesser, though a professed feminist, can think initially of nothing better for her golem than to make her into a maid, a domestic servant, a preparer of lunches, of soufflés even. Initially, then, Puttermesser remains faithful to her source, however flawed philosophically. It is perhaps ironic that it is not Puttermesser who finds a gender-neuter role for her golem. The golem herself will assert her intrinsic value. When brought to Puttermesser's office and seated at a typewriter, Xanthippe will of her own volition create a plan for the redemption of New York. Ozick's tale, through Ozick's golem, repairs its own flawed source.

So important to the structure of the narrative is the idea of repair that even the mode of Puttermesser's golem's self-destruction may be seen as a repair of Ozick's source. According to Scholem, the "golem has prodigious strength and grows beyond measure. He destroys the world, or in any case does a good deal of damage."[16] So too does Ozick's golem. She adds, however, another crucial element. The classical golem "had to be made without generative power or sexual urge."[17] Ozick's golem reveals voracious, Rabelaisian sexual appetites, and, moreover, like her creator who desires daughters, the golem "yearns hugely after the generative, the fructuous" (145). It appears then that Peter Brooks is right when he asserts that every narrative of desire contains within it what he calls the "desire for narrative," a wish to create fictions.[18]

The Generation of the Fiction. The generation of fiction in Ozick's case stems from a particular desire. Throughout the text Puttermesser notes that the world is in need of repair, like the world in which Judah Loew carried on his redemptive activity. There is a genetic connection between Prague and New York just as there is a genetic connection between Puttermesser and Xanthippe. Xanthippe claims not only to be Puttermesser's daughter but also to "express" her, to "copy" her, and "record" her. Xanthippe then is not a daughter but a literary text.

The time comes, as come it must, to destroy the golem. Unlike most fairy tales, which rush to a conclusion, the golem story rushes back to the beginning, seemingly as if nothing has happened. In order to destroy the golem, one must perform the rites of its creation backwards, or as Ozick says of Judah Loew in a crucial sentence, "Whatever he had early spiraled, he later unraveled" (155). Ozick's sentence here is not merely a retelling of the Prague myth but a commentary on it. Xanthippe names herself after Socrates' wife because she alone gainsaid the philosopher. "I mean to be a critic," Ozick's Xanthippe echoes. The choice of the word "critic" is not accidental, for Xanthippe's role in the final analysis is a literary one. Not only is the world in need of repair. So is the text.

It is a curious fact of Ozick's text that the narration of the creation of the golem is presented at a considerable remove temporally from the act of creating it, after the golem has already asserted her existence and is on the verge of performing her role of repair in the manner of historic golems.

It disturbs Puttermesser that "she did not recall *making* her" (106); "Ah, here was a stale and restless truth: that she did not recollect the actual fabrication of the golem, that she had helplessly, without volition, come upon Xanthippe in her bed as if the golem were some transient mirage, an aggressive imagining!" (121–122). It is in fact only inadvertently at first, and without intending it, that Puttermesser gives the golem its final form, repairs its flaws, and then brings the golem to life. True, she did circle several times around the bed in which the intruding creature lay, thinking that she was merely examining it. It turns out that she has circled the bed the exact number of times the treatises on mysticism say are required to animate a golem. But, initially, there is no desire for magic, no desire to create a supernatural being, no desire, in other words, to create a fictional text.

The "real" reason for creating the golem—repair of a flawed world—is supplied only retrospectively. The text adds a new dimension however. It now insists that Puttermesser had in mind all along to create a golem. *Hic iacet lepus:* Puttermesser created the golem inadvertently; Puttermesser created the golem willfully. Both are asserted as true. Can a story with such a blatant flaw stand? Ozick will somehow have to repair the text. As we shall see, repair, for Ozick, does not mean emendation.

Ozick would rather write a whole new story than go back and correct a single line. She insists on this method of writing in a description of her writing habits she gives in one of her interviews. "My habit is not to go on to the next sentence until I have perfected the one before it. . . . The inflexible principle of never turning back to revise or in any way fiddle with what I've already finished (in the sense of having given it 'finish,' that is burnishing) often enough gets me into a pickle. Rather than go back, I accept the fix I'm in, and accommodate the future to the immovable past. . . . I'm locked in and have to figure out how to escape. I weave loopholes; I unriddle; I decipher."[19] Ozick the writer therefore performs on her own text the job she has assigned to Xanthippe—that of the critic. She judges her own work, sees its flaws, and then proceeds to repair them. This repair takes place by "changing" the text retroactively.

The idea of sequence of events is crucial for the notion of repair of the text. The narrator insists that it is not an issue of remembering time past but of reimagining it: "Puttermesser re-imagined the electric moment exactly: the PLAN swimming like an inner cosmos into being, the mere solid golem an afterthought" (124). It is clear from this that there are two stories being told here: the story *in* the text and the story *of* the text. In the story in the text, the golem creates the means of redemption; in the story of the text the idea of redemption precedes the existence of the golem, as it preceded, no doubt, the creation of the story itself.

Ozick's method of repairing her flawed text is an act of redemption; it parallels her desire to redeem a flawed world, the world as given. (It will be remembered from the earlier story that Puttermesser is not an artifact but an essence, a given.) The golem itself is like a story. It must be woven out of an idea, and then, because in Ozick's value system stories are inherently dangerous, like golems, it must be unwoven. "Now," we are told, "all must be consciously reversed" (154).

While the creation of the work of fiction may have been inadvertent—that is, the desire to create was a subconscious one—the return to reality is a conscious return. The reason for this is clear from another metaphor found in "Puttermesser and Xanthippe," the theme of the emptying of the frame. Tooth decay is a concern for the fudge-eating Puttermesser. At the beginning of the story we learn the seemingly unimportant detail of Puttermesser's periodontal disease, a curse perhaps of late middle age. Ozick's presentation of the disease, however, supplies a clue that leads the reader to expect that the very meaning of the story will be tied to Puttermesser's teeth: "It was as if in the dread underworld below the visible gums, a volcano lay, watching for its moment of release" (79). At the beginning, therefore, there is expectation, and, moreover, dread of the potential destructive forces that lie under the surface. There is also a fear of closure.

During the course of her story we learn that history plays a central role for Puttermesser the autodidact, whose very skeleton is presented as the container of the history she has learned. But there can be too much history. "Puttermesser's intelligence, brambly with the confusion of too much history, was a private warted tract, rubbled over with primordial statuary. She was painfully anthropological. Civilizations rolled into her rib cage, stone after graven stone: cuneiform, rune, cipher" (99). History is first of all a written text, demanding to be deciphered. But history can also lead to an emptying out of the skeletal frame, to the observation that there is only emptiness. At the end of the story Puttermesser undergoes the periodontal surgery whose need was announced at the beginning: "When it is over, the roots of her teeth are exposed. Inside the secret hollow of her head, just below the eye sockets, on the lingual side, she is unendingly conscious of her own skeleton" (158).

All along the story, the narrator had expressed, not the desire for the end, but a fear of concluding. She knew that sooner or later the golem would destroy, first, the ideal society it had created and, then, its creator. The destruction of the creator of the fiction is apparently the only way out of the fiction. But there is a moment of ambiguity. As in the story "Levitation," where at the end a roomful of people continues living in the realm of the fantastic, Ozick's tale here refuses to return completely to the real world. Judah Loew's golem, so the legend goes, "lives on" in the attic of the *Altneuschul* (the Old–New Synagogue) in Prague. Puttermesser's golem, at the end, is buried in a flower bed behind Gracie Mansion, the mayor's residence, the grave adorned with red geraniums. Strangely, these geraniums retain the magic power to cause illness to anyone who, by picking them, will destroy their beauty.

Despite the fact that the golem did not succeed in repairing the decay of the world—"Nothing Happened"—something of value did go on. What went on was the creation of a work of art whose magical qualities will, for good or ill, reverberate into an eternal future. Like all of Ozick's fictional daughters, the narrative will have an intrinsic value; it will exist for its own sake. Like them as well, it will have an instrumental role to play, serving to exemplify the need to repair the world through the repair of the text.

Chapter Ten
The Redemption of the Book: *The Messiah of Stockholm*

Toward the end of 1976 Cynthia Ozick was asked by the *New York Times Book Review* to review Bruno Schulz's *The Street of Crocodiles*. The book had already appeared in English in the United States in 1963 and was now to form part of the Penguin Books paperback series "Writers from the Other Europe," edited by Philip Roth.[1] The purpose of the series, which publishes such authors as Milan Kundera and Tadeusz Borowski as well, is to make known to English-speaking readers influential works of fiction by Eastern European writers who are virtually unknown in the West. Obviously, the editors of the *Book Review* felt that the work of Bruno Schulz, a Polish-Jewish writer of phantasmagoria in the Kafka strain who flourished during the 1930s, would engage Ozick's interest. Certainly they could not have predicted where such a reviewing assignment would lead Ozick the novelist.

It was not only the stories *in* the book that would enthrall Ozick. The story of the writer *of* the book was also to fascinate her. Bruno Schulz (1892–1942), an art teacher in the Galician town of Drohobycz in Poland, had written two volumes of stories, published in Poland as *Cinnamon Stores* (1934) and *Sanatorium Under the Sign of the Hourglass* (1937), as well as a Polish translation of Franz Kafka's *The Trial* (1936). It was also rumored that he had begun work on another manuscript, a novel to be entitled *The Messiah*. This slender corpus of works had brought Schulz renown in the literary capitals of Europe but his fame did not tempt Schulz to abandon his provincial existence. In the 1940s, during the Nazi occupation of Poland, Schulz was protected by an S.S. officer who admired his art. However, he and other Jewish residents of the ghetto of Drohobycz were murdered by the Nazis on what has become known in local history as Black Thursday, 19 November 1942. When Bruno Schulz was gunned down by the S.S. officer who was a rival of his protector, the manuscript of *The Messiah* disappeared.

Ozick reports that in 1984, when her novel *The Cannibal Galaxy* was published in Sweden and she went to Stockholm for the launching of the book, she was swept up in the whirlwind of a city obsessed with serious literature.[2] Out of the blue she was startled by the rumor—totally untrue, of course—that the lost manuscript of Bruno Schulz's *Messiah* had surfaced in Stockholm, of all places. It was against such a background, colorful and entertaining, that Cynthia Ozick's critically acclaimed 1987 novel *The Messiah of Stockholm* came to be written.

There is a sense, however, in which this novel did not at all come to Ozick out of the blue. As has been demonstrated in earlier chapters of this study, Cynthia Ozick rewrites both herself and others as a matter of literary and moral principle. In the present chapter it will be demonstrated that *The Messiah of Stockholm* may be seen as a culmination of Ozick's rewriting activity and as the logical conclusion of much that she has written to date.

The title of Ozick's novel is ambiguous. *The Messiah of Stockholm* is at one and the same time an allusion to the lost and fictitiously found manuscript of Schulz's novel and to the character in this novel whose goal in life is to recall Schulz's murdered work to life. One is tempted to say that the title is also polyvalent, for it is also, much more meaningfully, a hidden allusion to Cynthia Ozick's attempt to repair Schulz's work and to bring redemption to the world by redeeming the book.

The Messiah's Story

The story revolves around Lars Andemening, the third-ranking book reviewer for the *Morgontörn,* one of Stockholm's less weighty daily newspapers. Lars's colleagues on the cultural page, Anders Fisknygel and Gunnar Hemlig, have cornered the market on popular American novels, spy thrillers, books about royalty and sports, and cookbooks. Thanks to the popularity of their subject matter and to the titillating style of their writing, Gunnar and Anders have an enormous following. Their columns appear on Wednesdays and Fridays, the days, so the book insists, most favored by the readers of the paper's cultural page. Lars has been left with Monday, the least favorable day.

He is not all unhappy with this situation, however, because having few readers means that he also has few responsibilities and is free to pursue his own literary interests. With utmost devotion and seriousness, he dedicates himself to difficult writers from Eastern Europe, literary artists largely ignored by Western readers.

Lars Andemening, forty-two years old in 1984, is free in another way as well. He is a war orphan who, having been rescued by unknown persons and passed from household to household until he reached the home of the widowed sister-in-law of his rescuer's cousin, is ignorant of the identity of both his mother and father. He lives with his foster parents until the age of sixteen when he runs away from home and acquires a job as a messenger boy on a newspaper. He also acquires an identity by giving it to himself. Either because he is of Polish-Jewish stock or because he imagines himself a marginal Jew, he gives himself an ambiguous Jewish name, Lazarus Baruch. This name, it is possible to conjecture, is an allusion to both the resurrected New Testament figure Lazarus and to the seventeenth-century Dutch-Jewish philosopher and theologian Baruch Spinoza, excommunicated for religious heresy by the Jewish community of Amsterdam. Lazarus Baruch decides to remain in Sweden, a country hospitable to refugees whom it nevertheless does not assimilate easily. He gives himself another name, a Scandinavian name, also made up out of the dictionary. Lazarus becomes Lars, a change easy enough to follow. Baruch, which is Hebrew for "blessed," is transformed by a mystical, cabbalistic route, into Andemening, from a Swedish word whose dictionary meaning carries the sense of "inspired."

Lars does not stop there, however. Just as he has reached into dictionaries and books of religious history to find himself names, Lars will dip into literary history to choose for himself an identity. Free to choose as he wishes, Lars adopts the Polish-Jewish writer Bruno Schulz as his father. Lars immerses himself in the exquisite inner life he has given himself, one that is in harmony with Schulz's published works, which, by force of reading and rereading, Lars has acquired by heart. Madly obsessed by his new identity, in which he by now firmly believes—the mask having stuck to his skin— Lars, after two failed marriages, yielding one child in whom Lars strains to perceive his father's artistic bent, sets about Stockholm in search of Schulz's unpublished correspondence, and, especially, in search of *The Messiah*.

Fortunately for Lars, Stockholm is a crossroads of literary Europe and gives domicile to booksellers who are able to obtain all sorts of literary exotica. Indeed, Lars comes upon a bookstore that is reminiscent of the Drohobycz "cinnamon shops" his adopted father has described. These are not stores that sell cinnamon but rather places that sell rare and spicy objects from far-off places, including books. Lars thus makes contact with Heidi Eklund, *Bokhandläre*. A refugee herself, Heidi supplies Lars with a Polish tutor—it is not clear whether a refugee princess or a milliner—so that he may read his father in the original. She also provides him with the Eastern European authors he craves, his Vaculiks and Hrabels, his Gombrowiczes and Konwickis. Because Lars has taken Mrs. Eklund into his confidence and has revealed his secret identity to her, Heidi, who nevertheless remains skeptical of his story, also furnishes Lars with one of his father's manuscript letters. How does she acquire these treasures? She is married to one Alter Eckstein, also a Jewish refugee, who now calls himself Dr. Olle Eklund. He passes himself off as either a psychoanalyst or a gastroenterologist, it is never clear which, but he may in truth be a dealer in forged passports and a smuggler. He travels frequently to Eastern Europe and, a master of theatrical plotting and intrigue, he succeeds, as Heidi says, in getting things out. He get things and people out, and, somehow, the people and things he gets out find refuge in hospitable Stockholm.

One day, Mrs. Eklund supplies Lars Andemening with the manuscript of Bruno Schulz's lost masterpiece, *The Messiah*. But it is not only the manuscript she gives him. She gives him a story as well, or rather a theatrical production. Dramatically, after a three-week absence from her shop, following a quarrel in which Heidi emphasized her unwillingness to fall in with Lars's game of paternity, Lars receives a telephone message at his newspaper: "Mrs. Eklund phoned about your sister." How could Lars have a sister? He does not even have a father. It appears that Mrs. Eklund wishes, by multiplying the illusions, to punish Lars for living the life of illusion. Lars nevertheless returns to Heidi's shop, where he is informed that a middle-aged woman has come into the shop claiming to be the daughter of Bruno Schulz. She not only mirrors Lars's story, she also mirrors his desire, for she claims to be in possession of the original Polish manuscript of Shulz's masterpiece, *The Messiah*. Lars protests: there is no sister. While Lars had passionately wanted the manuscript to exist, he did not wish to receive it in a way which would cast doubt on the life he had created for himself. He is therefore forced to deny that the manuscript is genuine.

But the drama that has been set in motion by Heidi and Olle Eklund has a momentum of its own and will continue to play itself out. Returning home to his drab bohemian apartment, Lars is accosted by a figure in a white beret carrying a white plastic bag, a figure who seems to be the source of her own light. Her name is Elsa Vaz and she claims to have arrived in Stockholm via São Paulo, Amsterdam, Budapest, Brussels, and Warsaw. She informs Lars not only that she is the illegitimate daughter that Bruno Schulz fathered with one of his fifteen-year-old art students in Drohobycz but, adding contempt to contumely, she tells him that her name is Adela, the name of the maid who tyrannizes the narrator's father in Schulz's fiction. The name Adela is a signal to Lars that he is being toyed with. He is being forced to disbelieve in "Adela's" story. Is it so that he might believe all the more firmly in the recovered manuscript? After Adela explains, in detail worthy of belief, how, by a circuitous route, she came into possession of the manuscript, she empties the pages of the manuscript onto Lars's bed. The scene resembles a religious ceremony and is interestingly reminiscent of the idol-worshiping scene in which Rosa prepares to open the box containing her daughter's shawl (see chapter 6).

Does Lars worship the work of Bruno Schulz? Can he be made to believe in the existence of a lost text? Giving in to temptation, he reaches for the manuscript, kicking Adela out of the way in the process. More agile than her opponent, Adela snatches the manuscript from his hands and rushes out the door, leaving a trail of whiteness—her beret—in her wake. Lars now knows that he has already lost something more essential to his life than the manuscript. His effort to create a false identity for himself has ended in failure. He is not the extraordinary person he had fashioned.

He will display his insufficiency by going to the offices of the *Morgontörn* in broad daylight—previously he had worked there only at night, among the ghosts and the mice. He chooses from a pile of books a novel by a popular and prolific Swedish writer to review. In two hours the book is read and the review is written. Nilsson the editor is pleased. For Lars, this has been a painful derogation. Previously, he would read a book, a work of true literary merit, and then sleep on it for a while. He would then awaken with an understanding of its deeper meaning, which he was permitted to see during the nap thanks to the fact that he had been visited by his father's perceptive eye. Henceforth the visitation, no longer necessary, will no longer occur. Having once succumbed to mediocrity, he has been abandoned by his father's eye.

The story does not end here however. In fact, we might say that it is just beginning. The text has been transformed into a new literary genre, what we might call a narrated drama. The curtain goes up on Heidi Eklund's bookshop, framed in the shadow of night. On stage are Heidi and the mysterious Dr. Eklund, returned from a secret voyage. They are waiting for someone—Lars or Adela—it seems. In fact, they have scripted the arrival of both of them. First comes Lars, who is shocked by his confrontation with Dr. Eklund's reality. Then Adela arrives, bearing the manuscript, not in a white plastic bag this time. Having become a priestess in some religious ceremony, she now carries it in a metal amphora. Elsa Vaz, the Brazilian vase-vessel of the drama, sprinkles the manuscript out on the floor. Dr. Eklund who in addition to everything else is a handwriting expert examines the manuscript and certifies that it is genuine.

Lars is now given the text to read for himself. He is not interested in the handwriting but in the writing's style and content. The story is very much in Schulz's style. Having nothing to do with chronology, it can be read in any order whatever. It does and does not contain Adela. It tells of the destruction of the human population of Drohobycz and of the occupation of the little village by idols. The idols themselves resemble Schulz's tailors' dummies (The most elaborate sequence in *The Street of Crocodiles* is called "Treatise on Tailors' Dummies") and idolatry being founded on death and the idols having no more humans for their sacrifices, the idols sacrifice each other. Chaos reigns.

Into this chaos intrudes the Messiah, an iconoclast who arrives to destroy the idols that "Schulz" had previously created. Who is this Messiah? The Messiah is not a who; it is an *it;* the Messiah that destroys the idols and brings redemption is a book. Is it Schulz's book? The exact nature of the book will be analyzed subsequently. For the moment it is sufficient to say that Lars's reading of the text has a strange effect on him. Probably because what the text says is further proof of his failed life, Lars stuffs the manuscript back into the amphora, lights a match, and sets it afire, thus destroying the *Messiah* of Stockholm.

Was the *Messiah* of Stockholm the *Messiah* of Drohobycz? Lars, apparently, thinks not. He sees that there is an essential difference between what Schulz might have written and what he has read. He therefore accuses Dr. Eklund of having forged the text in order to pass it off on some unsuspecting collector of rare manuscripts. Using his Monday column, where he has the reputation of being a disinterested belletrist who announces to the world from time to time his discovery of fine and exotic writings, Lars will, in Eklund's scheme, announce to the world the coming of the *Messiah*. Lars refuses to play the assigned role and the curtain comes down on this playlet as the defeated imposter, Dr. Eklund, kicks his daughter "Adela" in a rage at his failure.

The play is over. The novel, however, resumes seven months later. Lars has given up all pretensions at being extraordinary. He has moved out of his bohemian apartment into a more conventional setting, complete with home computer. At his newspaper, he has abandoned fine literature and has become a caterer to popular taste. He has become so popular a reviewer at the *Morgontörn* that he will soon expand from Mondays into Sundays and Tuesdays. He is becoming an industry. He has put Bruno Schulz and *The Messiah* behind him.

But in Ozick's world nothing is allowed to end with finality. Elsa Vaz, accompanied by a sick little boy, comes to pay Lars a visit at his office. She has come to tell Lars that he has caused irremediable damage to her father, Dr. Eklund, who, because of him, has left Stockholm with Heidi, forced to abandon her shop. Lars is cynical. He suspects that the old troupers have merely gone on to greener pastures, in search of more gullible victims. Elsa has returned to plant a seed of doubt in Lars's mind. Perhaps, she suggests, the manuscript was genuine after all.

Although Lars does not really believe Elsa's story, or believes it only at infrequent intervals, Elsa's most recent appearance has had an effect on him, perhaps even the desired effect. She has reminded the successful journalist Lars has become that there is still room in his life for the emotional angst and existential dread described by his formerly favorite authors. From time to time, henceforth, he will grieve. His grief does not come, however, from the loss of *The Messiah,* or even from his loss of the ability to see with Schulz's eye. His grief stems from another picture in his mind's eye, of a Polish-Jewish author, on the way to his martyrdom, seeking to preserve in the ground his treasured manuscript. At the end, Lars Andemening grieves as he remembers, not the author but the martyr. Lars finally becomes an agent of redemption, for, as Cynthia Ozick has written in *Trust*, "When we remember the martyrs we bring on the Messiah."[3]

Echoes in *The Messiah*

The novel *Trust* reverberates throughout *The Messiah of Stockholm*, although it is not the only Ozick text to do so. *The Messiah of Stockholm*, a culmination of Ozick's oeuvre, is characterized by a considerable amount of echoing, allusions bouncing from the present text to one of Ozick's previous texts, and then on to another. It is as though Ozick has made an effort here to put all of herself in her most recent work, as though *The Messiah of Stockholm* is meant to be a summing up, or a turning point.

The Swedish novel *Illusion*, imbricated in her text by Ozick in order to exemplify Lars Andemening's fall from reviewer's grace, is about a man who passes himself off as the creator of a body of artistic work by an older woman. The retelling of the plot of this novel constitutes a meaningful allusion to Ozick's own story "Virility," in which a similar story develops. It also echoes back to the present work, where the main character is living a life of literary illusion, and who can be saved only by an act of usurpation.

Lars Andemening, the character in search of an identity, reminds the careful reader of another Ozick "orphan," Allegra's daughter from *Trust*. "Trust," Lars says. "I want trust."[4] What he really wants is a hero figure to emulate, and, like Allegra's daughter, will come up against conflicting claims to his loyalty. The allusions to *Trust*, by the way, are at times ingenious. *Trust* is a novel in which punning takes place at an almost murderous pace. Jokingly, in one of the many stories told in the novel—we shall call them "stewpot stories"—Ozick tells how a mistranslation of the word "trust" into the Swedish word for "trussed" caused the heroine of a novel to go around tied up in knots.

"Usurpation" is another of Ozick's stories to reverberate in this one. What else is *The Messiah of Stockholm* if not the rewriting of "other people's stories"? It both contains usurpations (i.e., the plagiarism of a complete book of Swedish poetry, all the poems being translations of American poets first-named Robert) and is a usurpation of the writing of Bruno Schulz. And, as is being demonstrated here, the novel constitutes yet another example of self-mining by Cynthia Ozick.

Like Rappoport, Puttermesser's mysterious lover in "Puttermesser and Xanthippe," Dr. Eklund goes around the world getting people out. Lars himself is very much like Xanthippe, a golemlike figure arrested in earliness, as we shall see. The Messiah described here by Ozick has origins similar to those of the golem of Prague, described in her earlier story. Is not a golem also a messiahlike figure who, for a while, brings redemption, but whose redemption carries in its wake destruction?

Reverberating throughout this novel is, finally and most importantly, *The Cannibal Galaxy*. Joseph Brill is the brilliant headmaster who, like his name Brill, stops too soon and never becomes brilliant. Lars Andemening also has genius but he can sustain his genius for only a brief moment and is unable to bring it to a successful conclusion. And then there is Heidi Eklund, the woman whose name had, "in the last decades, begun to suit her" (22). It will be remembered that Hester Lilt's first name comes from the Hebrew word "to hide." Is not Heidi, pronounced "hidey," the mysterious character whose background is not vouchsafed to us and who is, like Hester Lilt, a writer of parables, of stories with hidden but necessary meanings? Like Hester, Heidi has a story to tell. Like the heroine of "Rosa," her background takes place in a Nazi concentration camp. It will be suggested that, like both Hester and Rosa, Heidi is a writer, the writer of *The Messiah* manuscript that surfaces in Stockholm, the writer of the book that redeems Bruno Schulz. Coincidentally—that is to say, simultaneously—Cynthia Ozick, who, throughout her writing career, has been concerned that her own fiction-making may be akin to idol-making, has finally brought redemption to her complete oeuvre.

The road to redemption in this novel takes many turns and is essentially that taken by Ozick's characters. Lars Andemening, at forty-two and despite his graying hair, looks as though he could still be taken for the messenger boy he was at sixteen. As Ozick puts it, "there was something in his face that opened into unripeness—a tentativeness, an unfinished tone" (4). Birgitta, Lars's first wife, used to complain that there was something "undigested" about him, and Lars sees himself as an "arrested soul." His very naïveté permits him to live the literary life he so cherishes. Childishness, with all its latency, gives Lars the freedom to chose both his names and his father. To be an orphan is still to be a child, and Lars "had an orphan's terrifying freedom to choose. He could become what he wished; no one could prohibit it, he could choose his own history. He could choose and he could relinquish. He was horribly, horribly free" (102).

At the newspaper as well, because he is so naive about the ways of the journalistic world, like Balzac's Lucien de Rubempré on the road to *Lost Illusions*,[5] he is able to review whatever authors he wishes: "Lars was unread, unmolested, unharrassed; he was free" (7). This childlike freedom is of course something greatly to be cherished. It bestows on its possessor the capacity to become extraordinary, to create utopias. The reader becomes aware of the potential for extraordinariness at the point during the novel when Lars becomes mediocre, when he decides to write reviews of popular novels: "Somehow he wasn't so much fixed in earliness as he used to be; you could tell at a glance he wasn't a boy. Impossible to mistake him now for anything but a man of middling years" (134). Anything middling, as we have learned in *The Cannibal Galaxy*, is mediocre. As Elsa Vaz, Lars's latest critic, puts it, "You've gotten just like the others. . . . You're an ordinary reviewer" (131).

Players in the Drama: Lars and Elsa

Lars loses his freedom as well as his youth. All along he had sought to provide himself with an identity that would give him a sense of self-worth. The Eklunds seek to deprive Lars of any intrinsic worth; they wish to make him into a mere instrument of their plotting. Ozick emphasizes this point by saying twice that in their presence Lars felt "there was something he was intended for" (118); "clearly they intended him for something" (119). They intend for Lars to serve as the Elijah for their *Messiah,* announcing its coming. That is, however, only the superficial meaning of Lars's function in the story. More importantly, Heidi Eklund intends to destroy Lars's fiction about himself, to make him see that he was wrong to have lived a life of fiction.

Apparently, Lars has acquired an extraordinary power, the power to approach a literary text with the eye of a visionary. Lars believes that he has been influenced by Bruno Schulz and it does not appear to matter to him whether the influence has been transmitted genetically or through Schulz's writing. In either case, the result is organic, that is to say necessary. Lars's talent is real, and awe-inspiring. He is more than a meticulous reader, however. He is a reader able to gain secret knowledge: "He drove through all the caged hypotheses of his author—some were overt and paced behind bars; others were camouflaged, . . . he penetrated everything" (8). Lars reads texts the way a serious reader is supposed to read texts.

The reader of Ozick's text apparently is being invited to do the same, to drive through the author's caged hypotheses, to penetrate her text in search of a camouflaged, if not hidden, meaning. Certainly *The Messiah of Stockholm* lends itself to such a reading, for Lars Andemening is more than what he seems. He is not merely a third-rate journalist with a benign eccentricity that affects no one. He is more dangerous than that. Lars "had long ago thrown himself on the altar of literature" (7) and has now become, in Ozick's terms, "an idolator." He has become, not a decoder of the universe but its consumer, a cannibalizer. He is not a prophet but a priest. His function is not to announce *The Messiah,* but to worship the text as an idol. Confronted with the manuscript, "he had swallowed it down like a priest, the priest of some passionate sect, for whom scripture is subordinate to the hour of sacral access" (117). Lars burns the manuscript of *The Messiah* because it indicts his very life.

Elsa Vaz is in many ways Lars Andemening's sister. She too is in her forties, and, like Lars, appears much younger than her years, a child. She too is free, a "bedouin," able to cross international borders without detection or hindrance. Like Lars she has a convoluted story. And, as her Portuguese name "Vaz" implies, she is a vessel, a person with a specific function. She is "Hebe the cup-bearer, messenger, deliverer" (101). She appears on the stage of life emanating a glow that bathes the entire stage in whiteness. When she sweeps through the doorway of Heidi Eklund's shop, wearing a white beret and carrying a white plastic bag, the place takes on "a wild morning brightness: snow-dazzle freakishly shot through with slashes of early sunlight, too sharp to bear. All that exaggerated whiteness seemed to be crowding into the narrow vestibule of the shop" (54). Is Elsa a supernatural being, or is she an actress creating an illusion? Lars himself, in Elsa's case, is able both to make a distinction and to conjecture: "It occurred to him that the woman in the white beret, in the morning's white brilliance, carrying a featherweight *Messiah* in a white bag was, if she wasn't an angel, a lie" (56). Elsa is a lie, one might say a white lie. She has come for Lars's good, to cure him of his madness, or, more precisely, she has come as the representative of the person who has taken it upon herself to redeem Lars Andemening.

The Mystery of Heidi Eklund

The most perplexing character of *The Messiah of Stockholm*, and the one to whom the reviewers, fooled by Ozick's camouflage, have paid the most scant attention, is the book dealer Heidi Eklund.[6] Heidi passes for the wife of Dr. Olle Eklund. She may indeed be his wife or she may be nothing more than the business partner of the former Alter Eckstein, merchant of forged documents. In a detective-story reading of the situation, Heidi's bookshop would be nothing more than a "front" for much shadier transactions. But there exists another, more literary, way of reading Heidi Eklund's text.

Heidi, it will be remembered, is hidden. If one lifts the camouflage material covering her person, one notices that Heidi is not so much the business associate of Olle Eklund as she is the literary partner of Lars Andemening. She has fallen in step with Lars's story and has taken an interest equal to his in Bruno Schulz's fate. She is, as Ozick says, "a kind of partner" to Lars Andemening. It is she and she alone who is able to understand how Lars would react to the discovery of his adoptive father's text. For Lars, Heidi is not merely a partner, not even a partner of desire; she is more than his equal; she, like Schulz, is a hero and worthy of being emulated: "It occurred to Lars that he would like to marry such a woman, independent, ungenial, private, old; *a kind of heroine*" (22; my italics).

Heidi is as devoted to literature as Lars is; she reads the books she sells, and she reads them with a concentration and penetration similar to his. In addition, she has the gesture of an oracle and is deemed to be, by Elsa, clairvoyant. She has the power to see beyond the surface of things. "She could see through to the skeleton," writes Ozick. "Skeletons. Everyone who walked by her. All her refugee customers. . . . And the tall infantile graying head of Lars Andemening: no more than a clean skull when she stared across at him" (40). Heidi knows things, and to Lars's great consternation, she is less interested in Bruno Schulz's stories than in the story of Bruno Schulz. She is particularly fascinated by the murder. Like a novelist of great talent, she is capable of rewriting that story. She is, in fact, capable of starting from any point in the story that Lars had told her about Schulz and bringing it to the "wild action" of that Black Thursday in 1942. Heidi-as-narrator like Schulz-as-writer transcends chronology. Heidi is interested less in Schulz's tales than in Schulz's death because she means to transcend fantasy as well as chronology. She finds reality much more engaging than fantasy. She is critical of those who write fiction for its own sake. She is a judge and a critic of all sorts of imposture, and she sees imposture all around her. She has seen people who claim to have been a famous professor in Warsaw, an ambassador to Argentina, or the one who got Sartre started on the Talmud. (She's met twenty-five of these last, she says mockingly.)

Heidi always returns Lars to Schulz's death because she means thereby to act as the one who brings punishment upon him, in the way that the narrator of "Usurpation" punishes the "goat" for his haughtiness. Lars's transgression has been nothing less than the wasting of his life in imitation. "You want to *be* him. . . . Mimicry. Posing in a mirror. What's the point of it? What will it bring you? You throw out your life" (41). Even when she speaks in a context of death, Heidi always comes down on the side of life, and therefore on the side of redemption.

Heidi is brutally frank. Try as Lars might, Heidi reminds him, he is not his adoptive father's literary equal. The beginning of Heidi's accusation against Lars is that he is not a worthy disciple of his master. He is merely a reviewer, not a writer. Even though his reviews sometimes read like Schulz—the reader sees only one phrase— she reminds him that "nobody gets the Nobel Prize for writing on Mondays" (41).

More importantly, and here we come to the heart of the matter, Heidi is critical of Bruno Schulz. In response to a line taken from Schulz's fiction that asserts, "Reality is as thin as paper and betrays with all its cracks its intuitive character," Heidi cries out: "Nincompoopery. Standing things on their head. What's real is real" (37). For Heidi, reality is not as thin as paper; the world is not made of literature. To stand things upright, one would have to say, rather, that literature must somehow be identical with life. Literature, for Heidi, must have the same type of meaning that life must have. She is critical not only of Lars's worshiping of Schulz. She is wary of Schulz's own idolatry: "She told Lars it was all madness.

Images in magnetic batches. She scolded him for turning his father into some sort of ceremonial mystification; there was a smoldering cultishness in all of it. His father's tales—animism, sacrifice, mortification, repugnance! Everything abnormal, everything wild" (33). Heidi, in her criticism of Schulz, sounds very much like the Ozick who reviewed Bruno Schulz's *The Street of the Crocodiles* in 1977. There, Ozick wrote:

What is being invented in the very drone of our passive literary expectations is Religion—not the taming religion of theology and morality, but the brute splendors of rite, gesture, phantasmagoric transfiguration, sacrifice, elevation, degradation, mortification, repugnance, terror, cult. The religion of animism in fact, where everything comes alive with an unpredictable and spiteful spirit-force, where even living tissue contains ghosts, where there is no pity.[7]

We know that for Cynthia Ozick the Second Commandment, the commandment against idol-making, is rooted in Judaism's insistence on pity in the world, the pity that denies the primordiality of death.

It is quite tempting here to bring forward for consideration, from the coincidence of Heidi Eklund's and Cynthia Ozick's literary and moral judgment of Bruno Schulz, the following conjecture: Is it not likely that the author of *The Messiah* that appears in Stockholm is not Dr. Olle Eklund, the forger of manuscripts, as it appears on the surface, but Heidi Eklund, the spokeswoman in the novel for the author of *The Messiah of Stockholm*? The *Messiah* that turns up in Stockholm is a forgery that could have been written only by someone who has penetrated to the heart of Schulz's writing, and disagrees with him. The author of the rewritten *Messiah*, the corrected *Messiah*, could only be Heidi Eklund, who will demonstrate to Lars what it is to redeem a text, by rewriting it.

It is very important not to confuse Heidi Eklund with Olle Eklund. The latter is also interested in reality. But he is attracted only to "original behavior," "curiosities," "tangled lives," "human oddity." He is also attracted to "the seduction, the magnetism of a sublime text" (95). But Dr. Eklund's attraction to a text is for the illusion it contains. He is devoted to tales for their own sakes.

Lars as much as admits that his story is a tale—a fairy tale at that. When confronted with the possibility that he may have a

sister, Lars blurts out, "There's no room in the story for another
child. It's not feasible. It can't be. You know the story as well as
I do" (53). For Lars, "story" is supreme and governs reality. Heidi
also has a story, one that she prefers not to reveal clearly. She claims
that during the war she lived outside the gates of a concentration
camp and would throw food over the fence at frequent intervals.
Because of Heidi's ability to describe what went on in the camp,
one may conclude that either she was indeed *inside* the fence, and
therefore is a liar, or, that she is an artist of the first rank, an artist
who writes with a moral purpose.

"Stewpot Stories"

There are many stories in *The Messiah of Stockholm,* many fictions
beyond those told about themselves by Lars Andemening, Elsa Vaz
and Olle and Heidi Eklund. There are in addition to these stories
another group of stories in *The Messiah of Stockholm,* what we call
here the "stewpot stories." These are the stories of literary gossip
that the novel says are universal to the book-reviewing departments
of the world's newspapers. The "stewpot" metaphor comes to Ozick
via Balzac's *Lost Illusions*[8] and appears as a leitmotiv throughout the
novel. *The Messiah of Stockholm,* for example, itself a story born out
of a piece of gossip, is also a stewpot story, a rewriting of the story
of the sudden appearance of Schulz's *Messiah,* overheard by Ozick
during a trip to Stockholm.

Several other stewpot stories are recounted within the novel. They
are all stories of literature and art and include tales about mistrans-
lations of literary works, the plagiarism of a complete book of verse,
and a retelling of the way Lars Andemening was hoodwinked by a
family of forgers. There is also the plot of the story that Lars reviews
on his way to popularity, a novel of illusion that touches on lust,
deceit, ambition, and death. Most importantly, it is a story about
someone who usurps the art of another for his own purposes.

Bruno Schulz: Not a Jewish Writer

Bruno Schulz's stories are admittedly works of great art. They
are full of symbols, and the effect these symbols produces is more
important than the things these stories describe. Schulz's stories,
as can be seen from the following are strangely reminiscent of Kafka.
"Savagely crafty nouns and verbs were set on a crooked road to take

on engorgements and transmogrifications: a bicycle ascends into the zodiac, rooms in houses are misplaced, wallpaper hisses, the calendar acquires a thirteenth month. Losses, metamorphoses, degradations. In one of the stories the father turns into a pincered crab; the mother boils it and serves it to the family on a dish" (32). Schulz is himself a usurper of Kafka. Ozick emphasizes that Schulz's creativity borders on the criminal in another way as well. She has chosen to set the tone of her novel by using as its epigraph an illuminating quotation taken from Bruno Schulz. Schulz writes of the creative process and of the methods at hand: "Even if the classical methods of creation should prove inaccessible for evermore, there still remain some illegal methods, an infinity of heretical and criminal methods." Schulz is a creative criminal because he is a creator of literary idols.

In her essay "Literature as Idol," Cynthia Ozick makes a distinction between the Terachs and the Abrahams of the literary world. In the story told in Genesis, and elaborated upon by the rabbis in their midrashic tales, Terach, Abraham's father creates and purveys idols. Abraham, the creator of monotheism, destroys them. The midrashic story contains both Terach and Abraham. In her essay, Ozick contends, "if there *can* be such a chimera as a 'Jewish writer,' it must be [a] kind of sphinx or gryphon (part one thing, part another) . . . sometimes purifying like Abraham, more often conjuring like Terach, and always knowing that they are icily, elegiacally at war."[9]

It appears that Bruno Schulz is himself *not* a Jewish writer in this sense. It is not that he rarely alludes to Jewish nationality. Nor is it even that Yiddish is a foreign language to this Polish Jew from Galicia, a center of Yiddish culture. As Ozick says so elegantly, "If he had ever sipped a word or two of Yiddish out of the air, it did not ride his spittle or his pen" (35). Bruno Schulz is a criminal creator because, in the context of the Jewish value system, he is a pagan writer. This is the reading Cynthia Ozick gives of Schulz's works. It is, moreover, the sense of the rewriting activity she engages in, reproducing a Schulz text she can only imagine.

Ozick's story of Schulz's *Messiah* is one of creation and redemption. It is the story of Schulz's creation and Ozick's redemption. It is, moreover, a story of Terach and Abraham, a midrash on that story, and a parable. It is a rewriting of Bruno Schulz for didactic purposes. The first half of the story is inspired by Terach, and that is why the village of Drohobycz, which has been emptied of humanity, is now peopled exclusively by idols. Where idolatry reigns there does death become a sacrament, even if it means the sacrifice of idols to each other. Until this point we are caught up in what both Heidi Eklund and Cynthia Ozick agree is the domain of Bruno Schulz. The story is worthy of Schulz, possessor of an infinity of heretical methods of creation, a Terach in the extreme.

Schulz's world is a flawed one, however. It is in need of repair and redemption. Terach needs an Abraham, an iconoclast, a Messiah. And at this point, Cynthia Ozick and Heidi Eklund take over. In reading the manuscript that the Eklunds wish to pass off as Bruno Schulz's, Lars Andemening, the insightful and incisive reader, realizes right away that something is rotten in the state neighboring Denmark. He knows that the text is a lie. But then he reorders his thinking. Something else—not a lie—is going on: "What was smoldering in this place was not so much a lie as a latency" (119). Lars realizes that there is another text hidden inside the "Schulz" text. The latter will be expanded. It will be made into a Jewish text by the addition of a new dimension. To Terach will be added Abraham.

Ozick insists that although there is a sequence of events in this narrative, chronology is not what is important:

The order of the pages did not matter. These poor battered sheets were erratically paginated, some not numbered at all, and one eddying flowed into another; there were sequences and consequences, parallels and paradoxes, however you shuffled them. . . . So it was with the intelligence of *The Messiah's* order and number and scheme of succession; everything voluminously overlapping, everything simultaneous and multiform. (106)

This text is not so much a rewriting of Schulz as it is an allusion to Heidi's ability to begin anywhere and yet to wind up at the point of Schulz's murder.

"When we remember the martyrs," Cynthia Ozick has written, "we bring on the Messiah." In *The Messiah of Stockholm* she demonstrates *how* one goes about bringing on the Messiah. For Ozick, the Messiah is not a person at all. It is a text that demands interpretation, because it contains within itself a message to be deciphered. It may, at first, be "impossible to say what this unreadable text might be proposing as its thesis or axiom" (110), because the text is written in a hitherto unknown alphabet, one that requires patient deciphering. If one looks at *The Messiah of Stockholm* long enough and creatively enough, one realizes that the book itself is not the idol it appears to be but the bringer of redemption. It brings redemption both to the creation of God and to the creations of man.

Chapter Eleven
"Genesis"

Cynthia Ozick's career as a published author spans more than three decades, from "The Sense of Europe," a thirteen-page piece excerpted in 1956 from the manuscript of *Mercy, Pity, Peace, and Love,* her unfinished and abandoned philosophical novel, to *The Messiah of Stockholm,* her 1987 novel that grew out of a projected short story. Ozick's oeuvre follows an itinerary of her mind. All along the road Ozick has been preoccupied with and has evolved an answer to one central question: May a Jew write stories and still remain an authentic Jew, a bearer of the Jewish idea, an opponent of idolatry? Is not the very term "Jewish writer" an oxymoron?

This is a question that Ozick has wrestled with in her stories and in her essays, in speeches and in interviews. Lately, beginning approximately with "Bialik's Hint," a talk she gave at the Bellagio Conference in 1982, Ozick has come to the conclusion that the Jewish idea is not the enemy of the imagination she had feared it was. To posit an incorporeal God, she now reasons, is to use the imagination for the highest of purposes. In *The Messiah of Stockholm,* a culminating work, as in *The Cannibal Galaxy,* "The Pagan Rabbi," and "Levitation," Ozick has demonstrated that there is such a thing as a Jewish fiction writer and that there is a type of fiction-making that may serve redemption.

Having more or less solved her life-long problem, where does Cynthia Ozick go from here? Will she continue to play the one-note melody that seems continuously to buzz in her ears? Or will she strike a new note? There are signs that Cynthia Ozick is mellowing, that she no longer needs to avenge her childhood hurts, that she no longer has to write "to punish," as the narrator of "Usurpation" says *she* did. In a 1987 interview in *Publishers Weekly,* Ozick expressed the hope that she would now move away from writing out of antipathy, that she could now begin "to explore the more sympathetic side of my temperament." The interview concludes with a startling confession by Ozick: "I want very much to acquire the sympathetic vision of life because I know that as a reader I don't want to read what I write."[1] All readers of Ozick will want to know how she means to approach this self-reformation, this new genesis. Several tactics suggest themselves.

Cynthia Ozick has often talked of bringing Ruth Puttermesser, the heroine of two of her stories, back for a third go. She has indicated that she would like to marry her off, to make her normal, to provide her with normal human entanglements. And indeed, Ozick has revealed that she is currently working on the story of a married Ruth Puttermesser.[2] Will the new, improved Puttermesser engage the reader's sympathies?

Cynthia Ozick is working on another novel as well, currently "in abeyance," due to more pressing writing commitments. The first chapter of that as yet untitled novel appeared as the story "At Fumicaro" in the 6 August 1984 *New Yorker.* The story is about an American Catholic radio journalist, Frank Castle, who, while attending a conference in Italy on "The Church and How It is Known"—Frank Castle's specialty is to interview converts—impulsively marries his chambermaid, Viviana, already pregnant by her mother's lover. According to Ozick's own admission, the part of the novel already published is "a part that completely misrepresents the whole." Frank Castle, it turns out, is Jewish. To *Publishers Weekly* she revealed that the novel is really about the children of intermarriage—half Gentiles, half Jews. From what Ozick has told her interviewer, the novel bids fair to be a realization, on a different plane, of the dual curriculum of the Edmond Fleg Primary School of *The Cannibal Galaxy:* "I wonder what it must be like to be thus divided. When you put together two essentially colliding natures, cultures, temperaments, histories, and then you have a child who's bound genetically and loyally to both, what happens in the mind of that child?"[3] The important fact to retain from Ozick's question is that she is thinking today not of what divides these two cultures, the Christian and the Jewish, but of how they can accommodate each other when by the very nature of things they are forced into a partnership.

Cynthia Ozick has written movingly of the Holocaust, although she has almost never herself used the word in print. She told *Paris Review* that she would prefer that the documents of the Holocaust— and not fiction—be enough to make witnesses to the destruction of European Jews and their civilization out of all of us: "I don't want to tamper or invent or imagine, and yet I have done it. I can't not do it. It comes, it invades."[4] Ozick's imagination has been invaded by survivors of the Holocaust who have come to America's shores from London and Paris as well as from the destroyed shtetlach of Eastern Europe. She has brought these Jews back to life in America's suburbs and has redeemed them, much in the manner America has done. Virtually all of the main characters of *The Messiah of Stockholm* are survivors of the Holocaust living in Europe, seeking redemption from a book. How will Ozick continue to write of the Holocaust?

Although she is a steadfast supporter of Israel, Ozick has not yet, in her fiction, set her feet firmly on the soil of the land of the Jewish redemption. Is it going too far to speculate that she will one day soon follow in the footsteps of Philip Roth, in his 1987 novel *The Counterlife*, and set a future tale of hers in Israel?

The speculative mode induces other questions about the future. Cynthia Ozick is a highly respected writer of essays, in which she gives free rein, not to her imagination, but to her citizenly impulses. Knopf is preparing to bring out a second volume of her essays, entitled *Metaphor & Memory*, after the title of her 1985 Phi Beta Kappa Oration delivered at Harvard University. Will Ozick now concentrate on the essay form to the detriment of her fiction? Despite all appearances that she may already be doing so, and despite the opinion of those who prefer her essays to her fiction, this is not at all likely. Ozick's real strength, as this book has labored to demonstrate, is as a maker of fictions. Moreover, the writing of fiction is not a matter of choice but of need. And Ozick has demonstrated, quite vividly, that she has that need.

Finally, although she believes, as she told her *Paris Review* interviewer, that "more can be found about a writer in any single sentence in a work of fiction . . . than in five or ten full-scale biographies,"[5] perhaps the time is ripe for an autobiography. Ozick has revealed recently that she has been keeping a diary since 1953. What is recorded there promises to be very revealing. Is it too much to speculate that Ozick will one day publish her own answers to her own questions about her own life?

These are some of the questions that cross a reader's mind as he thinks about the next phase in Cynthia Ozick's writing career. We may be certain that Ozick will continue to be "possessed" by writing and will continue to make a contribution to American letters. We may be no less certain that Ozick, as she writes, will continue to surprise and dazzle her readers and will enthrall them with the power of her language. Of one last thing we may above all be certain: We have not yet seen Ozick's masterpiece. When one of his old poems is praised as his best, Edelshtein, the poet of "Yiddish in America," responds, "The one on my table, in progress, is the best." Ozick's faithful readers await that work in progress with pleasant expectation.

Notes and References

Chapter One

1. Cynthia Ozick, "On Excellence," *Ms.*, January 1985, 44.
2. Letter from Cynthia Ozick to Joseph Lowin, 7 October 1983.
3. Cynthia Ozick, "Spells, Wishes, Goldfish, Old School Hurts," *New York Times Book Review*, 31 January 1982, 9, 24; reprinted as "A Drugstore in Winter," in *Art & Ardor* (New York: Knopf, 1983), 298–305.
4. Quoted from transcript of Bill Moyers, "Heritage Conversations," WNET-TV, New York, 3 April 1986, 32.
5. Elaine M. Kauvar, "An Interview with Cynthia Ozick," *Contemporary Literature* 26, no. 4 (1986):385–86.
6. Cynthia Ozick, "The First Day of School: Washington Square, 1946," *Harper's*, September 1985, 69–72.
7. Cynthia Ozick, "The Lesson of the Master," *New York Review of Books*, 12 August 1983; reprinted in *Art & Ardor*, 291–97.
8. Moyers, "Heritage Conversations," 41.
9. Catherine Rainwater and William J. Scheick, "An Interview with Cynthia Ozick [Summer 1982]," *Texas Studies in Literature and Language* 25, no. 2 (Summer 1983):257.
10. Cynthia Ozick, "Good Writers, Bad Citizens," *New York Times Book Review*, 15 February 1987, 13.
11. Quoted from statements made by Ozick in a "dialogue" with William Berkowitz at Alice Tully Hall, Lincoln Center for the Performing Arts, New York, 13 June 1984. *Shavuot* is the Feast of Weeks, a holiday celebrating the anniversary of the giving of the Torah on Mount Sinai seven weeks after the Exodus from Egypt.

Chapter Two

1. Letter from Ozick to Lowin, 25 December 1985.
2. Cynthia Ozick, "A Riddle," *Judaism* 14 (Fall 1965):436. (Reprinted by permission.)
3. Cynthia Ozick, "Toward a New Yiddish," in *Art & Ardor* (New York: Obelisk/Dutton, 1984), 155. The article originally was published as "America: Toward Yavneh," *Judaism* 19 (Summer 1970):264–82.
4. Alvin H. Rosenfeld, "Cynthia Ozick: Fiction and the Jewish Idea," *Midstream*, August/September 1977, 79.
5. Ibid., 79.

6. Cynthia Ozick, "Prayer Leader," *Prooftexts* 3 (1983):1–8.

7. *The Penguin Book of Yiddish Verse* (New York: Penguin, 1987), 422.

8. Letter from Ozick to Lowin, 17 September 1984. *Mamaloshn* is mother tongue; *Shekhine* (Shechinah) is identified in English dictionaries as "Jewish spirit."

9. Cynthia Ozick, "A Bintel Brief for Jacob Glatstein," *Jewish Heritage*, Spring 1972, 60.

10. Ibid., 60.

11. Jacob Glatstein, "The Fame of Bashevis Singer," *Congress Bi-Weekly*, 27 December 1965, 17–18.

12. Ibid., 17–18.

13. Cynthia Ozick, "Envy; or Yiddish in America," in *The Pagan Rabbi and Other Stories* (New York: Obelisk/Dutton, 1983), 99; cited hereafter in chapter 2 by page number. The story was originally published in *Commentary* 48 (November 1969):35–53.

14. In "Rosa," analyzed in chapter 8, Ozick requires us to act as though we are reading a letter in Polish. Amazingly, there also, she succeeds.

Chapter Three

1. Moyers, "Heritage Conversations," 23–25.

2. Victor Strandberg, "The Art of Cynthia Ozick," *Texas Studies in Literature and Language* 25, no. 2 (1983):267. Strandberg's appreciation of the novel's value is all the more remarkable because of the fact that, on publication, *Trust* was received as "hollow," "insubstantial," and "a performance from ambition." See, in this matter, Robert Taubman, "Allegra's Daughter," *New Statesman*, 20 January 1967, 85–86; and Eugene Goodheart, "Cynthia Ozick's *Trust*," *Critique* 9, no. 2 (Winter 1967–68). For a positive early review, see David L. Stevenson, "Daughter's Reprieve," *New York Times Book Review*, 17 July 1966. Remarkably, *Trust* has subsequently been largely neglected by both readers and critics who have gone out of their way to praise so many of Ozick's more recent works. Strandberg's essays and this chapter agree on one thing at least: *Trust* is worth the reader's effort.

3. Cynthia Ozick, preface to *Bloodshed and Three Novellas* (New York: Obelisk/Dutton, 1983), 4–5; originally published by Knopf in 1976.

4. Ibid., 5.

5. Curiously, at the time Ozick was writing *Trust*, Erik H. Erikson was publishing his series of essays on the ages of man. A comparison between Ozick's novel and Erikson's treatment of fidelity would be fascinating. See, in this matter, Erikson, "Youth: Fidelity and Diversity," *Daedalus* (1962):5–27.

6. Cynthia Ozick, *Trust* (New York: Obelisk/Dutton, 1983), 323; cited hereafter in chapter 3 by page number. Originally published by New American Library in 1966.

7. Strandberg, "The Art of Cynthia Ozick," 270. For an interesting argument contending that Ozick may indeed be a pagan whose beliefs are at odds with her fiction, see Haim Chertok, "Ozick's Hoofprints," *Modern Jewish Studies* 6 (1987):5–12.

8. Ibid., 277.

9. It seems futile to speculate about the name "Vand," which may refer to the past participle of the German verb *"winden"*—"to turn," "to bind." Is Enoch one who has "turned" to his tradition and "bound" himself to it? The idea may appear genial, but it is too speculative to build on.

10. Ozick uses neither the word "Holocaust" nor its Hebrew equivalent *"Shoah"* to talk about the destruction of Europe's Jews. She is nevertheless one of the most preeminent practitioners of Holocaust fiction.

11. Moyers, "Heritage Conversations," 35.

Chapter Four

1. Ozick, preface to *Bloodshed*, 4.

2. Ozick discusses several of the more famous love lyrics of Catullus. These same verses make their way into *The Cannibal Galaxy* as well. For all her Jewishness, Ozick is steeped in the Western cultural tradition.

3. Although Ozick says in her preface that "An Education" is a Jewish imitation of the Irish stories of Frank O'Connor, the story is not Jewish in the way *Trust* is in the end, or in the way many of Ozick's later stories are. It is extremely difficult to accept, moreover, Strandberg's assertation that "An Education" is about the loss of Jewish identity. Strandberg writes that "Chimes fails because, having renounced his Jewish birthright, he faces the dilemma of trying to write literature without any cultural roots whatever" ("The Art of Cynthia Ozick," 302). As will be seen, it is wrong to take Chimes so seriously, as either an intellectual or a writer.

4. Cynthia Ozick, "An Education," in *Bloodshed*, 126; cited hereafter in chapter 4 by page number. The story was originally published in *Esquire*, April 1972, 92–108.

5. Ruth Wisse, "American Jewish Writing, Act II," *Commentary* 61, no. 6 (June 1976):44.

6. Forty-year-olds, lawyers, and fund-raisers recur frequently in Ozick's work. Una Meyer is forty-two at the end of the story; Ruth Puttermesser is a lawyer of forty-six; Puttermesser's lover Rappoport is a fund-raiser. Bleilip, therefore, is signalled to us as a central character in Ozick's human comedy.

7. Cynthia Ozick, "Bloodshed," in *Bloodshed*, 59; cited hereafter in

chapter 4 by page number. The story was originally published in *Esquire* (January 1976):100, 130–38.

8. Cynthia Ozick, "The Riddle of the Ordinary," *Moment* 1 (July–August 1975):55.

9. Ozick, "Riddle," 59.

10. The meaning of *azazel* is anyone's guess. According to the most prestigious biblical lexicographers, both Jewish and non-Jewish, *azazel* means either "where the goat goes" or "entire removal." See Rabbi David Kimchi, *The Book of Roots* (in Hebrew) (Jerusalem: 1967), and *A Hebrew and English Lexicon of the Old Testament,* ed. Francis Brown, S. R. Driver, and Charles A. Briggs (Oxford: Clarendon Press, 1967).

11. James Russell Lowell, "A Fable for Critics," in *Lowell's Writings,* vol. 9 (Cambridge: Riverside Press, 1890), 85.

Chapter Five

1. Quoted by Eve Ottenberg, "The Rich Visions of Cynthia Ozick," *New York Times Magazine,* 10 April 1983, 65.

2. Cynthia Ozick, "Puttermesser and Xanthippe," in *Levitation: Five Fictions* (New York: Obelisk/Dutton, 1983), 99–104. The story was originally published in *Salmagundi* 55 (Winter 1982):163–255.

3. Tzvetan Todorov, *The Fantastic: A Structural Approach to a Literary Genre,* trans. Richard Howard (Ithaca, N.Y.: Cornell University Press, 1975).

4. See Sigmund Freud, "The Uncanny" (1919), in *Collected Papers,* vol. 4, trans. supervised by Joan Riviere (New York: Basic Books, 1959), 368–407. A psychoanalytic reading of Ozick's use of the fantastic would be fascinating. It is both beyond the scope of this chapter and the competence of this writer. It is nevertheless instructive to point out that Freud himself, who "collected" uncanny episodes from real life, including his own, recognized the extraordinary power of literature in this domain: "There are many more means of creating uncanny effects in fiction than there are in real life" (44).

5. Todorov, *The Fantastic,* 25.

6. Ibid., 173.

7. Ozick, "The Riddle of the Ordinary," 57–58.

8. Cynthia Ozick, "The Pagan Rabbi," in *The Pagan Rabbi,* 13; hereafter cited in chapter 5 by page number. The story was originally published in the *Hudson Review* 19 (Autumn 1966):425–56.

9. One thinks readily in this context of the talmudic Aggadah concerning the "Four who entered the Pleasure Garden" (B. Talmud, *Haggigah,* 14b). Without going into the details of the story, I may say fairly confidently that the rabbis themselves were concerned about the dangers of the mystical enterprise, which they related metaphorically to

the aesthetic appreciation of nature, to the world of the imagination, and, by extension, to storytelling.

10. *Mise en abyme*, as used here, is the technique of reproducing, within one work of art, another work of art. It has a mirroring function, effects a reverberation, and serves to enlarge the scope of an artistic text beyond its ostensible borders. The technique can be found in a variety of artistic texts—for example, the description of Hephaistos' shield in the *Iliad*, the players' scene in *Hamlet*, and the artist's canvas in Velasquez's *Las Meninas*. The technique is used extensively, and masterfully, by Ozick.

11. Todorov, *The Fantastic*, 41.

12. Rainwater and Scheick, "An Interview with Cynthia Ozick," 262–63.

13. Wisse, "American Jewish Writing, Act II," 43.

14. The term "key" is taken from Erving Goffman, *Frame Analysis* (New York: Harper & Row, 1974), 40–82. "In brief, a play keys life, a ceremony keys an event" (58). In a similar way, a title keys a story.

15. The terms are Freud's, who notes in "The Uncanny" that the uncanny and the canny are simultaneously in opposition and compatible. "What interests us most . . . is to find that among its different shades of meaning the word *heimlich* exhibits one which is identical with its opposite, *unheimlich*" (375). In Ozick's terms, the Ordinary becomes the Extraordinary. For us, the Jewish and the artistic—although they may sometimes exhibit opposite characteristics—do sometimes coalesce, most notably, as I am attempting to show here, in the literature of the fantastic.

16. Joseph Epstein, "Cynthia Ozick, Jewish Writer," *Commentary* 77, no. 3 (March 1984):68.

17. Ibid., 68.

18. Rainwater and Scheick, "An Interview with Cynthia Ozick," 256.

19. Jurij Lotman, *The Structure of the Artistic Text* (Ann Arbor, Mich.: Michigan Slavic Contributions, 1977), 212–13.

20. Cynthia Ozick, "Levitation," in *Levitation*, 3; hereafter cited in chapter 5 by page number. This story was originally published in the *Partisan Review* 46 (1979):391–405.

21. Cynthia Ozick returns to Italy and to the notion of an "erotics" of Christianity in her short story "At Fumicaro" (*New Yorker*, 6 August 1984, 32–58).

22. Epstein, "Cynthia Ozick, Jewish Writer," 67.

23. Ibid.

Chapter Six

1. Wisse, "American Jewish Writing, Act II," 45.

2. See Naomi B. Sokoloff, "Interpretation: Cynthia Ozick's *Can-*

nibal Galaxy," *Prooftexts* 6, no. 3 (1986):239–57, who finds the claim that Ozick has developed a characteristically Jewish mode of narrative "dubious." Of course writing need not resemble biblical prose in order to be in a Jewish mode.

3. Erich Auerbach, *Mimesis: The Representation of Reality in Western Literature* (New York: Doubleday, 1957), 489.

4. Ibid., 5.

5. Ibid., 10.

6. Ibid., 9.

7. Cynthia Ozick, "America: Toward Yavneh," *Judaism* 19 (1970):280; reprinted as "Toward a New Yiddish," in *Art & Ardor*, 154–77.

8. Harold Fisch, "Introducing Cynthia Ozick," *Response* 22 (1974):29.

9. Ottenberg, "The Rich Visions of Cynthia Ozick," 66.

10. Cynthia Ozick, *The Cannibal Galaxy* (New York: Knopf, 1983), 11; hereafter cited in chapter 6 by page number.

11. The idea of *t'shuva* ("repentance") as a motor of *The Cannibal Galaxy* comes from Ozick herself. In response to a review that I wrote of her novel, she writes: "I didn't realize this story is so much about pedagogy: I thought (i.e., the inner hum that set it going) of the idea of redemptiveness. The opposite of Greek fate: that if we can change ourselves, we can change our character, and if we change our character, we can change what appears to be our 'fate.' That destiny is not fixed. That Torah's gift is *t'shuva*. That the meek can grow strong. That there is hope for the worm" (letter from Ozick to Lowin, 7 October 1983).

Chapter Seven

1. Rainwater and Scheick, "An Interview with Cynthia Ozick," 262–63.

2. Cynthia Ozick, preface to *Bloodshed*, 4; hereafter, the preface and "Usurpation (Other People's Stories)" cited in chapter 7 by page number. "Usurpation" was originally published in *Esquire* 81 (May 1974):124–28, 158–175. Ozick's assertions in the preface to *Bloodshed*, it will be seen subsequently, need to be taken with a grain of proverbial salt. Nevertheless, from the inner evidence of her tales, one has ample reason to conclude that in this case the credo seems to accord with the practice.

3. In the preface we are told that the "famous writer" is Bernard Malamud; the story is "The Silver Crown."

4. The preface reveals that the story is also a real one: David Stern, "Agnon: A Story," *Response* 7 (1973):7–32. The narrator in "Usurpation" gives herself license to "enter into" the Stern story by noting, first, that its nature is ambiguous, and, second, that it demands interpretation. "It

was not clear to me whether this was fiction or not. The title suggested it was: 'A Story of Youth and Homage.' But the narrative was purposefully inconclusive. Moreover, the episodes could be interpreted on several 'levels.' Plainly it was not just a story, but meant something much more, and even that 'much more' itself meant much more" (138).

5. In "The Moral Necessity of Metaphor," *Harper's,* May 1986, 62–68, Ozick claims that metaphor is a Jewish tradition, "one of the chief agents of our moral nature." For an insight into what happens in the Jewish exegetical tradition when a metaphor is taken literally, see Warren Harvey, "The Pupil, the Harlot and the Fringe Benefits," *Prooftexts* 6 (1986):259–64.

6. Cynthia Ozick, "What Literature Means," *Partisan Review* 49, no. 2 (1982):296.

7. James L. Kugel, "Two Introductions to Midrash," in *Midrash and Literature,* ed. Geoffrey H. Hartman and Sanford Budick (New Haven, Conn.: Yale University Press, 1986), 92.

8. Note also that Isaac Kornfeld of "The Pagan Rabbi" and the Feingolds of "Levitation" are themselves writers. This point cannot be stressed enough.

9. Quoted in Eisig Silberschlag, *Saul Tchernikhovsky: Poet of Revolt* (Ithaca, N.Y.: Cornell University Press, 1968), 43–44.

10. Ibid.

11. The word "gassed" here is pregnant with meaning. To compare a levitating figure to a balloon filled with helium is one thing; to talk about the gassing of Jews is another. Both senses are eerily inherent in Ozick's usage.

12. Wisse, "American Jewish Writing, Act II," 43.

13. Rainwater and Scheick, "An Interview with Cynthia Ozick," 258.

14. Boris Uspensky, *A Poetics of Composition* (Berkeley: University of California Press, 1973), 139.

15. S. Y. Agnon, "Messiah," in *Ir Um'loah* [The city and all that are contained therein] (Jerusalem: Schocken, 1973), 22.

16. Babylonian Talmud, *Sotah,* 4b.

17. Religiously punctilious Jews refrain from pronouncing God's name, the Tetragrammaton. They even refrain from pronouncing its replacement, a word meaning "Lord." Instead, they replace that word with *Hashem,* a word meaning "the name."

18. Kauvar, "An Interview with Cynthia Ozick," 395. (The original has Deuteronomy 29:29, a nonexistent verse.)

19. Ibid., 394–95.

20. Ibid., 395.

Chapter Eight

1. Bernard Malamud, *God's Grace* (New York: Avon Books, 1982), 80.
2. Harold Bloom, *The Anxiety of Influence* (New York: Oxford University Press, 1973), 55.
3. Cynthia Ozick, "The Shawl," *New Yorker* 26 May 1980, 33–34; page numbers are not cited in the text.
4. Cynthia Ozick, "Rosa," in *Prize Stories 1984: The O. Henry Awards,* ed. William Abrahams (Garden City, N.Y.: Doubleday, 1984), 2; hereafter cited in chapter 8 by page number. This story was originally published in the *New Yorker,* 21 March 1983, 38–71.
5. Polish poet Julian Tuwim (1894–1953) represents one form of the symbiosis between enlightened Jewish and Western culture. His manifesto, *We Polish Jews* (1944) (Jerusalem: Magnes Press, 1984), is required reading in this connection.
6. In "The Riddle of the Ordinary" Ozick asserts that the mission of the Jews is to sanctify the ordinary.

Chapter Nine

1. Moyers, "Heritage Conversations," 33.
2. Cynthia Ozick, "Literature and the Politics of Sex: A Dissent," *Art & Ardor,* 284–85. This essay was originally published, under a different title, in *Ms.,* December 1977, 56, 79–81.
3. Ibid., 285.
4. Ibid., 285.
5. Kauvar, "An Interview with Cynthia Ozick," 387. Kauvar has also written on the Puttermesser stories ("Cynthia Ozick's Book of Creation: Puttermesser and Xanthippe," *Contemporary Literature* 26, no. 1 [1985]:40–54).
6. Ibid., 387.
7. Cynthia Ozick, "Notes Toward Finding the Right Question," *Forum* 35 (Spring–Summer 1979):37–60.
8. Cynthia Ozick, "Puttermesser: Her Work History, Her Ancestry, Her Afterlife," in *Levitation,* 31; hereafter cited in chapter 9 by page number. This story was originally published in the *New Yorker,* 9 May 1977, 38–44.
9. Lists, by the way, recur frequently in and add an epic dimension to "Puttermesser and Xanthippe."
10. See Ozick's essay on Scholem in *Art & Ardor,* 138–50.
11. Cynthia Ozick, "Puttermesser and Xanthippe," in *Levitation,* 84; hereafter cited in chapter 9 by page number.
12. Kauvar, "An Interview with Cynthia Ozick," 391–92.
13. They are of an intensity similar to that of the classic literary case

of seventeenth-century French *épistolière* Mme de Sévigné for her daughter, Mme de Grignan. The reference is far from gratuitous: Ozick refers to it expressly in describing Hester Lilt's attachment for Beulah. One might add that motherly attention to offspring is a general leitmotiv of *The Cannibal Galaxy.*

14. Peter Brooks, *Reading for the Plot* (New York: Knopf, 1984), 48.

15. Gershom Scholem, "The Idea of the Golem," in *On the Kabbalah and Its Symbolism* (New York: Schocken, 1969), 158–204. Scholem wrote at least two other pieces on the golem: one for the *Encyclopedia Judaica,* reprinted in his *Kabbalah* (Jerusalem: Keter, 1979), 351–356; the other was a speech delivered on the occasion of the installation of a computer (a modern golem) at the Weizmann Institute of Science in Rehovot, Israel, reprinted as "The Golem of Prague and the Golem of Rehovot," in *The Messianic Idea in Judaism* (New York: Schocken, 1971), 335–40.

16. Ibid., 202.

17. Ibid., 195, note 2.

18. Brooks, *Reading for the Plot,* 52.

19. Rainwater and Scheick, "An Interview with Cynthia Ozick," 258.

Chapter Ten

1. *The Messiah of Stockholm* is dedicated to Philip Roth, and this dedication is meaningful. It is not Roth the novelist to whom Ozick is paying homage but rather Roth the editor. The dedication therefore is to be read as an organic part of the novel, a key signature. Like the series edited by Philip Roth, *The Messiah of Stockholm* is devoted, at least in the beginning, to rescuing an important writer from oblivion.

2. In Mervyn Rothstein, "Cynthia Ozick's Rabbinical Approach to Literature," *New York Times,* 25 March 1987, C25.

3. Cynthia Ozick, *Trust,* 236.

4. Cynthia Ozick, *The Messiah of Stockholm* (New York: Knopf, 1987), 2; hereafter cited in chapter 10 by page number.

5. Balzac's novel is mentioned specifically in Ozick's text. While Balzac is only one of over forty authors—among them fifteen Nobel Laureates for Literature—whose names are sprinkled throughout *The Messiah of Stockholm,* the connection with Balzac's novel is an organic one. *The Messiah of Stockholm* may well be as much a rewriting of *Lost Illusions* as it is of Bruno Schulz's work.

6. Of the more than fifteen reviews of the novel that I possess, only Harold Bloom's "The Book of the Father" (*New York Times Book Review,* 22 May 1987) hints that the writer of *The Messiah* might be other than Olle Eklund. This chapter, which has taken much from Bloom's review, nevertheless disagrees with Bloom's assertion that *The Messiah of Stockholm* is "a very Schulzian book, in substance as well as in spirit" (36).

7. Cynthia Ozick. "The Phantasmagoria of Bruno Schulz," in *Art &
Ardor*, 227. This essay was originally published in the *New York Times
Book Review*, 13 February 1977, 4–5. See also Bruno Schulz, *The Street of
Crocodiles* (New York: Penguin Books, 1977).

8. On her return from Sweden in November 1984 Cynthia Ozick
wrote a letter to me in which she described the literary atmosphere in
Stockholm. Her choice of words in the following sentence is particularly
suggestive: "The literary community lives at a high competitive pitch: a
stewpot out of Balzac's *Lost Illusions*" (Letter from Ozick to Lowin, 9
November 1984).

9. Cynthia Ozick, "Literature as Idol: Harold Bloom," *Art & Ardor*,
198. This essay was originally published in *Commentary*, January 1979,
43–51. Much of the animosity Ozick displays toward critic Bloom in this
essay could have been directed at herself. Her positive conclusion—that
Bloom, the author of *Kabbalah and Criticism*, is a Jewish writer—is ap-
plicable to her as well. One need only adjust the Terach-Abraham pro-
portions. In his review of *The Messiah of Stockholm*, Bloom contends that
Ozick has modulated her anxieties about idolatry, anxieties of which Schulz
was, Bloom notes, innocent. As this chapter intends to show, Ozick may
be less strident here; she is no less firm.

Chapter Eleven

1. Peggy Kaganoff, "*PW* Interviews Cynthia Ozick," *Publishers Weekly*,
27 March 1987, 34.

2. Lowin, telephone interview with Ozick, 24 August 1987.

3. Kaganoff, "*PW* Interviews Cynthia Ozick," 34.

4. Tom Teicholz, "The *Paris Review* Interview with Cynthia Ozick,"
Paris Review 102 (Spring 1987):185.

5. Ibid., 169.

Selected Bibliography

PRIMARY SOURCES

1. Novels
Trust. New York: New American Library, 1966; New York: E.P. Dutton/
 Obelisk, 1983.
The Cannibal Galaxy. New York: Alfred A. Knopf, 1983; New York:
 E.P. Dutton/Obelisk, 1984.
The Messiah of Stockholm. New York: Alfred A. Knopf, 1987.

2. Collections of Stories
The Pagan Rabbi and Other Stories. New York: Alfred A. Knopf, 1971;
 New York: Schocken Books, 1976; New York: E.P. Dutton/Obelisk,
 1983. Contains "The Pagan Rabbi," "Envy; or Yiddish in America,"
 "The Suitcase," "The Dock Witch," "The Doctor's Wife," "The
 Butterfly and the Traffic Light," "Virility."
Bloodshed and Three Novellas. New York: Alfred A. Knopf, 1976; New
 York: E.P. Dutton/Obelisk, 1983. Contains "Preface," "A Merce-
 nary," "Bloodshed," "An Education," "Usurpation (Other People's
 Stories)."
Levitation: Five Fictions. New York: Alfred A. Knopf, 1982; New York:
 E.P. Dutton/Obelisk, 1983. Contains "Levitation," "Puttermesser:
 Her Work History, Her Ancestry, Her Afterlife," "Shots," "From a
 Refugee's Notebook," "Puttermesser and Xanthippe."

3. Collections of Essays
Art & Ardor: Essays. New York: Alfred A. Knopf, 1983; New York: E.P.
 Dutton/Obelisk, 1984. Contains "Foreword," "Justice (Again) to
 Edith Wharton," "Mrs. Virginia Woolf: A Madwoman and Her
 Nurse," "Diary-Keeping," "Morgan and Maurice: A Fairy Tale,"
 "Forster as Moralist: A Reply to Mrs. A. F.," "Truman Capote
 Reconsidered," "Literary Blacks and Jews," "Cultural Impersonation:
 1. Bech, Passing; 2. Esau as Jacob," "The Fourth Sparrow: The
 Magisterial Reach of Gershom Scholem," "Toward a New Yiddish,"
 "Literature as Idol: Harold Bloom," "The Riddle of the Ordinary,"
 "Remembering Maurice Samuel," "I. B. Singer's Book of Creation,"
 "The Phantasmagoria of Bruno Schulz," "Out of the Flames: The
 Recovery of Gertrud Kolmar," "The Biological Premises of Our Sad

Earth-Speck," "Innovation and Redemption: What Literature Means,"
"The Hole/Birth Catalogue," "Justice to Feminism: 1. Previsions of
the Demise of the Dancing Dog; 2. Literature and the Politics of Sex:
A Dissent," "The Lesson of the Master," "A Drugstore in Winter."

4. Uncollected Fiction

"The Shawl." *New Yorker,* 26 May 1980, 33–34. Reprinted in *Prize Stories
1981: The O. Henry Awards,* ed. William Abrahams. Garden City,
N.Y.: Doubleday, 1981, 15–19.

"The Laughter of Akiva." *New Yorker,* 10 November 1980, 50–73.

"Rosa." *New Yorker,* 21 March 1983, 38–71. Reprinted in *Prize Stories
1984: The O. Henry Awards,* ed. William Abrahams. Garden City,
N.Y.: Doubleday, 1984, 1–36.

"At Fumicaro." *New Yorker,* 6 August 1984, 32–58.

5. Uncollected Nonfiction

"The Evasive Jewish Story." *Midstream* 12 (February 1966):78–80.

"Full Stomachs and Empty Rites." *Congress Bi-Weekly* 34 (January 23,
1967):17–19.

"Four Questions of the Rabbis." *Reconstructionist* 38 (February 18, 1972):20–
23.

"Holiness and its Discontents," *Response* 15 (Fall 1972):87–93. Also in
Jewish Book Annual 30 (1972–73):6–11.

"A Bintel Brief for Jacob Glatstein." *Jewish Heritage* 14 (Spring 1972):

"Notes toward Finding the Right Question." *Forum* 35 (Spring–Summer
1979):37–60.

"Prayer Leader." *Prooftexts* 3 (1983):1–8.

"Bialik's Hint." *Commentary* 75, no. 2 (February 1983):22–28.

"Writers Domestic and Demonic." *New York Times Book Review,* 25 March
1984, 1, 30.

"Farcical Combat in a Busy World." *New York Times Book Review,* 20 May
1984, 1, 44–45.

"Torah as Feminism, Feminism as Torah." *Congress Monthly* (September–
October 1984):7–10.

"The Question of Our Speech: The Return to Aural Culture." *Partisan
Review* 51 (1984):755–773.

"On Excellence." *Ms.* 14 (January 1985):44–45.

"Fakery and Strong Truths." *New York Times Book Review,* 7 July 1985,
1, 18.

"The First Day of School: Washington Square, 1946." *Harper's,* September
1985, 69–72.

"Literature Lost." *New York Times,* January 1986.

"The Moral Necessity of Metaphor." *Harper's,* May 1986, 62–68.

"The Role an Author Plays in Jewish Communal Life." *The Jewish Week*, 11 July 1986, 19.

"The Muse, Postmodern and Homeless," *New York Times Book Review*, 18 January 1987, 9.

"Good Novelists, Bad Citizens." *New York Times Book Review*, 15 February 1987, 13.

"Where Orphans Can Still Become Heiresses." *New York Times Book Review*, 8 March 1987, 13.

"The Library of Non-Existent Classics." *New York Times Book Review*, 12 April 1987, 12.

"Science and Letters: God's Work—and Ours." *New York Times Book Review*, 27 September 1987, 3, 51.

"Reflections on Hanukkah." *New York Times Magazine*. Part 2. 15 November 1987, 44–45, 59–62.

"Ruth." In *Congregation: Contemporary Writers Read the Jewish Bible*. ed. David Rosenberg. New York: Harcourt Brace Jovanovich, 1987, 361–82.

6. Poetry and Poetry Translations in Anthologies and Periodicals

Virginia Quarterly Review. 38 (Winter 1962):99–100. Contains "Revisiting," "Stile," "Footnote to Lord Acton."

The Literary Review 5 (1962):403–06, 543–45. Contains "The Engineers," "To My Uncle, A Craftsman," "The Artist, Ha, Ha," "Short Historical Essay on Obtuseness," "The Coming," "The Arrest."

"Jewish Poetry and Poets," *Judaism* 14 (Fall 1965):432–36. Contains "The Wonder-Teacher," "Origins, Divergences," "Yom Kippur, 5726," "When That With Tragic Rapture Moses Stood," "A Riddle."

A Treasury of Yiddish Poetry, ed. Irving Howe and Eliezer Greenberg. New York: Holt, 1969. Contains Ozick's Translations of David Einhorn's "The Last to Sing," "And All of Them Are Gone," "A Prayer"; H. Leivick's "Sanatorium," "On the Road to Siberia," "God, A Boy," "A Voice," "Cain and Abel"; and Chaim Grade's "The Coat," "Elegy for Soviet Yiddish Writers."

Voices Within the Ark: The Modern Jewish Poets, ed. Howard Schwartz and Anthony Rudolf. Wainscott, N.Y.: Pushcart Press, 1980. Contains "A Riddle," "The Wonder-Teacher."

The Literary Review 25 (Summer 1982):611–16. Contains "Fire-Foe," "In the Yard," "Urn-Burial."

The Penguin Book of Yiddish Verse, ed. Irving Howe, Ruth Wisse, and Khone Shmeruk. New York: Penguin Books, 1987. Contains Ozick's translations of H. Leivick's "Sanatorium"; Jacob Glatstein's "1919," "Evening Bread," "Without Jews," "Mozart," "Old Age," "Genesis," "Yiddishkayt," "Sabbath," "Prayer," "Our Jewish Quarters," "Sunday Shtetl"; and Abraham Sutzkever's "Frozen Jews," "Poems from a Diary."

7. Other Poetry
"Apocalypse." *Commentary* 28 (September 1959):242.
"In the Synagogue." *Jewish Spectator* 35 (December 1970):9.
"The Seventeen Questions of Rabbi Zusya." *Midstream* 18 (Winter 1972):70.

8. Forthcoming
Metaphor & Memory: Essays. New York: Alfred A. Knopf.

SECONDARY SOURCES

1. Bibliography
Currier, Susan, and Daniel J. Cahill. "A Bibliography of the Writings of Cynthia Ozick." *Texas Studies in Literature and Language* 25, no. 2 (Summer 1983):313–21. A comprehensive listing of Ozick's work published to 1983, admittedly in need of revision, correction, and updating. An indispensable tool for anyone engaged in the serious study of Cynthia Ozick. I acknowledge considerable debt to this bibliography, which served as a virtual *vademecum* during the many months of research and writing. Contains more than 150 entries.

2. Books
Bloom, Harold, ed. *Cynthia Ozick: Modern Critical Views.* New York: Chelsea House, 1986. The best essays in this collection that deals with works to 1983 include an introduction by Bloom, in which he concludes that when Ozick's artistic and polemic writings seem to clash, one ought to trust the tale before the teller; a review essay on *Bloodshed and Three Novellas* by Ruth R. Wisse, in which she singles Ozick out as the leader in a new stage in American Jewish writing; and an essay by Victor Strandberg, in which he analyzes in detail the first four volumes of Ozick's work. The book's greatest drawback is that thirteen of the twenty pieces included are brief book reviews that are long on immediacy and short on in-depth analysis.
Pinsker, Sanford. *The Uncompromising Fiction of Cynthia Ozick.* Columbia: University of Missouri Press, 1987. A breezy overview, in chronological order, of six volumes by Ozick, from *Trust* through *The Cannibal Galaxy.* Contains, in addition, a brief survey of American-Jewish literature as context for Ozick's writings.
Walden, Daniel, ed. *The World of Cynthia Ozick. Studies in American Jewish Literature,* vol. 6. Kent, Ohio: Kent State University Press, 1987.

An invaluable "next step" for the student who proposes to approach Ozick's work seriously. Contains essays on some Ozick stories not covered in the present book, although it does not treat at length Ozick's poetry or latest novel. Fine writing throughout.

3. Articles and Essays

Apple, Max. "Wresting Life from the Void." *The New Leader* 66 (December 12, 1983):14–15. Sees *The Cannibal Galaxy* as a successful attempt by Ozick to understand the universe in the chaos of post-Holocaust Europe and in the desolation and emptiness of suburban American life and education. Reprinted in Bloom, *Modern Critical Views.*

Alexander, Edward. "Cynthia Ozick and the Idols of the Tribe." *Midstream* 30 (January 1984):54–55. A paean of praise for Ozick the essayist. Sees her as a critic, not so much of literature, but of history, society, and, above all, religion.

Bloom, Harold. "The Book of the Father." *New York Times Book Review,* 22 March 1987, 1, 36. A brilliant analysis of *The Messiah of Stockholm,* in which Bloom assesses the influence of Bernard Malamud and Philip Roth on Ozick's latest writing, mediated by Bruno Schulz. Sees *Messiah* as a work that breaks through Ozick's anxiety about writing as idolatry.

Chertok, Haim. "Ozick's Hoofprints." *Modern Jewish Studies* 6, no. 4 (1987):5–12. Analyzes "Shots." Contends that one must trust the life as well as the fiction, and that Ozick, when she creates fictions, is indeed practicing the idolatry she claims to shun.

Epstein, Joseph. "Cynthia Ozick, Jewish Writer." *Commentary* 77, no. 3 (March 1984):64–69. Article critical of Ozick's fantastic fiction, demonstrating a preference for her "stories written in a more realistic mode," and an even stronger preference for Ozick's essays.

Fisch, Harold. "Introducing Cynthia Ozick." *Response* 22 (1974):27–34. One of the earliest articles to recognize the artistry of Cynthia Ozick. Presents *Trust* and *The Pagan Rabbi* and makes the connection between the two.

Gertel, Elliot B. "Cynthia Ozick and the 'Jewish' Short Story." *Midstream* 29 (December 1983):43–47. An attempt, seemingly futile here, to define the short story and to exclude from the genre several of Ozick's shorter fictions. Searches for a paradigm, among the rest, of the "Jewish" short story.

Gittenstein, R. Barbara. "The Temptation of Apollo and the Loss of Yiddish in Cynthia Ozick's Fiction." *Studies in American Jewish Literature* 3 (1983):194–201. Asserts but fails to demonstrate that Ozick's fiction is characterized by a vague yearning for Yiddish.

Harap, Louis. "The Religious Art of Cynthia Ozick." *Judaism* 33

(1984):353–63. Traces Ozick's development as "a passionate expo-
nent of literature in English which aims to be Jewish in its essence."

Kauvar, Elaine M. "Cynthia Ozick's Book of Creation: *Puttermesser and
Xanthippe.*" *Contemporary Literature* 26, no. 1 (1985):40–54. Sche-
matic attempt to show a formal link between Ozick's story and the
Kabbalistic work *Sefer Yetsirah,* or *Book of Creation.* Reprinted in
Bloom, *Modern Critical Views.*

Lowin, Joseph. "Cynthia Ozick's Mimesis." *Jewish Book Annual* 42 (1984–
85):79–90.

————. "Cynthia Ozick and the Jewish Fantastic." In *Identity and Ethos,*
ed. Mark H. Gelber. Bern: Peter Lang, 1986, 311–23.

————. "Cynthia Ozick, Rewriting Herself: The Road from 'The Shawl'
to 'Rosa.' " In *Since Flannery O'Connor: Essays on the Contemporary
American Short Story,* ed. Loren Logsdon and Charles W. Mayer. Ma-
comb: Western Illinois University Press, 1987 (*Essays in Literature*
book series).

Mort, Jo-Ann. "Cynthia Ozick and the Future of American Jewish Literature." *Jewish Frontier* 52 (January 1985):20–21, 26. A review essay
in which we are given a brief tour of Ozick's "odd creations," characters who are "hardly a lineup of positive role models depicting
Jewish life in America."

Rosenfeld, Alvin H. "Cynthia Ozick: Fiction and the Jewish Idea." *Midstream* 23 (August–September 1977):76–81. One of the most articulate, eloquent, and insightful critics of Jewish literature examines
the meaning of Ozick's term "The Jewish Idea" and comments on
her insistence that the artist has an ethical function.

————. "The Education of Joseph Brill." *Midstream* 30 (February 1984):58–
59. Review of *The Cannibal Galaxy.*

Sokoloff, Naomi B. "Interpretation: Cynthia Ozick's *Cananibal Galaxy.*"
Prooftexts 6, no. 3 (1986):239–57. Presents Ozick's novel as a "fable
of interpretation," in which context confers meaning and in which
change of setting calls for reinterpretation.

Strandberg, Victor. "The Art of Cynthia Ozick." *Texas Studies in Literature
and Language* 25, no. 2 (1983):266–311. Although one might with
justice quarrel with some of Strandberg's interpretations, one is grateful for the fine overviews he gives of each of Ozick's first four books.
Especially useful is his extensive treatment of *Trust.* Reprinted in
Bloom, *Modern Critical Views.*

Wisse, Ruth R. "American Jewish Writing, Act II." *Commentary* 61, no.
6 (June 1976):40–45. An accurate reading of the state of American
Jewish literature at the time of the essay's publication and an assessment of Ozick's role as a leader of the movement among American
Jewish writers toward the use of Judaism in their writings. Extremely

useful and thought-provoking. Reprinted in Bloom, *Modern Critical Views*.

4. Interviews and Feature Articles

Grossman, Edward. "Trust the Teller." *Jerusalem Post Magazine,* 19 September 1986, 6–7.

Kaganoff, Peggy. "*PW* Interviews Cynthia Ozick." *Publishers Weekly,* 27 March 1987, 33–34.

Kauvar, Elaine M. "An Interview with Cynthia Ozick." *Contemporary Literature* 26, no. 4 (1985):376–401.

Moyers, Bill. "Heritage Conversation with Cynthia Ozick." Transcript, WNET-TV, New York, 3 April 1986.

Ottenberg, Eve. "The Rich Visions of Cynthia Ozick." *New York Times Magazine,* 10 April 1983, 47, 62–66.

Rainwater, Catherine, and William J. Scheick. "An Interview with Cynthia Ozick [Summer 1982]." *Texas Studies in Literature and Language* 25, no. 2 (Summer 1983):255–65.

Teicholz, Tom. "[*Paris Review*] Interview with] Cynthia Ozick." *Paris Review* 102 (Spring 1987):154–90.

Index